DEAR PRIME MINISTER

MARTYN LYONS is Emeritus Professor of History at the University of New South Wales. He has published many books and articles on the history of reading and writing in Europe and Australia, including *A History of Reading and Writing in the Western World* (2010) and *The Writing Culture of Ordinary People in Europe, c.1860–c.1920* (2013).

DEAR PRIME MINISTER

LETTERS TO ROBERT MENZIES
1949–1966

MARTYN LYONS

UNSW PRESS

A UNSW Press book

Published by
NewSouth Publishing
University of New South Wales Press Ltd
University of New South Wales
Sydney NSW 2052
AUSTRALIA
newsouthpublishing.com

© Martyn Lyons 2021
First published 2021

10 9 8 7 6 5 4 3 2 1

This book is copyright. Apart from any fair dealing for the purpose of private study, research, criticism or review, as permitted under the Copyright Act, no part of this book may be reproduced by any process without written permission. Inquiries should be addressed to the publisher.

A catalogue record for this book is available from the National Library of Australia

ISBN   9781742237305 (paperback)
           9781742249957 (ebook)
           9781742249926 (ePDF)

Internal design Josephine Pajor-Markus
Cover design Luke Causby, Blue Cork
Cover image Portrait of Prime Minister Sir Robert Menzies at his desk, Canberra, November 1951 by Max Dupain. *Mitchell Library, State Library of New South Wales*
Printer Griffin Press

All reasonable efforts were taken to obtain permission to use copyright material reproduced in this book, but in some cases copyright could not be traced. The author welcomes information in this regard.

CONTENTS

Acknowledgments		vi
1	*'I want so much to let you know how we ordinary folk feel'*: Menzies' Forgotten People	1
2	*'Dear Mr Ming'*: The profile of the ordinary writer	25
3	*'You are the only saviour of the country'*: Fan mail and congratulations	41
4	*'If you want anything <u>done</u>, go to the top'*: The personal hotline	62
5	*'Please don't think I'm a crackpot'*: The rhetoric of apology	81
6	*'I am sir [sure] you will act as human bean'*: The cry of the distressed pensioner	103
7	*'Much as I love our little Queen, I think she needs a spanking'*: Britain and the Empire	123
8	*'A Commonwealth Citizen in every woodpile'*: Immigration and the White Australia Policy	148
9	*'Mr Khrushchev is planning something big'*: The changing face of anti-communism	163
10	*'People will weep tears of blood'*: Angry letters and political protest	188
11	*'The Kingdom of God is nigh'*: Paranoid letters	205
12	Structures of belief	218
Notes		230
Bibliography		251
Index		257

ACKNOWLEDGMENTS

I would like to thank Humphrey McQueen for bringing the existence of the Menzies letters to my attention in the first place, and then for inviting me to continue and complete an investigation which he had barely begun but whose importance he was the first to recognise.

I am grateful to the Faculty of Arts and Social Sciences at the University of New South Wales for two small Emeriti support grants, which sadly had no sequel.

I thank my Canberra landlord, Victor Speranski, for being considerate, generous and responsive, and Mina for commenting on extracts from the book.

1

'I want so much to let you know how we ordinary folk feel'

MENZIES' FORGOTTEN PEOPLE

The Menzies years

On Boxing Day 1949, Reg Longden of Ballarat (Victoria) was driving home through South Australia when his car broke down, and he found himself stranded for several days near Riverton. He was about 700 kilometres from home, with very little money. He telephoned his friends and family in Ballarat, but they were away from home and could not help him. Who could he turn to? Who *does* one turn to, in a tight spot with little money and no immediate assistance in sight? Reg turned to his prime minister. He sent him a letter appealing for emergency assistance, hoping for a good response since he had driven a car for his local Liberal Party branch at the recent general election. He wrote:

> No doubt you will be surprised to hear from me in this way, but the fact is I am in one hell of a mess.

> I have had car trouble at the above [he gave an address in Riverton], and have to hang on here until Wed or Thurs with exactly 4 pounds.

DEAR PRIME MINISTER

> Would you be good enough to wire me at Riverton Post Office
> 8 pounds until my affects are clear [*sic*].[1]

Reg Longden did not receive the eight pounds he wanted, but he did get a reply in which the prime minister hoped he had successfully returned home. Today, when public trust in politicians throughout the Western world has sunk below sea level, it is to say the least unusual to find an individual appealing directly to his prime minister in a personal emergency during the Christmas holiday period. The prime minister in question was Robert Menzies, and Reg Longden's letter was one among thousands which Menzies received, answered, carefully filed and eventually left to the National Library of Australia in Canberra.

Robert Gordon Menzies was the longest-serving prime minister in Australian history. He did not come from a privileged background, but was born in the tiny township of Jeparit in western Victoria, where his father ran the general store. He was a student at Wesley College in Melbourne and then at Melbourne University, where he studied law. He became a leading light of the Melbourne Bar and entered state politics in 1928. Several correspondents evoked their common background with Menzies during those early years in the legal profession, Wesley College and even Jeparit. In 1934, Menzies became federal member for the safe UAP (United Australia Party) seat of Kooyong in central Melbourne. He boasted Scottish ancestry on his father's side, and this was a well-advertised aspect of his life. He was a Presbyterian although a tolerant one, and he deplored the virulent sectarianism of his time. In 1920, he married Pattie Leckie in Kew, where they lived. In 1954, she was appointed Dame of the Order of the British Empire. Menzies' correspondents frequently referred to 'Dame Pattie' with respect and affection.

Menzies became prime minister for the first time in 1939 on the sudden death of Joseph Lyons, but he led a divided party and an uneasy coalition with the Country Party. In 1941, he spent several months in

London as a member of Churchill's War Cabinet. Correspondents would frequently bracket Menzies' name with Churchill's, no doubt intending this as a compliment but perhaps forgetting that he had described Churchill as a menace and a publicity-seeker, and found Churchill's leadership too authoritarian.[2] Factions within the coalition distrusted Menzies and feared that his manner was too distant and superior ever to win an election. In 1941, they forced his resignation, but two years later the UAP was heavily defeated at the polls. Menzies devoted his time out of office to establishing the modern Liberal Party as a mass party based on the principles of free enterprise and individual freedom.

The effort invested in rebuilding the party paid off. Menzies returned to power in 1949, after a strike wave and profiting from the unpopularity of the Labor Party's (ALP) proposals to extend state control over the banking sector and to prolong petrol rationing. This was the first of Menzies' seven consecutive election victories for the coalition of Liberal and Country parties. At first Menzies enjoyed a healthy majority of 27 in the lower house and, in 1951, the coalition also gained control of the Senate. After a subsequent swing to Labor, the coalition's primary vote fell below 50 per cent, but Menzies defied predictions to scrape home again in 1954 with a majority of seven. Thereafter his fortunes were secured by divisions within the Labor Party. A breakaway anti-communist group seceded from the ALP to form the Democratic Labor Party, and the majority of its supporters gave their electoral preferences to the Liberals. Menzies was then able to win the federal elections of 1955, 1961 (albeit with a majority of only two) and 1963.

He served two terms as prime minister, the first from 1939 to 1941, and the second, with which this book is primarily concerned, between 1949 and 1966. His longevity in office is exceptional and indeed legendary. In cricketing terms – and Menzies was very fond of the game – he spanned generations, taking office at the close of the Bradman era just as Lindsay Hassett began as Australian captain, and stepping down well into the modern period under the cricketing reign of Bob Simpson. He presided over significant social, economic and political change. Some of it, like the mass immigration programme, was engineered by the government. Other changes, like the switch to decimal currency in 1966 or the declining influence of Britain, happened in spite of it. The Menzies years were a time of post-war reconstruction and rising prosperity against the background of the Cold War.

Australian politicians have battled for control of the historical memory of the 1950s. John Howard recognised Menzies not merely as the founder the Liberal Party, but also as the ideological fountain which constantly replenished the deep wells of Australian conservatism. In Howard's eyes, these years were a golden age of calm and prosperity during which the unbroken supremacy of the Liberal Party laid the foundation of modern Australia.[3] Howard selected what he needed from the past in order to construct a Liberal role model and an influential political tradition. For Paul Keating, on the other hand, these were years of complacency and cultural stagnation, soon to be shaken by mass immigration and the declining relevance of the White Australia Policy. Keating berated Liberal nostalgia for the 1950s as 'fogeyism' and condemned in particular its 'cultural cringe' towards Britain and its monarchy.[4] Keating was committing the sin of historical anachronism, judging the 1950s against the values of the present. The popular royalism which he and many others ridiculed was nevertheless a potent force in 1950s Australia.

Neither of the partisan visions articulated by Howard and Keating took any notice of the substantial correspondence Menzies received from ordinary voters. Even Allan Martin, author of a detailed and fundamentally sympathetic biography of Menzies, only dipped into the corpus occasionally and only then in search of letters from leading political figures.[5] Troy Bramston's more balanced account found Menzies guilty of 'policy ossification' and above all underlined his failure to develop a succession strategy, but it failed to subject the incoming correspondence to any systematic analysis.[6]

The Menzies years are conventionally interpreted as a period of prosperity and growing consumerism. It would be dangerous, however, to read the story of rising material prosperity too far back into the past. Historian John Murphy argued that the so-called post-war boom did not begin until 1954–55, making the conclusion of the decade very different from its beginnings. Those early years were tormented by economic crisis and high inflation. Perhaps even Murphy was putting too early a date on the arrival of good times, which depended on a mining boom which in 1955 still lay over the horizon. The consumer society of the 1960s was not yet evident. In 1956 about one quarter of private homes in Melbourne, Sydney and Brisbane still had no fridge and two-thirds of them still had no running hot water in the bathroom.[7]

Historians of the Cold War would endorse a periodisation which recognises the peculiar intensity of global tensions in the immediate post-war years as a whole. They envisage the years between the Berlin Blockade of 1948 and the mid-1950s as having a distinctive unity of their own.[8] This perspective implies some continuity between the Chifley Labor government of 1945–49 and the Menzies governments of 1949 and beyond. Indeed, Chifley and Menzies dealt with similar issues and concerns – anti-communism, the need to increase immigration, British nuclear testing on Australian soil, the beginning of the Snowy Mountains hydro-electric scheme, and so on. Nevertheless, voters who wrote to Menzies saw his arrival in power as a turning-point. But this is not a book about Menzies, and it does not set out to analyse his persona, assess his achievement or inventory his failings. Although Menzies is a central character in this book, he is largely a passive one, because instead I focus on the thousands of ordinary people who wrote to him.

Writing upwards

This book, then, is about the purpose and significance of letter-writing, and it uses letters to present a new 'history from below'.[9] Historians have long plundered correspondence for valuable personal testimony in domains in which official archives are often unhelpful. But they have sometimes been guilty of taking their sources for granted, and they have been slow to consider all the codes and conventions which have historically conditioned epistolary writing. Italian palaeographer and cultural historian Armando Petrucci outlined the essential elements of a different approach which guides my investigation. To put any letters into their historical context, we must first know who wrote them and to whom they were addressed. We need to know why they were written, why they were sent, and ultimately why they have been preserved. A further line of inquiry goes deeper than these rather obvious questions: how, Petrucci asked in his magisterial history of correspondence, with what techniques and instruments, in what spaces and according to what rules of graphic and textual organisation were letters conceived and written?[10] Letters are not merely texts, they are also material objects and they represent a social practice. Their physical characteristics, as well as the social grammar which informs their structure and form, need to be elucidated.

Letters to Menzies are examples of a specific genre of correspondence — namely, 'writing upwards'. Throughout history, ordinary subjects have collectively petitioned their rulers or written individually to them, workers have written to their bosses, impoverished refugees have written seeking help from aid relief committees and parishioners have written to their clergy. They often sought some personal gain, but this was not necessarily their only motive and sometimes their objective was not self-interest but simply reassurance. They wrote to denounce a corrupt official, or to congratulate a superior on achieving something of which they approved. They put their faith in letter-writing to cut through bureaucratic obstacles and directly reach out to a higher source of power. Sometimes their language was obsequious and self-effacing – a common tactic of the weak seeking the favour of the mighty. They borrowed and reproduced the language of their superiors, possibly unconsciously, in order to ingratiate themselves. Letters from ordinary voters to Menzies belong to and also enrich the history of this enduring scribal phenomenon.

Historians of popular writing have found a fruitful source in letters to eminent political leaders. Maarten van Ginderachter, for instance, analysed thousands of letters sent between 1865 and 1934 to the Belgian royal family. Most asked for some assistance, and normally the monarch obliged by sending a small gift, which showed that the strategy could be productive.[11] Hitler's Reich Chancellery received thousands of letters addressed to the Führer, and Hitler designated officials to reply to some of them. In Henrik Eberle's published selection, letters of protest to the Führer were initially present but gradually dwindled leaving an unremitting stream of veneration and birthday congratulations.[12] In 1934 alone he received 10 000 birthday letters. Mussolini also created a special office to deal with such correspondence. Anne Wingenter studied letters sent to Mussolini by surviving families of Italian soldiers killed in Ethiopia, in which desperate pleas for help were mingled with crude imitations of the heroic language of Fascist sacrifice, designed to demonstrate the writer's loyalty.[13] The regime published a carefully edited selection of them to confirm Italians' alleged devotion to their leader.

Scholars have also scrutinised writing to French presidents. Sudhir Hazareesingh interpreted Charles de Gaulle's incoming correspondence from the 1950s onwards as an important component in the cultivation of a personal myth of the providential saviour of the French people.[14] François Mitterrand received about 1000 letters daily during his presidency of France, and staff replied to almost every one of them in rapid time, although the requests they submitted were not granted. According to Béatrice Fraenkel, 110 standard responses were available to the presidential secretariat.[15] Such cases illustrate the persistence of popular belief in the personal benevolence of the ruler, and in the writer's ability to reach him personally, in spite of the inevitable bureaucratisation of official correspondence in the cases mentioned. When incoming correspondence was processed by dedicated office staff, the question arises: who actually replied to letters to the president? The same question will be asked of the Menzies correspondence.

Compared to the enormous quantity of letters received by François Mitterrand, the 22 000 letters sent to Menzies seem an almost trivial number, which explains why he needed far fewer secretaries to deal with them. The size of Menzies' own secretariat fluctuated, as more casual staff were hired when business expanded, but at any time the essential core personnel numbered only two. Those who dealt most closely with incoming correspondence were, in chronological order, Eileen Linehan, Everil Wilkinson, Hazel Craig, Geoffrey Yeend, William Heseltine, Les Moore and Frank Jennings. Perhaps the most influential of all was Craig, who served many years, continuing as Menzies' private secretary after his retirement from office. She developed a certain familiarity with several regular letter-writers. As chapter 4 will stress, these were all public servants who served several masters in turn, and maintained a traditional public service neutrality through changes of government and regardless of disagreement between parties. They made sure that a large number of correspondents received a reply to their letters.

The selection of letters to US President Barack Obama presented by Jeanne Marie Laskas is the most recent incarnation of the genre of writing to political leaders.[16] Obama received about 10 000 letters daily, and every day he read ten of them, carefully selected by his staff. The Office of Presidential Correspondence employed 50 staff members, 36 interns and 300 rotating volunteers, completely dwarfing Menzies' secretariat. The writers who replied to them, channelling the president's voice, included literature graduates sensitive to his tone and language – which was not the case with replies to the Menzies letters, penned by private secretaries who were not trying to imitate the prime minister's style.[17] Nor were Menzies' secretaries offered counselling, as Obama's staff were, when they had to deal with particularly traumatic letters.[18] Laskas' moving book is sympathetic to Obama, as a man of compassion who cared deeply about ordinary people's problems. I do not seek to emulate Laskas here: this book is not intended as a homage to Menzies.

In some ways, writing to a political leader in a constitutional democracy was slightly different from petitioning a dictator or an absolute ruler like the Tsar of Russia. For one thing, the leader had been elected, and the individual correspondent knew that his or her vote counted for something. This gave them an ounce of power, which perhaps led some of them to adopt a very familiar or even hectoring tone. Nevertheless, there was some continuity between letters received by elected leaders like Mitterrand, Menzies and Obama and those received under other, less democratic regimes. Correspondents all thought writing was an important medium; they all assumed that their leader was accessible and could remedy their personal wants and grievances.

The Menzies letters share some features of the correspondence received by all the 20th- and 21st-century leaders I have mentioned. Menzies, like his counterparts, had a special secretariat to deal with his incoming correspondence and, like François Mitterrand, he tried to reply to them all. His replies were inevitably standardised, even if he often departed from conventional protocol and made his own personal interventions. Although many of the leaders studied, including Menzies, made good use of public radio broadcasts, they all, again like Menzies, relied heavily on the written word as a means of cultivating their support base. The letters they received belong to a particular genre – the genre of writing upwards, embracing any kind of correspondence or petitions addressed to employers, church authorities or politicians.[19]

Writing upwards describes the multiple ways in which poor, desperate or indignant people addressed their superiors. The description implies nothing about the tone of the letters, which as this book shows could be grovelling, supplicatory or menacing; it refers simply to an inequality of status, between a prime minister and an ordinary citizen. 'Deference, Demands, Supplication' – this was how Camillo Zadra and Gianluigi Fait summarised their collection of studies on writing to the powerful.[20] Letters to authorities usually adopted a deferential tone which recognised their own inferior status, they often sought some personal advantage and sometimes they did so in begging or grovelling language. But this was not always the case. Writings to the powerful might be abusive or obsequious, or they could denounce neighbours, conspirators and corrupt officials. Occasionally they demanded nothing, but seem simply to have been a cry for attention or a plea for reassurance. Sometimes the writer assumed a network of reciprocal obligations and reminded a superior authority of its duty to fulfil earlier promises. The underlying condition of all writing upwards was social or political inequality between the correspondents. For poor people addressing powerful forces, it was wise to be deferential and cautious. As James C Scott has argued, however, expressions of loyalty and obedience should not be taken at their face value, because deferential language could disguise a deeper insubordination.[21]

The 'Forgotten People'

In his early career, Menzies was known for his sharp intelligence, but also for an undue sense of his own intellectual superiority. He liked debates that showcased his wit and repartee, but he frequently adopted an aggressive, adversarial stance that made him unpopular. Although he was a master of sarcasm and the cruel retort, he badly lacked the common touch, and did not convince his colleagues that he could win elections.²² After the humiliation of being ousted from office in 1941, Menzies licked his wounds and devoted his energies to the formation of the Liberal Party. At the same time, he needed to make himself more 'electable' and therefore made an effort to modify his public image.

In 1941 and 1942, he began a series of weekly talks on Sydney radio station 2UE, in which he explained his political philosophy and that of liberalism in general. On 22 May 1942, he addressed his broadcast to the 'Forgotten People' of Australia, those he believed were under-represented in the political system, and unprotected either by the interest groups of large-scale capitalism on one hand, or by the organised labour movement on the other. Menzies appealed to all those in between, a broadly based middle class whom he described as 'nameless and unadvertised', and who were usually taken for granted.²³ Their values, centred around the home, thrift and independence, were vital to the nation. In writing to the prime minister, Menzies' Forgotten People had an opportunity to express themselves and respond to Menzies' emphasis on patriotism, the home and self-sacrifice.

Menzies' overture to the Forgotten People was therefore an offer of government support for their values of thrift and self-reliance, and a promise to promote their aspirations to marriage, a secure family life and a house in the suburbs. He advanced a domestic ideal, based on traditional gender relations and a secure economic future (even though this took years to materialise). All this would be possible in a cohesive society, without divisive social tensions or racial friction. As Murphy argues, this was an age in which citizens retreated into a private and domestic realm, and when home ownership itself became a marker of full Australian citizenship.²⁴ Menzies' Australian vision was of a society which was homogeneous, conformist and, above all, white. The correspondence he received allows us to analyse more deeply the beliefs and assumptions of his constituency.

The Forgotten People were only vaguely defined in sociological terms. In historian Judith Brett's analysis, Menzies' radio talk was not directed solely at the middle class, but at a wider constituency, which he outlined as 'salary earners, shopkeepers, skilled artisans, professional men and women, farmers'.[25] His target audience (on radio and later television) was wide enough to embrace a lower middle class which resented the power of trade unions and did not like to see its taxes spent on welfare payments to those it considered shirkers and people who took scant responsibility for their own future. Those who wrote to Menzies rarely identified themselves as his Forgotten People – in fact only three letters explicitly used the phrase. One accused Menzies himself of forgetting the old age pensioners.[26] Another demanded the reform of the Lunacy Laws, referring to the forgotten inmates of New South Wales asylums – not exactly the audience Menzies had in mind.[27] Another was from author Zora Cross, seeking funds to promote her books in Britain, and pleading 'I am only one of the Prime Minister's "Forgotten People"'.[28] Perhaps she did not represent Menzies' main target, either. Nevertheless, as we shall see, the echoes of Menzies' 1942 speech reverberate through the correspondence he received, in attacks on compulsory unionism or cries for help from people on fixed incomes in a time of high inflation. In their letters, the Forgotten People had their say. As one Brisbane correspondent explained to Menzies:

> I want so much to let you know how we ordinary folk feel – and after all – we're a big percentage of the voters. Unfortunately we're so inarticulate or uninterested, we complain and criticise on the tennis court, on trains and in the office and that's futile I feel.[29]

Writing, on the other hand, was far from futile; it was a powerful medium, and those who used it were sometimes not quite as inarticulate as this writer disingenuously claimed.

Historians have become expert at examining indirect sources for writing the history of the silent masses, the 'forgotten people' of history. But the forgotten people are not always silent. The policeman's wife from Woy Woy (New South Wales) who told Menzies about her garden and the need to write felt by poor people with little education; the Melbourne pensioner dining on raisin bread and a soup cube, down to her last spoonful of tea: their voices and many others like them, neglected by histories of this period, cry out eloquently to be heard in the Menzies letters.[30] An alternative title for this book might be: 'The Forgotten People Write Back'.

The Menzies letters reflect their underlying anxieties. Australia certainly experienced a growing prosperity introduced by the first mining boom, and Liberals were justifiably confident about holding on to power against an opposition paralysed by its own divisions. Beyond these comforting developments, however, a deeper malaise surfaced in the correspondence to Menzies. There were concerns, fuelled by Menzies himself, that some of the certainties of Australian life were under threat from communist subversion and Asian hostility. The global importance of the British Empire, on which Australia had for so long relied, was shrinking. There were fears that the whiteness of White Australia could not be maintained in all its purity for ever. Meanwhile, the persistent level of poverty undermined official complacency about Australia's growing economy. The undeniable achievements of the age were accomplished in a polarised world in which there seemed to be a high risk of confrontation between superpowers. Meanwhile, over and above all those achievements loomed a mushroom-shaped vision of unparalleled destruction.

The power of writing

Writing, it was assumed, was the way to reach the prime minister and engage him in the kind of personal conversation which both geographical distance and his busy schedule made impossible in real time. Writers thought that letters were their best chance of bringing grievances to his notice, and of influencing government policy. There was often a strong dose of self-interest involved as well; writers hoped to secure some personal advantage, either for themselves or at least for the group to which they belonged. Menzies would surely listen because the writers had a claim on him: they, after all, were the voters who had put him into power and his political survival depended on them. For this reason alone, their letters counted for something and could not be ignored. In writing, they could alert Menzies to where he was going wrong, as well as congratulate and thank him for his successes. Writing was empowering, especially when writers used the letter as a pulpit from which to preach to Menzies about the salvation of his soul and of Australia generally.

In the course of his second term as prime minister, Menzies received about 22 000 letters, an average of over 1300 per year. In this number, I include all incoming postal items, including telegrams and air letters, 'with compliments' slips that often have a short message on them, greetings cards with handwritten messages inscribed, and cards acknowledging condolence letters. The material form of all these missives of different species is important; but so too is the mere fact that in each case a member of the public thought it worthwhile to send a message to Menzies. This study also embraces letters sent to Menzies' secretaries by name, as well as those addressed to Mrs and Miss Menzies (their daughter Heather), where they were ultimately destined for the prime minister and were filed accordingly.

He received letters from widows and war veterans, school students all over the world, political leaders, homespun philosophers, clairvoyants and prophets. Every British citizen had a constitutional right to petition the Crown and in Australia the custom was similarly recognised. As Menzies' private secretary, Hazel Craig, assured one tentative correspondent: 'It is the right of every citizen to write to the Prime Minister should they desire information, and he is only too happy to do his best for them'.[31] But correspondents did not entirely accept the limited contract which Hazel Craig was offering them. They wrote for many purposes besides simply seeking information.

While some submitted deferential inquiries and accepted the response, many sought a more personal connection, if not a platform from which they could browbeat the prime minister. They were not necessarily satisfied with the exchange of a single letter – like Joyce Atkinson of Nambour (Queensland), who sent Menzies 22 letters in 1958 alone, on the subject of any newspaper report which happened to spark her interest.[32] Australian businessmen sent him their annual company reports and foreign businessmen sought an interview to discuss investment possibilities. Correspondents sent him ties and handkerchiefs, and the Filipino ambassador sent huge cigars. People wrote to air grievances, to send congratulations and to comment on speeches they had heard on the radio. They wrote to support Menzies' policies, to request an interview or a photograph or to send him a book or a newspaper article they thought would interest him. Menzies had literary interests and, although his tastes were canonical and conventional, this was unusual in an Australian politician. Perhaps his literary interests encouraged amateur poets to send him their work. They lectured him, quoted Shakespeare and the Bible at him, and they sent him their verses, while revering him as a quasi-messianic saviour. A few letters were from complete eccentrics.

Writers confided with Menzies on an infinite range of topics from asking for permission to import exotic birds from New Guinea to sending him advice on how to eliminate the rabbit problem (more than ten billion feral rabbits multiplied freely in Australia, and were a menace to agriculture and the environment).[33] One inventor was perfecting a flying saucer to be used in aerial bombardments; another correspondent offered to demonstrate the benefits of yoga.[34] An English schoolboy asked Menzies to replace his broken boomerang with 'a true one' (Hazel Craig recommended a shop in London).[35] One woman was desperate to find out whether water-skiing was permitted on Canberra's newly inaugurated Lake Burley Griffin.[36] They wrote on plain or coloured paper, in ink, biro or pencil. Some showed a high degree of epistolary literacy with a firm command of the straight line, regular paragraph indentation and margins, while others were composed by writers with limited literacy skills and little epistolary experience. A few had problems with the correct form of address for an eminent politician, hence the uncertain mixture of familiarity and formality in the formula 'Dear Mr Ming' (Ming being one of Menzies' nicknames, probably derived from the Scottish pronunciation of his name as 'Ming-ies').[37] This study surveys their difficulties and examines the purpose and the function of their letters to Menzies. It examines why they wrote, what they hoped to achieve, and the fundamental assumptions which guided their written thoughts. Remarkably, the vast majority received a reply from the prime minister's secretariat.

Not all the letters Menzies received were from unknown or forgotten people. A certain proportion came from lobby groups and non-government organisations, such as the Protestant Council of New South Wales, or the People's Union, an anti-communist lobbying group based in Sydney. Others were communications, warnings and advice sent up the line from Liberal Party branches. I have reviewed them all, and I draw on letters from influential politicians and businesspeople as well as from ordinary citizens.

The letters were not all from Australia, either; in fact in 1950 almost a quarter of the corpus consisted of letters from overseas. As with anybody's correspondence taken as a whole, the letters allow us to map all the networks in which Menzies was enmeshed and which defined his social identity. Menzies' networks were multi-layered and reflected both his private and global interests: his epistolary connections were party-political, professional, familial (with his sister Belle and his brother Frank), ancestral (the Scottish connection), social (in clubs like the Savage Club), local (in the state of Victoria and especially his own constituency of Kooyong), global (especially across the countries of the British Commonwealth) and religious (the Presbyterian Church). In fact, the letters themselves played a major role in sustaining and performing those networks. Menzies, as well as his many correspondents, needed these letters. They kept him connected to the social groups which made him who he was.

Five types of correspondence

Broadly speaking, I have identified five types of letters which dominate Menzies' correspondence. These are the congratulatory letter, the letter of anger or protest, the supplicatory letter, the political letter and the paranoid letter. I have not attempted to quantify the presence of each of these categories within the corpus, because they frequently overlap. We find different registers combined within the same letter, and even a single paragraph may contain congratulations, a complaint, a request for a favour as well as general advice. My typology therefore outlines general themes running through the correspondence, without trying to allot exclusive labels to a mass of hybrid letters.

The congratulatory tone was most common in the letters and telegrams which flooded in after a successful election result. Liberal Party supporters also congratulated their leader on a telling speech, and this was a way in which they expressed solidarity with the party's cause. Menzies received a certain amount of personal fan mail, asking for an autograph or complimenting him on his dignified bearing in the presence of Her Majesty the Queen, on the tone of a recent radio speech and his intelligent common sense. There were gift-bonding messages, accompanying offerings with which correspondents showed their appreciation of Menzies and expressed personal sympathy with him. Writers sent cigars, knitted scarves or a portrait of Donald Bradman. This type of personal fan mail is discussed in chapter 3.

At the same time, there were letters of anger and protest, although they were always in a minority compared to the powerful tide of letters of praise and congratulation. There were protests above all against the government's pension policy (or the lack of one) and against the concessions Menzies was allegedly making to the demands of the Catholic Church. There were even a few isolated protests against the government's anti-communist policy. These will be considered in chapter 10.

The supplicatory letter asked for a personal favour. Menzies dealt with or evaded requests from businesses for tax exemptions and import licences. Businesses sent advertising materials, and a certain number of letters lobbied Menzies on behalf of a particular interest group. They were pitching for a government contract, or they sent a share prospectus inviting him to invest. For example, the Stanhope Hotel in New York sent a brochure inviting Menzies to stay there on his next visit.[38] They usually received a very non-committal acknowledgment. He received requests for letters of introduction, while constituents asked him to accelerate their connection to the telephone network. His correspondents include many tales of personal hardship from struggling old age pensioners, and these will be discussed in chapter 6.

The fourth type of letter contained political advice and warnings, often from Liberal Party MPs and local branches who were worried that government policy was alienating voters. These cries of alarm were written from the political grassroots, to urge a particular policy on the prime minister, or to advise him how to secure some electoral advantage over the Labor Party. Warnings might arrive in the form of 'tribune letters', from correspondents who claimed to represent the voice of the people, appointing themselves as tribunes or spokespersons of general discontent, sometimes prophesying doom, Cassandra-style.

The paranoid letter, the last type of letter identified here, expressed irrational fears and a sense of catastrophe. Religious fanatics prophesied an imminent Armageddon and bombarded Menzies with sermons. Neurotic individuals wrote above all of their fear of communism, and their paranoia exposes the irrational underside of

Cold War mentalities. They were paranoid about other perceived threats as well, usually from a Roman Catholic world conspiracy and, more rarely, from Jews or Freemasons. The most extreme of these paranoid letters were the ones that Menzies did not consider worthy of a response.

Letters to Menzies' could therefore be laudatory, supplicatory, homiletic, millenarian or cautionary. Frequently, they adopted several of these epistolary modes at once, blending congratulations with a warning, or mixing a request with political advice. Pledges of loyal political support could be interlaced with seething discontent. Whatever the fundamental purpose of the letter, the writer needed a strategy to capture Menzies' attention and to make sure he listened to its message. In his study of letters from paupers to the Poor Law overseers in England and Wales between 1750 and the 1830s, Steven King examined what he called the 'anchoring rhetorics' which formed the building blocks of the correspondence, and shaped the basis of the dialogue and negotiation between those seeking poor relief and the administrators responsible for distributing it.[39] The rhetoric deployed by those writing upwards to higher authorities was grounded, or 'anchored' in King's term, in common values or structures of belief which were shared reciprocally by writer and recipient. The effectiveness of any appeal depended on its ability to sound the right notes in order to draw a meaningful response, and a letter could only achieve this if it was rooted in ideas which were mutually appreciated, such as the values of Christian philanthropy, or reference to Australia's British heritage. Without these moorings in common values, a letter would lose direction; it would drift free and make little impact. Similarly, in the Menzies correspondence, I search for the 'anchoring rhetorics' which aimed to draw on Menzies' sympathy and attention.

Writers approached Menzies hesitantly and they used the rhetoric of apology for using up his valuable time. They frequently apologised for their deficient writing skills and even for the fact that they were writing at all. Examples of the apologetic mode are discussed in chapter 5.

Correspondents drew on the rhetoric of affinity, a device used to signal to Menzies that he and the writer shared a common geography, religion or ancestry. Members of his Kooyong constituency, for example, appealed to his obligations as their local member. The rhetoric of the Scottish connection was another way of claiming affinity with Menzies. Writers insisted they were, like him, passionate Liberal Party supporters, fellow Scots, Presbyterians, or else they had common friends or shared distant relations. These were all essential preludes to a request, identifying the writer's credentials for encroaching on the prime minister's time and patience.

The rhetoric of patriotism and Empire was deployed to enlist Menzies' support. Writers professed their loyalty to Britain, and they praised Menzies for his own attachment to British law and institutions. The enormous correspondence relating to the royal visit of the young Queen Elizabeth to Australia in 1954 was one sign of the depth of pro-British sentiment, which Menzies shared and on which he capitalised. Writers did not fail to appeal to Menzies as veterans (and perhaps as wounded veterans) of the First or Second World Wars, if not both. Menzies himself had never enlisted, which opponents often held against him, so this was not a claim to affinity but rather a demonstration of patriotism which deserved a hearing. In addition to such ordinary writers, Menzies had a strong British Commonwealth network, corresponding with fellow politicians across the world and British organisations interested in imperial trade preferences. The Commonwealth, or the Empire as he preferred to call it, was one of Menzies' most important global networks.

Anti-communism was a pervasive 'anchoring rhetoric', important enough to be treated in a chapter of its own (chapter 9). As we shall see, it became almost *de rigueur* in the 1950s for writers to mobilise a few anti-communist phrases, no matter what the purpose of their letter. Anti-communism could be invoked to justify almost anything:

one writer invited Menzies to launch a basketball match involving the touring Harlem Globetrotters, urging that the tour would be an antidote to the spread of communist propaganda.[40] Writers learned to feed the government's own anti-communist language back to Menzies. After Menzies referred in a radio broadcast to the struggle against communism as 'A spiritual war against diabolical subtlety', correspondents repeated his words parrot-fashion, pouring out their hatred of 'devilish' conspiracies and the forces of darkness. They faithfully echoed the language of demonisation to demonstrate their loyalty. Anti-communism, however, was neither uniform nor immutable. Our analysis must consider how it changed over time, particularly in response to the Petrov Affair in 1954, when the defection of a Soviet intelligence agent raised concern about Soviet espionage activities in Australia, and about the possible pro-communist sympathies of the Labor Party, its leader Herbert Evatt, and certain members of his staff.

In considering this rough typology of the correspondence and the rhetorical strategies which underpinned it, we are also identifying the common linguistic platforms shared between Menzies and his letter-writers. At times they shared common assumptions rooted in Christian philanthropy; at others, they evoked the rhetoric of sacrifice for the nation in time of war. Occasionally, they appealed to a common sense of 'British justice'. Their rhetoric was rooted in the 'schizophrenic nationalism' of the period, when to identify with Britain was an integral part of being a patriotic Australian. At other times, the linguistic platform reflected a common Scottish or Presbyterian ancestry, and writers might even shift into Scottish dialect to demonstrate their authentic bond with this tradition. In order to reinforce the desired linguistic register, writers used borrowed language, in the form of the enclosures they urged upon Menzies in their letters – press cuttings, brochures or religious tracts. Menzies regularly received books and articles designed to educate him on topics ranging from Moral Re-Armament[41] to cricket, and including the fate of Indigenous peoples. All communications like this reveal shared assumptions and a desire to stake a claim to the prime minister's attention and consideration.

An alternative history

Two discussions run in parallel throughout this book. One is concerned with the letters as *letters*, as an unusual phenomenon of scribal culture, which testifies to the importance and power of writing itself. This discussion will take note of the material form of the letters, their length, the quality of the paper, the writing instruments used and physical evidence of the writer's grasp of the rudiments of the genre — polite forms of address, indented paragraphs, clear margins and the like. The second parallel and concurrent discussion examines the letters as *texts*, in other words it elucidates the rich contents of the correspondence. In spite of the variety of correspondents represented here, the letters from ordinary and even semi-literate writers provide a unique window on the attitudes and unconscious assumptions of grassroots Liberal Party supporters in this period. They can tell us what ordinary people were thinking, in a way that a politician's best guesses or anonymous election results cannot. I cannot claim that the letters constitute a representative sample of 'public opinion'. Most of them were penned by Liberal supporters and as a result a large section of the political spectrum is not represented here. On the other hand, they were not blandly conformist and, although a majority of their authors were Liberal voters, they were Liberals with a grievance or a warning. Those grievances are themselves indicative of their unspoken beliefs.

Potentially, letters from ordinary citizens to any political leader open up an alternative history contrasting with conventional top-down political narratives. Textbook histories of the period may, if their scope embraces international affairs, underline the world-historical importance of events like the Korean War, the death of Stalin or the Suez crisis. Authoritative surveys with a more specifically Australian focus would perhaps emphasise a different set of landmarks – the Petrov Affair, the disastrous split in the Australian Labor Party, the perceived implications of Indonesian designs on New Guinea.[42] Ordinary writers absorbed and reflected the significance of some of these events, but remained completely indifferent to others. They had their own historical perspective and followed an autonomous historical calendar. They were most strongly moved, for example, by the royal visit of 1954, or Parliament's decision to increase the remuneration of its own members, or the provisions of a forthcoming annual budget. The concerns of their letters did not necessarily mirror conventional or official views of the period. Instead, they offer an alternative history of the Menzies years. For instance, the most persistent issue running through the Menzies correspondence was neither, as might perhaps be assumed, the future of the British Empire, nor even anti-communism, powerful as these themes were. The topic that exercised writers most regularly was rather the level of the old age pension and the difficulty of trying to live on it. Constant cries of distress on this point echo throughout the correspondence. At the same time, many issues rarely surfaced at all in the letters; discussion of Aboriginal affairs was notably absent.

Anthropologist James C Scott distinguished between the public transcript, representing a visible and possibly ritualised expression of conformity to official ideology, and the hidden transcript, referring to the private 'off-stage' conversations of citizens in which a more subversive discourse may be concealed.[43] When Menzies' correspondents (or at least most of them) went to the polls to vote Liberal, they were performing a public transcript of loyalty to Menzies and their political cause; in their personal letters, however, they expressed the hidden transcript of their misgivings and demands for change.

Menzies had some inkling of the historical importance of his own correspondence. He replied on one occasion to Lady Emily Lutyens:

'What a pity we have so substantially abandoned the art of the letter; all the more to be called "art", because of its unselfconsciousness, and its importance (unexpected at the time) as a source of social history!'[44] Historians can only endorse the prime minister's sentiments, and they apply to the thousands of letters he received from ordinary Australians. Their cries of pain, their anxieties, prejudices and unspoken assumptions form the subject of this book. In what follows, I will dissect the main themes of the correspondence, the rhetorical strategies employed to capture the prime minister's attention and sympathy, and the structures of belief which they reveal. Firstly, however, the corpus of letters itself must be presented.

2

'Dear Mr Ming'

THE PROFILE OF THE ORDINARY WRITER

Twenty-two thousand letters

There is much more to letters than the words inscribed on their pages. Beyond the content, the physical features of correspondence also give us clues about the level of familiarity or formality which correspondents assumed or desired between themselves and the prime minister. This is true of any epistolary exchange: its character, rhythm and duration are dictated not just by the subject matter, but also by such factors as the forms of address and farewell, the length of the message and the quality, colour and size of the paper. These aspects in turn express the social status of each writer, and the status gap between writer and sender. The material qualities of letters often indicate the unwritten reciprocal assumptions shared between correspondents about the exchange itself and how it should be conducted. These assumptions make up the social grammar of letter-writing, and they both bring the exchange into being and govern its progress. They form the substance of a tacit 'epistolary pact' between correspondents. Naturally, in the case of writing upwards, the inequalities between addressee and recipient guarantee that in practice reciprocity is very limited. Even, however, when writers only sent Menzies a single letter with little hope of a reply, their choice of paper as well as their choice of words signalled the kind of relationship they desired to have with the prime minister.

Who, then, wrote to Menzies? Where did they come from and what particular moments inspired them to write? This chapter aims to sketch a broad statistical profile of the correspondents, the rhythm and frequency of their letters, as well as the materials they chose for the task. It will suggest that ordinary writers expected to be on surprisingly familiar terms with their prime minister; but, at the same time, the letters also expressed due deference to Menzies and his illustrious titles. In order to outline a profile of the ordinary writer, and the choices of paper and materials which he or she made, a foray into quantitative methods is necessary.

The main archival series of 88 document boxes contains inward correspondence to Menzies during his second term of office as prime minister, and beyond. These were the letters worth bringing to Menzies' attention and which possibly demanded a response. Sometimes they required further action, for example they were referred to a minister or government department. Sometimes they just needed to be filed for reference. Just occasionally, they contained information so disturbing as to warrant referral to ASIO (Australian Security Intelligence Organisation). These are the letters I have analysed in this study. Altogether, they amount to over 19 000 items. Even this does not give us a complete picture of Menzies' mailbag. There are additional files of 70th birthday wishes, as well as collections of congratulations and get-well messages. The total correspondence archive includes further files marked 'no reply' which consist mainly of letters from eccentrics and religious fanatics. If we add all this documentation together, the corpus of the Menzies correspondence analysed here consists of 19 363 letters. I have counted, read or reviewed all of them and I draw on them throughout this book. On top of this, there are hundreds of letters which Menzies received on his elevation in 1963 to the Knighthood of the Thistle – an ancient order into which many Scottish aristocrats had been inducted as well as, in more recent years, members of the royal family such as Prince Philip, Prince Charles, Princess Anne and Prince William, Duke of Cambridge. Finally, there are dozens more boxes of invitations which Menzies usually declined. I have included neither the 'Thistle' letters nor the invitations in my analysis, but if I had done so, they would probably bring the total up to 22 000 items or more.

Menzies' incoming correspondence was exquisitely filed by his highly professional staff. In the main archival series, it was classified year by year, sorted alphabetically by the surname of the sender, and stapled to a carbon copy of the reply, always on green paper.

The correspondence includes letters of all sizes, telegrams, air letters, 'with compliments' slips and cards for different occasions – for birthdays, Christmas, Easter, *bon voyage* cards, welcome home cards and small visiting cards bearing a scribbled message. Ordinary writers did not always obey the standard rules of epistolary etiquette, and they exploited any material which came to hand. In Queensland, Lawrence Johnston received a letter from Menzies about his pension, and used the blank spaces on the page for his reply, writing his own message in purple ink all around the typed text of the ministerial letter.[1] Some correspondents simply tore a page from a ruled exercise book. Bill Newling, a former bus conductor, wrote to Menzies on a piece of brown wrapping paper.[2] The archive is a great leveller: missives like Bill Newling's piece of brown paper sit side by side with the occasional telegram from Her Majesty Queen Elizabeth II.

The graph overleaf shows the annual distribution of the 19 363 letters in the main archival series.

After a stuttering start, the incoming tide of letters reached its highest water mark in 1954 (2470 letters), the year not only of the Petrov Affair but also of the royal visit of the Queen and Prince Philip. Then, after two more uncertain years in 1956 and 1957, the correspondence settled down to a regular rhythm of between 1000 and 1500 letters received annually. The totals are naturally low for 1949 (106 letters), since Menzies assumed office only in December of

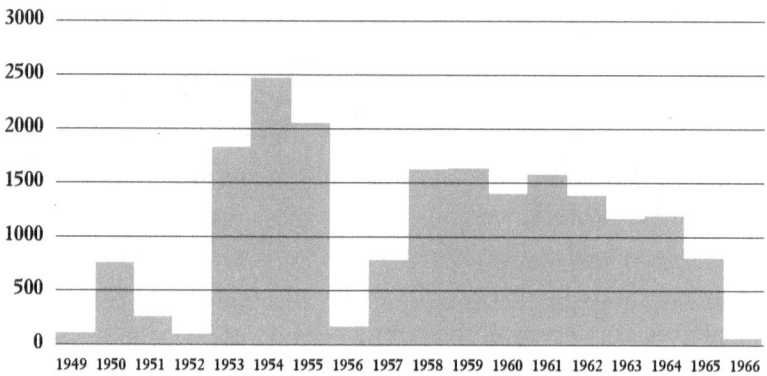

Letters to Menzies: Annual Volume

that year, and also for 1966 (64 letters), when he retired on Australia Day, 26 January. I have only taken account of correspondence received during his tenure of office as prime minister. The low totals of letters for 1952 and 1956 (101 and 173 letters respectively) are surprising and harder to explain. One possible explanation is that neither of these was an election year – an unusual event since there was a legislative election of one kind or another in almost every year of Menzies' term, and elections always acted as a spur to correspondents. This remains a weak explanation, however, because 1959 and 1960 were also election-free years, and correspondents nevertheless remained very active in those years. I speculate that some letters from 1956 are missing from the otherwise immaculate archive, possibly because Menzies was out of the country for an unusually long time. He remained overseas for four months after the Suez crisis forced him to extend his regular trip to Britain for the Commonwealth Prime Ministers' Conference. In other years, he would receive letters wherever he might be in the world, and they eventually found their way back into the files; perhaps this time some went missing in transit.[3]

My qualitative commentary on the correspondence is based on my reading of all 19 363 letters; there has been no triage or selection.

THE PROFILE OF THE ORDINARY WRITER

Some questions, however, demand statistical answers and for this quantitative part of my analysis some sampling has been necessary. To this end, I have conducted a simple statistical survey of three sample years, one at the beginning of the period (1949–1950, 863 letters), one in the middle (1958, 1623 letters) and one near the end (1964, 1195 letters). Altogether, these three years provide a total of 3681 letters, which is a solid sample of about 19 per cent of the main series of correspondence. The figures cited below are based on an analysis of these years, and the chronological span they cover allows a glimpse of one or two significant developments in the correspondence over the 16 years of Menzies' unbroken term.

The ordinary writer in profile

Menzies received many letters from collective or institutional bodies – ministries, embassies, government departments, businesses, churches and other non-government organisations. These collective letters regularly accounted for about 30 per cent of the correspondence (29.9 to be precise). This study does not neglect these sources of letters, but I am more interested in the letters from private individuals which made up the remaining 70 per cent (2579 letters in the three-year sample). These individual letters are where the Forgotten People expressed their grievances and aspirations, and where ordinary writers embarked on the unfamiliar challenge of writing personally to the prime minister.

Men wrote most of the letters, perpetuating an imbalance which has probably existed since the very beginnings of all written communication. It reflects the historical male domination of politics, public administration and capitalist enterprise. Even if we only consider letters from private individuals, 71.7 per cent were written by men, compared to 28.8 per cent by women, with a small residue of cases where the author's gender cannot be determined.[4] This disproportion remained fairly consistent across the years. The first characteristic of the ordinary writer's profile thus emerges: the writer was more than twice as likely to be a man than a woman.

There was a strong overseas presence in the Menzies correspondence. The number of overseas correspondents fluctuated, but overall they were responsible for one in five of all letters (21.3 per cent). 'Londoners love Mr Menzies', reported Norma Norris when she returned home to Warburton (Victoria) after her holiday in England in 1964, and British correspondents regularly addressed Menzies on a range of topics, including the possibility of an assisted passage to Australia.[5] British correspondents, some from Conservative Party circles and others from would-be emigrants, dominated the cohort of overseas writers, accounting for 45.4 per cent of all letters of foreign origin and rising to over 50 per cent of them in two out of the three sampled years. The USA produced just 22 per cent, and British Commonwealth countries like New Zealand and Canada dominated the rest. In fact almost two-thirds (64 per cent) of overseas letters originated from Britain or the Commonwealth, which is a good indication of Menzies' personal network as well as of his general world view.

Letters with an Australian postmark outnumbered overseas letters by about three to one, accounting for 76.9 per cent of the sample. They originated overwhelmingly from Victoria (35.2 per cent of Australian letters) or New South Wales (30.5 per cent), although Victoria's share was in slow decline. A rising proportion of letters came from Canberra (14 per cent), for example from government departments and parliamentarians. This change illustrates the slow bureaucratisation of the correspondence, in the sense that the direct and personal contact with Menzies to which correspondents eagerly aspired in 1949–50 was gradually interrupted and partially superseded in the corpus by epistolary conversations between public servants. Since almost 80 per cent of the Australian letters came from Victoria, New South Wales or the Australian Capital Territory, voices from other states were much more rarely heard. As a result, Menzies was far more likely to receive a letter from England than one from either Queensland, South Australia, Western Australia, Tasmania or the Northern Territory, which between them accounted for 19 per cent of Australian letters. Among the Victorian correspondents who loomed so large among ordinary writers, there was always a kernel of constituents from Menzies' own Kooyong electorate. 'Kooyong letters' made up 10.2 per cent of the Australian total, although their number fell at the end of the period, when the flow of requests for a faster local telephone connection dried up.

A fragile epistolary literacy

Menzies had a few very persistent correspondents, but the vast majority of ordinary writers (81.9 per cent) sent only a single letter each. About one in eight of them (12.6 per cent) wrote a second letter and a small minority (5.5 per cent) sent three or more. Their letters were usually short: 59 per cent of them were confined to a single page, not counting numerous telegrams and cards carrying very brief messages. They chose a wide variety of paper sizes, and there were many available, since Australia did not adopt A4 as the standard paper size until 1971. Nevertheless, 64 per cent of letters were on medium-sized paper, encompassing A4, US letter and variations on both. A substantial minority of 29.2 per cent of letters used a more intimate and smaller size, close to today's A5. A large paper size, foolscap or US Legal, was favoured by government departments and accounts for 6.7 per cent of letters.

The majority of letters had a formal letterhead, perhaps an individual's address (printed or cheaply embossed), a business address, or occasionally the letterhead of a ship or a hotel. On the whole, however, the correspondence is distinguished by a high degree of informality, especially from untutored hands. Individual and inexperienced writers often used lined paper, which accounted for over 20 per cent of all letters in 1949–50, although the proportion fell to 11.5 per cent by 1964. Over six per cent preferred coloured paper, almost always blue, although a lighter shade of grey was fashionable in 1964. Neither lined nor coloured paper can be considered conventional materials for formal letters. Sometimes they came from commonly available, small format notepads – the kind of paper one might use to jot down a note or make a list.

A few letters were even written in pencil, although more often they were handwritten in ink or typed. Although the correspondence certainly illustrates the inexorable rise of the typewriter, handwriting retained an enduring popularity. Some considered a handwritten letter more personal and informal than a letter typed on a machine. GD McKinnon of the Victorian Presbyterian Church wanted to send a letter with a personal touch, and explained: 'Having posted a typewritten letter to you this morning – somewhat hurriedly – second thoughts suggest that it smacked of being too "official"'. He rectified the situation by sending a handwritten letter.[6] Archbishop O'Brien (of Canberra and Goulburn) was under the mistaken impression that a handwritten letter was more likely to receive Menzies' exclusive attention, and he wrote, 'I have written, rather than typed, this letter, because I want it to be personal and not subject to the observation of others'.[7] In the 1949–50 sample, letters composed by hand were even in the majority, but this did not last long and overall handwriting was the preferred method for 43.4 per cent of all letters. Within this number, the domination of the biro over the fountain pen was secure. Biro was used for 62 per cent of manuscript letters in 1964.[8]

Many writers showed that they were not entirely familiar with the letter-writing process and its protocols. In other words, their level of 'epistolary literacy' was weak. By far the most common signs of inexperience and departures from the norm were the lack of any margins and a complete absence of paragraph indentation. More than a quarter of all manuscript letters (28.15 per cent) showed signs of one or another of these characteristics, and they usually went hand in hand. A few more writers failed to keep a straight line and others wrote either in a very cramped script or a very large one – both signs of unfamiliarity with the medium and poor control of the *mise-en-page*. Several writers had a shaky or scrawly hand, in some cases due to old age and natural frailty. A handful of letters used cross-writing, which is normally considered a sign of familiarity between friends, but frowned upon in more formal business correspondence. A couple were written entirely in block capitals. Fifteen letters exhibited symptoms of poor epistolary competence to the point of being virtually unintelligible. These included letters penned by inmates of mental institutions; their incomprehensible letters were dutifully forwarded to the prime minister in recognition of every citizen's right to petition Parliament. Using a typewriter, of course, was not necessarily any guarantee of accuracy or good epistolary literacy. Even accomplished poet Mary Gilmore typed a letter full of errors, when she wrote to recommend the work of Byram Mansell, an artist who used Aboriginal motifs and materials.[9] Overall, the combination of a biro and lined paper in small or medium format was a popular choice and this suggested an informal approach to Menzies.

Many letters demonstrated an imperfect grasp of English and spelling errors were abundant, in this age before automatic spell-checks. Capital letters might be distributed throughout the text quite indiscriminately. As with examples of 'writing from below' encountered in other contexts, the letters were also uncertain about punctuation and sometimes liberated themselves completely from the rules of grammar.[10] GH Parry of Merrylands (New South Wales), to take one example, who apparently thought somebody had been forging his signature, wrote:

> I saw Mr Ryan head of police Parramatta he told me to see my solicitor but he said case was to big for him Police and soluitons wont help so I thougt case for bigger man

This case is long over due it time some one dine about it [...]

your faifully, GH Parry.[11]

Writers with a grievance wanted to be 'compassated', or they complained that the attitudes of 'offissialdom' were far from 'addiquett'. They wrote 'leased' for least, 'sincear' for sincere, 'ledgeslation' for legislation or 'hole' for whole. They were frustrated if a request was 'refewsed'. Staunch Liberal supporters detested Labor 'polatishons', and especially denounced the 'hipocery' of Labor leader Evatt. They often had difficulty with names of foreign places and individuals. The correct English spelling of Khrushchev often defeated them, but in fairness it would have challenged any scholar. For one writer, however, Khrushchev's base was in 'Mossgow' – which conjured up an imaginary New South Wales town somewhere between Moss Vale and Lithgow. 'Mr K' was not all Menzies had to watch out for: there could be trouble from 'Chiner' and the 'Japanease' as well.

Greetings and farewells

A combination of familiarity and deference surfaced in the choice of forms of address and farewell, two key moments of any letter which both illustrate and shape the relationship (actual or desired) between writer and recipient. The combination appears in condensed form in 'Dear Mr Ming', in which Lillias Griffiths neatly incorporated Menzies' intimate nickname into a polite form of address.[12] The wide variety of forms of address – over 60 of them were adopted in 1958 and the same number in 1964 – indicates some difficulty, both in Australia and overseas, in deciding how to approach a prime minister of Australia. 'Honorable Sir', wrote Mrs Rogers of Perth, 'You will have to excuse me for the way I have addressed this note to you as I really do not know how to go about it', and she added, 'Please don't make this note public, as I know it is not properly written'.[13] Writing to prime ministers was not an everyday activity.

In formulating a suitable greeting, writers chose one of five main options, listed here in rough order of importance: 'the 'remote' option, the 'orthodox' option, the 'surname' option, a greeting addressed directly to a secretary and lastly the 'friendly' option. The 'remote' option was favoured by over a third (34.2 per cent) of letter-writers, who opted for a 'Dear Sir', an 'Honorable Sir' or a 'Highly respected Sir'. This was a deferential and usually impersonal method of approach. 'Honorable Sir' was particularly characteristic of Indonesian correspondents, but when they signed off 'Honorable from me' it became clear that the writer had not fully understood the English phrase. The 'remote' category includes the 'Your Excellency' formula to which uncertain overseas correspondents sometimes resorted. It also includes the 'Dear Highness' extravagantly offered by one correspondent, and 'Your Majesty', obsequiously used by one Indian woman seeking mint postage stamps for charities.[14] However low she might bow before the royal Menzies, her request was nevertheless denied. The figures are skewed, however, in 1964, after Menzies had received a knighthood. Writers seized on the opportunity to bow before his new title. 'Dear Sir Robert' now became by far the most popular form of address. Together with other forms using the title 'sir', it utterly eclipsed 'Dear Mr Menzies', which had now fallen into almost complete disuse. Instead of becoming more friendly as time went on, forms of address thus grew more deferential, highlighting Menzies' status and his honorific title.

The 'orthodox' method of addressing Menzies, by which I mean references to his prime ministerial office, was adopted by exactly 20 per cent of all letters. 'Dear Prime Minister' or 'My Dear Prime Minister', with a few variations, played upon his eminent position but remained distant. This was the mode especially favoured by cabinet colleagues and subordinates in the public service. I include here the formula 'Monsieur le président de la république australienne', which probably raised at least one of Menzies' famous eyebrows, and was especially used in 1958 by a group of French schoolchildren from the Aisne department.

The third 'surname' option, in which correspondents opened with 'Dear Mr Menzies' or variations thereof, led the field at the start (36.3 per cent of letters in 1949–50) but, as already noted, virtually disappeared after Menzies was knighted. Upper-class British friends were inclined to write simply 'Dear Menzies' in English public-school style. It sounded abrupt, but in a British upper-class context, it can be taken as a friendly greeting. 'Dear Mr Meengus' was another variation, clearly an attempt to capture the Scottish pronunciation of his surname.

A rising proportion of letters were addressed to one of Menzies' secretaries by name, and this form appeared in 9.2 per cent of all letters. Normally one of the main purposes of writing upwards was to establish direct personal contact with a supreme authority, and to by-pass secretaries and officialdom altogether. This notion of a personal hotline to the top is discussed in chapter 4. An increasing number of letters to the secretary suggests once more that the correspondence was experiencing a subtle process of bureaucratisation, in which more correspondents were learning to play the system rather than try to sidestep it completely. Letters to secretaries were not always accurately addressed. As far as the public was concerned, the secretaries still remained shadowy figures and their names and genders were not widely publicised. Hence Hazel Craig was mistakenly addressed as 'Dear Mr Craig', and Frank Jennings as 'Dear Miss Jennings'. In spite of such errors, a steadily increasing number of ordinary writers began to see the secretary not as an obstacle but an essential intermediary whose support might prove valuable. He or she was a potential accomplice 'on the inside' in the task of winning Menzies' confidence.

As well as the 'remote', the 'orthodox', the 'surname' options and letters addressed to a secretary, about 10 per cent of all letters

(9.9 precisely) struck a much more friendly register. These were the 'Dear Bob' or 'Dear R.G.' letters, and these forms were used not only by acquaintances but sometimes by complete strangers. If they felt slightly embarrassed by it, they put it in inverted commas, thus: 'Dear "Bob"'. I include here the 'Dear old friend' letters, sent by Menzies' fellow cricket enthusiast and journalist from Ceylon, Peter Foenander. For him, the friendly form of address was a way of ingratiating himself by recalling former meetings with Menzies, and he used the friendship to seek permission to emigrate to Australia for Ceylonese Burgher (i.e. mixed race) families.[15] His overtures usually failed, victims of a restrictive immigration policy which discriminated against coloured people. I include here a small number of letters from Menzies' relatives, not forgetting the man from Honolulu Cricket Club who began casually with 'aloha', and the angry pensioner who greeted the prime minister as 'Bro Menzie' – in this case a deliberately provocative form of familiarity.[16]

Forms of greeting began to register the presence of Menzies' wife Pattie and daughter Heather, as 'Dame Pattie' was included in the greeting and occasionally letters were addressed to her in her own right. Although such instances barely exceeded one per cent of all letters overall, they testify to her public presence.

If we turn to common forms of concluding a letter and farewelling Menzies, it is banal to record the overwhelming victory of 'Yours sincerely' and its variations.[17] This form left 'Yours faithfully' and 'Yours truly' utterly defeated in its wake, accounting for a clear majority (59.6 per cent) of all conclusions. 'Dear Sir Robert', together with 'Yours sincerely' eventually became the normal and conventional way to greet and farewell Menzies. It is more interesting to record the enormous range of other farewells adopted, in which writers resisted the forces of standardisation represented by 'Yours sincerely', in order to express individual feelings and more idiosyncratic concerns. They often felt deferential, offering Menzies their regards and esteem, not to mention their admiration and obedience, expressions of an enthusiastic self-abasement. Over 20 correspondents of the old school still signed 'Your (most) obedient servant'. Others signed 'Yours respectfully', or perhaps they just intended to do so in the case of 'Yours respectively'. They signed gratefully or hopefully and, once again, some very familiar farewells intruded among the floor-scraping, as correspondents sent good wishes, affection, love and sometimes lots of it. In the 1964 sample, there were no fewer than 98 different forms of farewell.

There was a Christian style of farewell, as in 'Yours in Christ' or 'Yours devotedly in God's vineyard', which tried to make Menzies complicit in the writers' Christian agendas. At the same time, there was room for the angry farewell ('Yours in deep anger'), the disgusted farewell ('Yours in disgust') and also the heart-wrenching, as in 'Yours so very sad at heart', from a recently bereaved widow. The yoga exponent who wanted to visit Menzies to explain the benefits of his craft signed with 'Yours in Yoga', while Thelma Saunders, who regularly cast Menzies as her imaginary father, signed 'Your daughter Thelma'.[18] There was a Scottish farewell ('Yours aye') and a patriot's farewell, as demonstrated by the correspondent who concluded with a rallying cry 'For God, the Queen and sanity'.[19] The farewell could always be used to claim Menzies' attention by signalling a past affiliation or shared experience, as in 'your old Jeparit pal', a reference to the village in western Victoria where Menzies had grown up.

An identikit portrait of a typical Menzies correspondent would show him as a male, living in Victoria or New South Wales, although significant numbers of writers were women, and British. Correspondents did not always divulge their age, so all we can say on this topic is that they ranged from nine to 90 years old – from young schoolchildren asking for an autograph or help with a school assignment, to very elderly women struggling on a pension or just reminiscing about the politics of a bygone era. It is unfortunately impossible to give an exact overall account of writers' social status, even though a few offered plentiful autobiographical information.

THE PROFILE OF THE ORDINARY WRITER

They wrote at specific times and in specific places. Harold Wright in Brisbane wrote in the midst of family duties, apologising because his young daughter had scribbled on the page while he was out of the room.[20] Many writers took advantage of a period of enforced idleness, writing from a hospital bed. 'I've typed this in bed with a temperature of 101 – what a bore!' wrote the High Commissioner for South Africa.[21] Far away in Devon, one correspondent hurried to sign off because 'my nurse is due to give me injection etc.'.[22] They wrote on ocean liners, using the ship's letterhead, and on long-distance flights. Sir Philip Hay, on his way to Singapore, recorded that his message was 'written in an aircraft somewhere above Simpson's Desert'.[23]

There was a great deal of immediacy about Joyce Atkinson's prolific series of letters which she very often timed, usually in the early hours of the morning. 'I shall now bid you Goodmorning [...] Its 2.15 am', she specified, perhaps enjoying a rare moment of peaceful solitude on her Queensland dairy farm to deliver another harangue.[24] She timed other letters at midnight, 2.40 am or a little later. 'It is somewhat early in the morn', she wrote in December 1955. 'Round about the 5.30 am mark on this eventful day.'[25] This was election day, when the Labor Party split and Democratic Labor Party preferences would deliver an unexpected victory for Menzies. Writers like Mrs Atkinson described their surroundings and added details of the times and places of writing which invited the reader to visualise them at their task, and to appreciate the effort they were making to communicate with the prime minister.

Throughout the correspondence a gradual trend towards greater bureaucratisation can be detected. Canberra and the sources of government provided a growing element in the correspondence, thereby reducing the share of letters received from private individuals and from other parts of the country. At the same time, correspondents began to recognise the presence of secretaries and their power to filter communication between the citizen and Menzies. The fiction of personal and direct access to the leader was effectively abandoned by an increasing number of writers. In spite of this, the myth of the personal hotline to the top continued to inspire ordinary writers to pick up their biros.

3

'You are the only saviour of the country'

FAN MAIL AND CONGRATULATIONS

The saviour of the country

Letters and telegrams of congratulation expressed the joy and relief of Liberal supporters whenever Menzies scored a political success, which he did with unprecedented regularity. An election victory, a successful speech or a significant anniversary stimulated followers to write their appreciation and admiration for their leader. One (male) supporter recorded that 'Listening to your Policy Speech last Tuesday I was so impressed that the tears rolled down my cheek with joy'.[1] In the hands of Menzies, politics was a drama which could move and inspire its audience. Letters of praise and adoration cast him as a hero and a providential saviour. Menzies was respected, loved as a son, and revered as an oracle and a source of inspiration.

Of course, this was not the only kind of letter in his mailbox, but this chapter will examine only the positive messages Menzies received, leaving letters of protest and dissent to be considered elsewhere. Congratulatory letters referred mainly to Menzies' achievements, but a significant body of letter-writers was interested in Menzies personally, his appearance, his tastes, his family and his health. It may seem incongruous to associate Menzies with the kind of celebrity today reserved only for film stars and popular singers, since by reputation he was aloof rather than engaging, and never aspired to the common touch. Nevertheless, his supporters wrote some genuine fan mail. Gordon Richardson bought a tartan tie donated by Menzies to a fund-raising auction on behalf of Sydney Grammar Preparatory School. Why did he want it? It was an urge 'comparable with the mob clawing for the crockery and bed linen used by the Beatles in America'.[2] Women fetishised the letters he sent them. One woman in a Presbyterian Home for the Elderly confessed, 'I keep your two letters […] in a private drawer, and read them over again, when down in the dumps, and they have a very beneficial effect […] You have such admirers here, 47 auld women!'[3] Menzies was unfamiliar with this kind of personal attention, which surfaced immediately after his 1949 election win, and he took a little time to adjust to it. But before long he was taking it in his stride, and successfully exploiting both radio and the new medium of television to enhance his personal appeal.

Each election victory produced a flood of congratulations but none, perhaps, was sweeter for Liberal supporters than the first which brought Menzies and the newly formed Liberal Party to power in December 1949. Religious voters perceived the win as a Christian victory, and voters thanked the Almighty for Menzies' success. Mrs Lawrence of Turramurra (New South Wales) saw the victory as a response to prayers for divine intervention, and added:

> Remembering God's Goodness through days of prayer
> during the war, we would like to see our new Government
> begin its reign by calling the Churches to a day of prayer and
> thanksgiving to our Omnipotent, Omniscient God, for all His
> wonderful goodness, including our wool and wheat harvest.[4]

There were several requests for special prayers to be recited in churches and in Parliament itself, but behind them lay the spirit of Protestant sectarianism and a fear that God would punish the sins of Australia's recent past. Bert de Plater, a member of the machine room staff on the Sydney *Sun*, suggested that parliamentary proceedings should open with a daily prayer, and wrote congratulating Menzies on the injection of some spirituality into politics. 'Australia', he said, 'has been paying the price of her national sins, or shall I say "lack of spirituality", and no nation or individual can afford to do just that and get away with it'.[5] Christians and Christian organisations responded to those of Menzies' speeches which had envisaged restoring a sense of spirituality to Australian politics. Mr Skerman praised Menzies' 'inheritant [sic] versatility in statesmanship' and urged him to revive his 'dormant spirit of righteousness' to help suffering people escape from captivity and bondage.[6]

As this biblical vocabulary suggests, Menzies was hailed as the Australian Moses leading his people out of slavery in Egypt. There was a similar reaction to the Liberal success in the Senate elections of May 1953, even though the results showed a swing to Labor. Norman O'Brien turned to Exodus chapter 13 to characterise Menzies as 'A pillar of cloud by day and a pillar of fire by night you have led Australia out of the wilderness'.[7] 'The battle is the Lord's and He will fight for you', Miss Shayler of Eastwood (New South Wales) assured him.[8] Menzies was a national saviour and, in spite of evil threats, the Israelites were on track to find the Promised Land. 'God bless and keep you to victory', wrote a Catholic voter in the aftermath of the Petrov Affair when the fear of communism loomed large, 'you are the only saviour of the country and our children every one seems to have turned away from God, and we must fall'.[9] Churches promised to hold prayers for a coalition victory and, once it was achieved, writers wrote homilies to keep Menzies humble and urge him to remain steadfast in the faith.

Menzies received congratulations on his election victories, on his continuing term of office, which broke all records for longevity, and on the appearance of his book of speeches entitled *Speech is of Time*, published in 1958. He was regularly complimented on distinguished orations (the Newland Oration in 1958, the Smuts Memorial Lecture in Cambridge in 1961, the Jefferson Oration in 1963), and each time writers asked for a copy of his text. He was patted on the back for political speeches where he disposed of hecklers, and for media appearances where he was judged to have defeated the journalists' attacks. Professor Harry Messel at Sydney University sent a long telegram congratulating the government on accepting the Murray report on increased funding for higher education. Menzies, he said, will usher in a new era for universities just as the Soviet Sputnik ushered in a new era for science.[10] 'Dear Friend', wrote a Melbourne woman at the time of the Liberals' 1958 election win, 'Once again the year is drawing to a close. I think of you as I have done of years gone by. I was so very happy knowing once again such a clear good soul as you was returned to us again'.[11] She concluded with wishes for the good health of Menzies and his wife Dame Pattie – a personal touch which was a frequent addition to political messages.

On several occasions, congratulations took the form of an extended cricketing metaphor. Menzies had had a splendid innings and was still not out. He had already made a good score but nobody wanted him to retire to the pavilion and take off his pads just yet. The bowling side would undoubtedly test him with some 'curly ones' and his skill was still required. The opposition, though, was no match for him, and one fan lamented: 'What a pity old Chif is not still leading the other side, It would make a better game. He could lead a team well. He only had Reserves and he made it a winning side. [...] The game lost a Star Player when he retired'.[12] Menzies respected Chifley and might have agreed. Cricketing fans now assured him that the current opposition eleven would struggle to avoid the follow-on (in other words, they were facing a crushing defeat).

FAN MAIL AND CONGRATULATIONS

In 1963, Menzies was elevated to the Knighthood of the Thistle, an ancient and relatively obscure Scottish order, which produced a torrent of over 3000 congratulatory messages and telegrams from all parts of the world (my estimate).[13] Australians clearly identified this honour as Scottish, but they also saw it as a recognition of Australia as a whole, not just of Menzies personally. DS Caithness of Sydney saw it as adding 'another rung to the ladder of Australian history'.[14] The event gave rise to a spate of feeble thistle jokes, warning Menzies to beware of the prickles and reminding him that the thistle was classed as a noxious weed.

A procession of notable anniversaries fell in 1964, drawing ever more congratulations: it was 30 years since Menzies first entered federal Parliament, 25 years since he first took office as prime minister, and on top of all that he reached another milestone – his 70th birthday. This would have been the *annus mirabilis* of Menzies congratulations, if not for the ill health, which, among other things, forced the cancellation of his intended visit to Israel. The secretariat was busy. Not only did elections and the Commonwealth Prime Ministers' Conference keep Menzies from dealing with his personal correspondence, but influenza also gave the secretaries extra work explaining that Menzies was too ill to respond to all letters in person. How long could he go on? 'Take it easy, old boy, we need you', advised Frank Packer in a letter from London.[15]

Fan mail

The fan mail began to arrive in 1950, almost immediately after the electoral success of the previous December. Complete strangers asked him for an autographed photograph of himself. At first, Menzies ignored them, and in fact the secretariat had none to distribute, but by August 1951, he was complying.[16] A 13-year-old admirer from Brisbane wrote to ask for one in very careful and accurate handwriting. She demonstrated her precocious political knowledge of Menzies' legislation plans and confessed her ambition to become a Liberal member for Brisbane. Her father framed the photograph that Menzies sent and she hung it in her room. Menzies hoped she would fulfil her ambitions.[17] He nevertheless made it a general rule that photo-portraits would only be autographed for people he knew.

As well as the requests for a photo of Menzies, a multitude of personal gifts arrived from followers everywhere. After a visit to South Africa, a well-wisher there sent him elephant tusks as a souvenir.[18] From Queensland, a supporter sent mangoes for Christmas.[19] Mary Morgan, a centenarian from South Australia, sent Menzies a piece of her 100th birthday cake.[20] Sister Mary of Brisbane sent a miraculous medallion and advised Menzies to put it in his inside pocket to guarantee Our Blessed Lady's protection.[21] The news of Menzies' fragile health had evidently circulated because, at exactly the same time in winter 1954, another concerned Catholic sent a St Christopher medal, which Menzies presumably never used because it remains pinned to the correspondence.[22] Irene Bilinsky recommended that the Liberal Party should actively promote a personality cult around Menzies.[23] After all, she argued, it had worked for Gandhi, Hitler and Stalin, but these were not exactly encouraging precedents for Menzies.

Supporters sent a constant flow of their poems, to mark royal occasions and to celebrate the beauties of Australia. Frances Lambert in England sent her verse on 'Your Beautiful Land, Australia' even though she had never actually visited the country. She had suffered writer's block after the death of her husband, but after three years she was suddenly inspired to write 45 poems and songs. Menzies was a lucky beneficiary (or victim?) of her new-found inspiration.[24] Writers sent poems about 'Winston', British bulldog poems, 'Lest We Forget' poems that mythologised the Anzacs, and there were inevitably poems about Menzies himself. Mrs Balfour wrote one defending Menzies' dress sense which had come under fire,[25] and Beth Stanger wittily saw Menzies as the safety valve for all Australia's ills, in her memorable tongue-in-cheek ballad, 'Put the Blame on Menzies':

> Don't worry any longer when things are going wrong,
> – When your wisdom tooth is aching, or the summer seems too long –
> It will make you feel much better, and relieve your own distress,
> If you put the blame on Menzies, when your world is in a mess.
>
> So if the country wobbles, and its wheels begin to squeak,
> If the level of production isn't always at its peak,
> If your baby gets the measles, or your terrier has fleas,
> Don't ponder on the reasons – just blame the credit squeeze.[26]

Unfortunately, popular poets rarely reached this level of verve and humour. Stanger later went on to self-publish more of her work.

What correspondents wanted most of all was to meet Menzies in person, and he received several invitations to visit the homes of his fans. One was Gertrude Hart, a serial correspondent, who invited Menzies to tea, and obligingly gave him directions to her home Afterglow in Victoria's Dandenongs:

> And you won't forget that you promised to one day bring Mrs Menzies up for afternoon tea? Yes, I know – every hour must be packed with two hours' work [...] but I should feel as if Royalty had been Afterglow is very easily found – turn off the Main Road at the Viola Café, Sassafras – drive down till you come to the fourth block; and there will be a big welcome.[27]

When Menzies left for an overseas trip, he received 'bon voyage' cards and when he returned, there were messages to welcome him home. Birthday and Christmas cards arrived, and congratulations on the wedding of his daughter Heather in May 1955. Sometimes the mail expressed the desire for an even more intensely personal relationship with Menzies. For instance, a recent Hungarian immigrant asked Menzies to act as godfather to his son, but Menzies declined.[28] Writing from aboard the SS *Orcades*, a Mrs Ashby told Menzies that she had named her Siamese cat 'Ming' – Menzies' confidential nickname.[29] The prime minister's reaction to this intended compliment is unknown. In 1959 a minor debate surfaced about Menzies' fashion sense. He favoured double-breasted suits, which the press decided was highly unfashionable, although the clothing industry leapt to the prime minister's defence.[30] A supporter noted that one journalist who criticised Menzies' suits was 'probably of Jewish descent' – a rare example of antisemitism in the correspondence, to which I will return in chapter 11.[31]

The private details of his life were no longer private. Celebrity created a general interest in all things Menzies. A student of Newington College in Sydney begged for a lock of the prime minister's hair.[32] The *Women's Mirror* wanted to know what Menzies had been like as a baby: at what time of day was he born? How much did he weigh at birth? When did he learn to walk and talk? – the kind of questions for which Menzies had a low threshold of tolerance.[33] He had more important issues to consider than what seemed to be domestic trivia and he did not cooperate with the *Women's Mirror*'s inquiry. Ron Caldwell of Adelaide wrote of his visit to Canberra and of his delight at catching a glimpse of Menzies driving away in a car. He did not fail to visit the Lodge, 'and my wife took some photos of your house which we both thought was very pretty'.[34] Menzies' home, his family and his wardrobe were now subjected to public scrutiny.

So, too, was his kitchen, when fans asked for recipes. The Women's College of the University of Queensland was preparing a cookery book for fundraising purposes and invited Menzies to contribute his favourite recipe. Private secretary Everil Wilkinson passed this on with a cautious message: 'I imagine that

FAN MAIL AND CONGRATULATIONS

your knowledge of recipes is confined to those for cocktails and it is doubtful if it would please your Presbyterian friends if such appeared as your choice'. The solution was to defer to his wife, who was eventually persuaded to provide a recipe for salmon and pickle loaf.[35] This request, received in 1951, was the first of its kind, and the exchange between Wilkinson and the Menzies family suggests a sincere attempt to oblige. But at this stage Menzies was still feeling his way with his unexpected fan base. When further requests for recipes followed in future years, he would simply decline them.

How had Menzies achieved so much? Fans were eager to discover the secret of his success. Neville Glancy was attending a bank training course in 1957 and consulted his oracle for tips on how to make it to the top. Secretary William Heseltine replied for Menzies in conventional fashion: 'There is no short cut to success. Success can only be achieved by hard work and willingness to apply oneself to the task in hand'.[36] Such advice was absolutely consistent with Menzies' own pragmatism and Protestant work ethic.

Menzies' personal following was very concerned about the prime minister's state of health, especially when the press publicised an operation or an attack of influenza. The maternal impulse was to send him a woollen scarf, especially if he was travelling to the northern winter. Dagmar Levy wrote on New Year's Day 1953: 'But oh we do feel impelled to implore you to take care of your health & even if it meant such a calamity as your resignation from politics, that your life is of far greater importance to your family & all of us'.[37] He had indeed been ill at the end of the previous year, and he was to worry his followers again in 1957, when he collapsed after an exhausting trip to Asia, and a few months later was forced to undergo a tonsillectomy while in England. Menzies, however, was a determined survivor, and unlikely to be stopped for long by illness. He received plenty of motherly advice. 'Please remember and avoid the cold', instructed Edith Thomas as Menzies was preparing to leave for Britain, 'because it got the best of your strength last visit'.[38]

Mrs Eales was also disturbed to hear that Menzies had been sick, and urged him to look after himself on such trips because if anything he commanded even more personal respect in Britain than he did at home (as chapter 2 demonstrated, Menzies had a solid fan base in Britain). She added a short *curriculum vitae* to support her request for a job as maid to Dame Pattie.[39] As so often occurred in the Menzies correspondence, the affection and concern of a fan were spiked with a self-interested demand. In hybrid letters like this one, praise and compliments were the necessary prelude to the request for personal assistance.

Fan mail arrived from school students the world over. They asked for a photograph, an autograph or for some Australian stamps. Menzies' secretariat always sent them some material, and enclosed a few used stamps if they asked for them for a stamp collection. Such was Menzies' global fame that requests were received from many countries in western Europe and South America, as well as New Zealand, the USA, Canada, India, Indonesia and the Philippines. Students asked for assistance with a history or social sciences project. A Canadian schoolgirl wanted to know which way the water ran down the plughole when you emptied the bath in the southern hemisphere, and secretary Hazel Craig gave her a very serious response.[40]

The statesman and the orator

Letters praised Menzies for his perceived personal qualities, especially his dignity and courage in face of his enemies. He seemed every inch a statesman, with noble objectives, unselfish and high-minded. The Archbishop of Brisbane told him that 'I have always admired your loftiness of character and your repudiation of shams'.[41] 'I am sure', wrote another admirer at greater length, 'that you will gain greater distinction in History Books than any other living Australian of today', and he credited Menzies with foresight, bold decision-making and leadership which would 'awaken the People of Australia to their great destiny'. This writer's eulogy was not yet complete; he also remarked on 'your obvious contempt for self-gain; your Education and Breeding; your amazing powers of Oratory'.[42] All this was evident to the writer even though Menzies had not yet completed a full year in office. References to Menzies' 'breeding' and good manners suggest that his remoteness and elegant language, which alienated some voters, had great appeal for others. Emotional self-control and a 'culture of restraint' characterised the code of masculine behaviour in British politics, as historian Martin Francis has argued, and the idea can be extended to Australia.[43] Supporters contrasted Menzies' statesmanlike gravitas with the approach of the Labor Party, which they perceived as vulgar and demagogic.

Menzies had the courage to defy the evils of communism, which writers felt showed exceptional fighting spirit. Herbert Bake congratulated Menzies on standing up to the waterside workers in 1953: 'May I congratulate you on your courage in facing up to these "beggars" as no one previously has ever done in my 33 years in Australia. You are a Man! Long may you reign in office'.[44] After the coalition's post-Petrov election win of 1954, Menzies stocks reached a new peak. WW Drayton of Sydney concluded that 'Whatever faults Mr Menzies may possess – and if he possesses any, he keeps them well hidden – cowardice, moral nor physical has not been among them'.[45] Menzies, it was considered, was one of the bulldog breed, a quality often attributed to Winston Churchill. Walter Henderson pursued the canine metaphor, viewing Menzies as 'a bull-dog with the sagacity of a canny old sheep-dog, and a man with the qualities of of [sic] bold action, thought, patience, and infinite courage'.[46]

Menzies was often compared to Churchill, although he never got the better of the comparison. A 13-year-old school student from Ceylon kept Menzies abreast of his current standing among international political leaders, writing: 'I admire you as a statesman of great quality. And in my rankings for the "Man of the Year 1953",

I have ranked you a very close second to sir Winston Churchill, and president Eisenhower, who is 3rd'.[47] This was a highly competitive league to play in, but Menzies may not have been overjoyed at the frequency with which he came second, especially considering his differences with Churchill in London during the war years.

Fans praised his bravery and *sang-froid* under attack. 'I know that if I was in a shell-hole there are few I would rather have with me than you', wrote Harry McCurrie in 1958.[48] In his courage and dignity, Menzies matched a certain ideal of masculinity. He defiantly challenged an enemy (communism) renowned among his supporters for being devious, cunning and duplicitous. He had a reputation for remaining calm and detached, focusing on broad horizons rather than petty, everyday squabbles. At the same time, he was chivalrous according to the expectations of the 1950s, showing exactly the right measure of respect, deference and politeness to the opposite sex. This was particularly evident to some in his treatment of the young Queen Elizabeth during her visit of 1954. Women appreciated the way in which Menzies offered her his guidance and protection. 'How she would lean on your balanced judgment', wrote one female admirer, 'your polished good breeding [...] how she would enjoy your brilliant wit!'[49] Menzies was complimented not just as a political leader, but also as a man.

Menzies was appreciated as an impressive orator, and he was familiar with the very best literary models. Menzies' affection for Shakespeare was well known: he kept a copy of Shakespeare's complete works in his prime ministerial office, and it was not there just for display.[50] His private secretary Frank Jennings recalled his reading Shakespeare alone for half an hour to calm himself down during a particularly turbulent cabinet meeting.[51] Whenever he was in London, he would take the opportunity to see a Shakespeare performance at the Old Vic theatre.[52] Perhaps Menzies' well-advertised literary interests encouraged correspondents to believe that he valued the written word, and that he would appreciate their

FAN MAIL AND CONGRATULATIONS

poetry. Writers encouraged him with suitable quotations. In 1950, at the outset of Menzies' unsuccessful campaign to ban the Australian Communist Party (further discussed in chapter 9), Sir Norman Kater sent him an airletter from London which contained nothing but this text:

My dear Bob

Beware of entrance to a quarrel, but being in bear't that the opposed may beware of thee

Good luck to you.

The secretariat correctly identified the origin of this citation in *Hamlet*, Act 1, Scene 3, line 65, and Menzies replied that he would bear it in mind in times of strife.[53] The trade in Shakespeare citations was reciprocated; Menzies also supplied business executives with suitable phrases with which they could enhance their company reports.[54] At some point in his past, Menzies had rewritten the court scene from *The Merchant of Venice* as it might have taken place following modern legal procedure. Several correspondents were curious and probed him about this, but Menzies declined to divulge the text to them. Eventually, however, the fans got their way. When Kenneth Slessor approached Menzies with a view to publishing it in the quarterly *Southerly*, he relented and accepted the invitation.[55]

His appearance at a televised press conference broadcast by the BBC in 1955 won more supporters for his calm and well-spoken command of the debate. Seeing politicians being grilled by journalists on the silver screen was still a novelty, but supporters were delighted with Menzies' performance. 'You seemed somehow an imperturbable and unruffled giant among a group of rather scruffy pygmies!' enthused one English viewer.[56] Miss Fagnani of Bristol (UK) was greatly reassured by his TV performance, writing: 'With men like you and our <u>Dear Old Bulldog</u> Skipper [i.e. Churchill], there's great hope for the world, Humanity and Peace'.[57] Menzies' *alter ego* Churchill was haunting him once again. After his early reluctance, Menzies developed some skill in the art of television interviews. Frances McNicoll of Elizabeth Bay (New South Wales) certainly thought so, after watching his appearance on the *Press Conference* programme in 1964.

> By now, Sir, if I may say so, she wrote, you are an absolute master of television technique. The goodhumoured mastery of every reply is as engaging as it is impressive; while the little quizzical smiles and lifts of the eyebrow are irresistible – the unseen audience is thereby taken into your confidence, sharing the sardonic joke.[58]

Her initial phrase 'By now' suggested that this had been a learning curve which Menzies had successfully scaled.

Another viewer responded to one of his broadcasts in the self-deprecating style common to many ordinary writers of modest social status. 'Mainly I consider myself to be an average middle class housewife and mother', Mrs Brooks of Heidelberg (Victoria) began, 'and although not the most brilliant pupil of Ivanhoe Girls Grammar School, I also consider I have average intelligence'. Apart from insisting on her averagism, Mrs Brooks also emphasised her complete obscurity, continuing with:

> Mr Menzies although you don't know me and probably never will, you are most terribly important to me, to my son, my husband and everyone I love so dearly including Australia [...] you should give many more talks to the people of Australia much more regularly. Last night you explained everything simply and fully and to me this is important for the people of Australia to hear you and see you much more frequently.

FAN MAIL AND CONGRATULATIONS

She concluded that Menzies on television was indispensable to the country:

> As much as you are important to me, I am also important to you, because I must have the average opinion of so many other people. You see I cannot tolerate the thought of you not being the Prime Minister of Australia. The mere thought makes me quite ill.[59]

Through television Menzies could reach the Forgotten People, and some like Mrs Brooks were inspired to write back.

Radio, however, was his best medium and, until television became widespread, this was how he made personal contact with his many followers. Elderly women in particular valued his reassuring presence and clear oratory in wireless broadcasts. Gertrude Hart welcomed Menzies home from his coronation trip in 1953: 'My – but it's good to have you back with us, and to hear the first electric utterances [...] It isn't only the oratory – and the charm of voice and chosen word [...] but the balanced pronouncements of the Statesman!'[60]

In the eyes of his fans, Menzies stood head and shoulders above his parliamentary rivals. One pensioner from Chatswood (New South Wales) lamented the abysmal standard of public debate: 'If God made some humans there's been sabatage [sic] since [...] I'm using my willpower to wish on some opposition members, a prolonged attack of Laryngitis!'[61] Even the speeches of other members of the coalition, like Treasurer and Country Party leader Arthur (Artie) Fadden, seemed uncouth beside Menzies' well-educated delivery. Sister McGrath wrote to deplore Fadden's undignified way of responding to interjectors. He was ungentlemanly. 'One never stoops to their level', she wrote. '<u>You</u> never do.'[62]

This distinction between Menzies the gentleman and the rabble-rousing remainder derived in part from his radio broadcasts. 'I like to listen to you speak', wrote Dulcie Burns in Brisbane, 'but I switch off some of the drawley [sic] illiterate voices'.⁶³ The recordings of those Menzies' speeches conserved in the Australian National Library testify that he spoke clearly and accurately, and in a voice that was not heavily accented, unlike those dismissed by Dulcie Burns as 'illiterate voices'. Michael Sawtell, a disillusioned and repentant socialist, was extremely impressed. 'We now have a Prime Minister', he exclaimed in capital letters, 'who is an orator, who can quote Shakespeare and speaks the KING'S ENGLISH'.⁶⁴ His radio speeches gave Leonora Hall the greatest pleasure, because of his command of English and his extensive memory. What was the secret of this fluency? she asked. Menzies replied that it simply took a lot of practice.⁶⁵

In 1953, Menzies gave a series of radio broadcasts, entitled 'Man to Man', which drew very favourable comments. 'We always enjoy your high-toned addresses', wrote Lieutenant-Colonel Imrie and his wife, from Sydney.⁶⁶ Another listener to these talks in Hobart found Menzies' reasoning sound and his expression brilliant.⁶⁷ Examples of such compliments could be repeated *ad nauseam*, but here it is simply worth noting the special appeal of the radio broadcast to women listening at home, often alone. In spite of the 'Man to Man' title of the 1953 broadcast series, 'Man to Woman' would be a more appropriate indication of Menzies' appeal as a radio orator. The radio enabled Menzies to speak to this female constituency personally and directly. Rhoda Payne in Chatswood was blind, but managed to write with some difficulty of her appreciation of Menzies' radio talks:

> it gives me a nice, safe, warm feeling to know that your wisdom and restraining influence will be guiding our nation […] I list [sic] with great pleasure and pride to all of your election broadcasts I could find […] yo [sic] spoke to the people so openly and fearlessly, and without malice or personal invective.

At this point there appears to be some text missing from her letter, but Payne then apologised for the typed signature on a handwritten

FAN MAIL AND CONGRATULATIONS

letter, and told him that 'the only way I could write clearly enough for you to understand would be in Braille'. Menzies knew exactly how to reply to this kind of fan. When broadcasting in future, he assured her, 'I will be wondering whether you are one of my warm-hearted listeners'.[68] Writing to Menzies was always an attempt to establish direct personal contact with him, but radio talks enabled him to give listeners something back. They provided the illusion that he was present in their home, speaking to each of them individually.

In the late 1950s, Menzies was getting accustomed to more frequent television appearances. One friendly viewer offered some very positive feedback on the medium's capacity for creating an intimate conversation:

> I know you had an aversion to T.V.; but you need not have from now on.
>
> We – you and I – have just had a lovely yarn in our little flat – just you and I – or so it seemed: except that you did all the talking, and I listened with rapt attention to you, as I invariably do, – and with great profit.
>
> Do please use this new medium of talking, as an individual to individuals in their homes, as often as you can, Bob, particularly in N.S.W. You 'came over' extraordinarily well and your 'stuff' was awfully good.[69]

Television, however, was not yet present in every home, and some supporters were frustrated that they were missing his televised talks. They relied on the radio, which still reached a wider audience.

Mrs Brown congratulated Menzies on one broadcast in 1958, and told him that his speeches 'rank only second to Sir Winston Churchill's "We have the honour to stand alone" and "we will fight them on the beaches"'.[70] If these comparisons ever rankled with Menzies, he never showed it. They implied that he and Churchill had common aims and personalities, and they were compliments to his oratorical talents. Alma Isaacs in Melbourne praised his 'Bull Dog tenacity', and another writer in Sydney looked forward to some 'good Australian "Bull Dog Breed" legislation'.[71] 'I don't think even Mr Churchill could have done better', wrote a Melbourne supporter.[72] Finally Gertrude Hart praised Menzies for braving 'the slings and arrows of outrageous fortune', and for showing his excellent breeding and gallantry. 'There are two great men in the world at the moment', she concluded, 'Winston Churchill – and Robert Menzies!'[73] There was always room for two idols on the exalted pedestal erected by Menzies' loyal devotees.

Menzies in the pantheon of history

Followers looked to posterity to confirm Menzies' eminent status as a statesman, and they did so more frequently when it became clear that he was contemplating retirement from public life. This in itself was a highly disturbing prospect to them. 'You must go out as a "Champ" not as a "Has been"', advised Miss Hannan in 1962.[74] The news of his imminent retirement could prove devastating. At the New Zealand High Commission, Anita Hazlett expressed her shock thus: 'I have heard it said by some people that Canberra is a city without a soul – [...] I have never felt this while you were at the Lodge but I now feel that the bottom has dropped out of everything!'[75] In the mid-1960s there was a growing sense among correspondents of the closing of an era.

Thoughts turned to how Menzies would be judged by history. Leonard Siegel from Ohio, asking for an autograph and photograph, knew the answer: 'I believe [...] that when the final chapter is written to the history of the 20th century Asia [sic] your name will be ranked as among the very greatest of all times'.[76] Hyperbole was common

FAN MAIL AND CONGRATULATIONS

from autograph-seekers, but Thomas Bengtsson sought nothing in return for his sober assessment that the Menzies years were

> the bridge years between a nervous, distraught, undecided Australia and a nation restored to health after taking its medicine. Today, our country is alive. Our people know where they are going. They are eager, industrious, but at the same time conscious of the forces of disruption which, in the past, have held them back.[77]

Menzies was seen as a historical turning-point, leading to prosperity and national self-confidence.

One way to immortalise Menzies was to paint his portrait. In the early 1960s, would-be biographers continually hovered in the correspondence, while people asked to paint Menzies' portrait or sculpt his bust, and English publishers lined up inviting him to publish almost anything with them. The William Dobell portrait, which was reproduced on the cover of *Time* magazine in April 1960, did not quite achieve the desired resonance. In fact, it was highly unpopular with Menzies' supporters. Dobell presented Menzies as a man in power, and comfortable in the role. His portrait managed to capture some of Menzies' legendary aloofness. He showed Menzies with outsize hands, greenish skin and extraordinary eyebrows. Dobell only had a fortnight to prepare the image, and it was based on just two sittings. It severely disappointed Menzies followers, even though many of them asked for a signed copy of the *Time* cover.

Correspondents saw little resemblance between the Menzies they knew and Dobell's portrait. It appeared 'an outrageous caricature', a 'travesty' or 'an atrocity'. Perhaps they expected something more reverential, more statuesque. From Alice Springs, Eddie Connellan telegrammed: 'HAVE JUST SEEN DOBELOSITY NIL BASTARDO CARBORUNDUM', mangling the dog-latin phrase *Nolite te bastardes carborundorum* (Don't let the bastards grind you down).[78] Menzies said very little about the portrait but he did confide to one correspondent: 'I can't say I feel kindly towards the picture on the cover. I must say I am very happy that my friends have stuck to me and recognised there is no relation between the painting and the subject'.[79] The Dobell portrait seemed too idiosyncratic to be a satisfactory memorial to Menzies.

Nevertheless, he looked to posterity for praise and affirmation. This corresponded in spirit with Menzies' own view of history and history-writing, in which great individuals were the primary agents of change. He discussed his notion of history in a revealing letter to British historian AL Rowse, who had sent Menzies a copy of his recent book *The Later Churchills*. First of all, Menzies dismissed the pedantic style of schoolboy history on which he had been weaned: 'When I was a boy', he told Rowse,

> the chief function of the historian seemed to be to hammer home a long series of dates and dynasties. This, no doubt, had some merit though at the time we thought it an abomination of desolation. Later on, my own studies seemed to involve a concentration upon the history of wars and other lesser events. I am not sure that Winston is not currently the greatest surviving member of this school.

Then he went on to dismiss the fashion of attributing historical developments to unseen economic forces – a materialist interpretation of history which he attributed to Marxist influence. The true answer lay in the role of the great individual, always gendered masculine. Menzies went on:

> I have long since come to the conclusion that Diogenes was right and that at all stages and under all circumstances we must look for a man.

FAN MAIL AND CONGRATULATIONS

> Individuals have affected the course of history in the most astonishing degree. To understand history and to learn its constantly fresh lessons, therefore, involves the study of men and not of 'blue books'.[80]

It is hard to avoid the thought that he was referring to himself as a subject worthy of historical study. The Great Man theory of history involved a search beyond superficial propaganda to understand the personality of the hero.

When Thomas Lilley wrote in 1964 to congratulate Menzies on completing 30 years as member for Kooyong, and on his 70th birthday, he placed Menzies' long term of office in a historical perspective close to the prime minister's heart, in these words:

> At the death of Queen Victoria there were middle-aged subjects of Her Majesty who had never known another reigning monarch, and in Australia today there are young electors who have known none but you as the Prime Minister in office during their lifetime. We must look to the career of Pitt the Younger for a satisfying comparison.[81]

This flattered Menzies in a historical register which he greatly appreciated, not least because Lilley's historical pantheon was British. Menzies was affected by this deeply enough to reply:

> I receive thousands of letters in the course of the year – some favourable, some unfavourable and some indifferent. But I hasten to tell you that no letter I have received for a long time has given me such encouragement as yours. I would like to believe that I was even partly worthy of your generous sentiments.

Even the greatest idols have feet of clay, and they are easily softened by the fragrant oil of flattery.

4

'If you want anything _done_, go to the top'

THE PERSONAL HOTLINE

Direct access to the prime minister

One fundamental assumption of writing upwards was that ordinary people had a right to direct personal access to their superiors. Their previous efforts to solve a problem might have run into difficulty with the authorities, or they may have been frustrated by bureaucratic delays and obfuscation. Menzies' local constituents from Kooyong, for example, reported their failures to persuade the Postmaster-General's office to extend a new telephone line to their premises; would-be emigrants had hit a brick wall in their approaches to the Australian High Commission in London to secure approval for an assisted passage; applicants for a war or a disability pension had initially been refused by the relevant ministry. George Reeves, a Lancashire man trying to get an assisted passage to Australia, described a common situation very succinctly: 'After many weary years of waiting', he wrote, 'I now attempt to side step red tape and present my case'.[1] Writers implicitly believed that if they could reach a higher authority in person, they would receive humane treatment and a sympathetic hearing. Writing upwards, then, strove for a personal connection with the leader and assumed it was possible.

THE PERSONAL HOTLINE

Correspondents desired an unmediated connection with the leader, without filters or interpreters. One member of François Mitterrand's staff labelled this a 'monarchist' vision of the world.[2] In such a vision, the citizen imagined that if the sovereign could only be made aware of the heartlessness of his subordinate officials, he would right all wrongs, ensure that his subjects were no longer mistreated and in this way justice would prevail. In the bureaucratised world of the twentieth century, this might have seemed a throwback to a pre-modern age, if political leaders had not themselves seen some advantage in encouraging citizens to write to them.

This assumption that a personal epistolary hotline was available ran counter to the practical realities of government. Writers became exasperated when their requests got lost in red tape at the hands of government officials who stood between themselves and Menzies, but these intermediaries could not always be avoided. In practice, of course, Menzies himself diverted private requests to the appropriate public organisation responsible for dealing with them. Even if correspondents knew full well that this would happen, they continued to believe that a word of support from Menzies himself would fix their problem. Menzies had his own private secretariat to deal with the correspondence he received, and the role of the secretary will be examined in this chapter.

Menzies, it was assumed, was accessible to all and sundry. 'I have been told', wrote Arthur Smellie from London, 'that you are great enough as a statesman and a man, for the humblest to seek and obtain your ear.'[3] Mrs Radcliffe, writing from South Africa, began with a standard apology before insisting on addressing the highest authority:

> Please forgive me writing to you: my father used to say to me as a child 'If you want anything <u>done</u> go to the top' and I don't feel it would be nice if this were picked over by endless people and perhaps never reaching you at all.[4]

The personal hotline was activated to secure an understanding and effective response.

The assumption that Menzies was accessible to all was evident in the material signs of intimacy in the letters. As noted in chapter 2, the use of decorated or coloured paper, together with coloured inks, usually purple, green or red, indicated a close rather than a formal relationship. We even find examples of cross-writing, when a correspondent filled a page portrait-style, then turned it 90 degrees and continued writing the message at right-angles over the previous text. In the 19th century, cross-writing was a way of saving paper, but it was something only acceptable between friends. Familiar forms of address like 'Dear Bob' also assumed a close relationship between Menzies and the writer. There was a widespread feeling among correspondents that Menzies 'belonged' to his public, as a letter from Alice Hann indicated: 'Please forgive me if I presume too much but I feel my Prime Minister belongs to me as to all his other loyal constituents and I would be so happy to meet you and Mrs Menzies'.[5] Writers imagined that they could nullify the status gap between themselves and the prime minister, making even a personal meeting possible.

Correspondents needed to ensure that their letter found its way into Menzies' own hands. They feared that a secretary would intervene and interrupt their personal communication route to him, like John Mason in Sydney who wanted to attack compulsory unionism, and told Menzies, 'I am writing this to you hoping that you shall read it yourself and not office staff or screw it up and throw it away in the dust bin, until you have read it yourself'.[6] Professor Warren Carey of the University of Tasmania had something to say about the nationality of the next Governor-General, and did not see why the office should be the exclusive preserve of Australians and Britishers. Unable to see Menzies in person, he put his arguments in writing to Menzies' secretary William Heseltine, commenting for his benefit: 'It will not suffer by being left unopened for a while, but it is not a matter which should be bandied about in the department before it has gone to the Prime Minister'.[7] Many just did not anticipate the role of a secretary to filter the mail and respond to it, and reacted angrily when they received a message from the secretary telling them he or she would bring the matter to the prime minister's attention. Some naively believed that by marking their letter 'Private', they would guarantee its swift passage to the prime minister. Sydney Moss peppered the prime minister's office with letters about pension increases, and wrote to William Heseltine:

> Whilst I thank you for yours under date the 26th inst., in answer to my "PRIVATE" letter to Mr Menzies of the 20th [...] I am at a loss to understand why my letter was not received by Mr Menzies himself, being addressed 'Private' and why you, Sir, should state 'you will bring it under his notice etc'
>
> It is far too important a matter to be shelved, as thousands of poor unfed Pensioners are suffering though [sic] lack of the Governments interest or action, on their behalf, and I shall look for some explanation, as to why so urgent a mater [sic] was not dealt with by the Prime Minister himself, and opened by him.[8]

A few writers imagined that the secret of direct access was to address the letter appropriately, like John McConville who sent his letter to Menzies' private residence, because in his words, 'I feel if I sent it to Parliament house it would just be dealt with by your Secretary and you might never see it'.[9] His letter protested against salary rises for members of Parliament, and Heseltine sent him a reply. Mr Roberts from Menzies' Kooyong constituency also hoped to bypass bureaucratic obstruction to make a similar protest, writing: 'in the hope that this communication survives the sometimes impenetrable barrier of secretaries our politicians have erected at our expense, I wish to voice an emphatic protest at the shameless salary grab in which you are about to participate'.[10] But it was more productive to curry favour with the secretaries rather than insult them.

This discussion is primarily devoted to writers who made a direct and personal approach to Menzies. For those more aware of the paths their letters actually followed, however, it was politic to address the secretaries themselves, perhaps to ask them to intervene on the writer's behalf. From Wales, Joan Lewis only realised the true mediated nature of the epistolary exchange when she received an unexpected reply from Menzies' office, and immediately understood that she owed this as much to the secretary as to Menzies himself. She wrote again, this time to private secretary Hazel Craig herself, to express her surprise and gratitude for the reply, referring to 'Your letter from the Prime Minister Mr Menzies', which seems an excellent formulation of the collective work of the secretariat. She was amazed that Menzies had taken the time to attend to her questions, and wrote, 'I don't really know how to start to thank you', referring to Craig.[11]

One Englishman invited Hazel Craig to visit him in Devon, promising her a room with a view of the sea,[12] but a better example of epistolary dialogue between a correspondent and a secretary is Mrs Thisseu, an elderly woman with restricted mobility. Mrs Thisseu explained to Hazel Craig that she had not been out of her house in Swansea (New South Wales) for years. She related her life story and asked for a food parcel and an autograph. She, too, addressed herself to Hazel Craig, pleading: 'Do you think you could write me a letter sometimes Miss Craig, and help to make my life a little brighter by reading something of what you do, its very lonely sometimes!' Mrs Thisseu was exceptional in that she clearly would have liked to strike up a relationship with Craig and establish a hotline with her rather than with Menzies. Her plea illustrates one of the rarely articulated motives for writing to a public figure: the sheer loneliness of the elderly.[13]

For almost everybody, however, access to Menzies himself was the prime objective. One ruse adopted to activate the hotline was to address the letter to Mrs Menzies. This was predominantly a female strategy: out of 11 correspondents in the corpus who addressed their letters directly to Dame Pattie Menzies in the sampled years of 1949–50, 1958 and 1964, eight were from women, two were from men and one was from a company selling encyclopaedias. Joyce Atkinson wrote inviting Pattie Menzies to have a 'back-stage chat' but fully expected her to 'pass the information on to hubby for me [...] please'.[14] Adele Vandenberg tried to reach Menzies by this roundabout route with an apologetic and flattering request:

Dear Dame Pattie,

<u>Please forgive me</u> for passing this on to you, but I feel that by doing so, I will genuinely get in touch with (our dear Prime Minister) – your husband.[15]

Another female correspondent also sent New Year greetings and congratulations to the prime minister via his wife, adding in a postscript:

I am addressing this to Mrs Menzies as I feel there is more likelihood of your reading it, than if a secretary had to decide an important enough epistle for you to spend your time on.

But naturally I think it is very important!![16]

Gladys Kennedy wrote about the Moral Re-Armament World Summit, and addressed her letter to Mrs Menzies because 'I want to reach the heart of Australia and I thought of no better way than to write to you – the Prime Minister's wife'.[17] She received a reply, but from Hazel Craig. None of these tactics stood any chance of avoiding the usual secretarial screening.

The secretariat and the art of the evasive reply

Menzies' private secretaries had to demonstrate a high level of technical competence, and they enjoyed the advantage of being close to the prime minister. In spite of this, they had little power to resolve problems; usually they simply had to know the best person to whom they should *refer* problems. A referral from the prime minister's office was a strong incentive to a minister or official to examine an individual dossier very carefully. The prime minister's secretaries, then, were not administrators with the capacity to make decisions. Referrals to a ministry or a department never pressed for any particular outcome – they just asked for a report. Once the report was received, the secretariat had to relay an administrative decision back to the correspondent, and it was often unfavourable. This required a skilful reply which intermingled bureaucratic explanations with a dose of compassion.

Leaving aside the prime minister's press secretary, who was not directly concerned with his personal correspondence, there were always at least two staff members responsible for receiving and responding to personal letters, and at very busy times more were hired on a casual basis. Over the course of Menzies' record-breaking run as prime minister, several of them had a significant presence in the correspondence.

Eileen G Linehan, known as 'Lennie', was one of the first, but she had already had a long public service career before joining Menzies' staff. After moving to Canberra from South Australia, she had served as stenographer to Treasurer Richard Casey, then as private secretary to Prime Minister Joseph Lyons, breaking into a world which was hitherto male-dominated. The media described her as 'a cheery brunette with a brisk, energetic manner and an insatiable appetite for hard work'.[18] She first worked for Menzies in 1939, after Lyons' death. When Menzies joined the War Cabinet in London during the

Second World War, he took Linehan with him. She followed Menzies into opposition and then accompanied him through the formation years of the Liberal Party. In 1950, her health was deteriorating, and she took sick leave in the middle of that year, being replaced by Everil Wilkinson. In fact Linehan went on a trip to Britain, with her friend and counterpart Hazel Craig, who was then secretary to the leader of the opposition, Ben Chifley. Correspondents were confused by this unexpected female presence in the correspondence chain. When they addressed themselves to the secretary by name, they were inclined to assume mistakenly that Everil Wilkinson was a man.

Hazel Craig, who became private secretary to Menzies in 1951, was Linehan's close friend. Craig was the daughter of a carpenter, born in Bankstown in southwest Sydney in 1914. She came to Canberra in 1934 as a 19-year-old junior typist.[19] Before joining Menzies' staff, she worked for Chifley, but this was no bar to employment by his political adversaries. Officially, prime ministerial secretaries never expressed private opinions, but worked as dedicated public servants who embodied a public service ethic of impartial service and confidentiality. But this is not to say they had no opinions at all. Craig confessed in a later interview that she could never have worked for Labor leader HV Evatt. Evatt, she felt, was always outshone by Menzies, and in the end 'he was just absolutely berserk'.[20] She travelled almost annually with Menzies to Commonwealth Prime Ministers' Conferences in London, and later even stayed in a flat in Walmer Castle on the Kent coast with Menzies and his wife after he was appointed Warden of the Cinque Ports (a sinecure conferring nominal guardianship of the English Channel coast).[21] Her loyalty and dedication over many years were rewarded by the MBE, OBE and CBE, as well as the retirement gift of a silver tray from Menzies and his wife, inscribed to 'A splendid secretary and a faithful friend'.[22]

Geoffrey Yeend acted as Menzies' principal private secretary between 1953 and 1955 and injected his own brand of common-sense professionalism into dealing with the personal correspondence. After his death in 1994, Liberal Senator James Short paid him a warm tribute in a speech to the Senate, emphasising his impartiality and integrity.[23] Yeend was replaced by William Heseltine until 1959, with a brief interruption in 1957, after Heseltine's wife was killed in an accident, when their car was hit by a train between Melbourne and Canberra. Heseltine went on to an even more distinguished career as private secretary to Queen Elizabeth II.

In 1963, Frank Jennings became Menzies' private secretary. Jennings was the son of a timber mill worker from Ballina (New South Wales), and he ended up in the post almost by accident. He was trained as an industrial chemist but had a secret ambition to do missionary work in Papua New Guinea. When he applied to enter the public service, he intended to work for the Minister for Territories. But once he arrived in Canberra, he was shunted into the prime minister's office. Jennings worked as private secretary to Sir Allen Brown, head of the Prime Minister's Department, and then for Treasurer Harold Holt, so he came to the job of private secretary to Menzies from the highest echelons of government. When he recalled his work in a later interview, he revealed how unsatisfying he had found it. He disliked filing letters and did not feel that acknowledging them was a very useful occupation. Perhaps some of this reluctance spilled over into the way letters to Menzies were dealt with during his regime in Menzies' concluding years. Jennings considered that Menzies' successor, Harold Holt, was foolish when, on becoming prime minister, he wanted to reply to every congratulatory message he received. Jennings' job, as he recalled it, was to prioritise the paper flow, leaving Hazel Craig to take care of 'really personal stuff'. Menzies called him 'laddie', approved almost all of the draft letters he composed, and would invite him for a drink at the end of the day. He testified to Menzies' dislike of the media, the television and the telephone, and to his scrupulous insistence that documents should be drafted in accurate English.[24]

These public servants formed the small group of hard-working,

THE PERSONAL HOTLINE

experienced and politically neutral secretaries who mediated the epistolary hotline between Menzies and his correspondents. They gave incoming correspondence three red stamps, as appropriate. Firstly, letters were stamped 'Received', with the date of reception. A selection of letters was stamped 'Personal', when the letter was from a personal friend of Menzies and a personal reply was required. A further selection was stamped 'Seen by the Prime Minister', when it was considered important enough to be brought to his attention. Menzies, in other words, did not see every letter, although he was virtually present in all the replies they received. To this extent, the personal hotline to which correspondents aspired was an illusion.

In most cases, the secretaries would send a noncommittal reply thanking the sender, and they would draft this on their own initiative. Some letters bear a typed or handwritten note: 'ack.', with the date, indicating when a simple acknowledgment of receipt had been sent. A proportion of letters would be referred to an appropriate ministry or government department. In some of these cases where the original letter has been forwarded, only the reply remains on file. We have to deduce the contents of the original from the prime minister's response.

There were inevitably occasions when the secretary needed to confer with Menzies before drafting a suitable reply, and the correspondence bears the traces of their dialogue. In straightforward cases, the secretary would forward the letter to Menzies and write in pencil in the margin – 'anything wanted?' and Menzies would write back in pencil: 'No, RG'. Sometimes the letter was illegible and incomprehensible, and the secretary would type a transcription for Menzies to read easily. If a letter arrived in a foreign language, a secretary would find an expert to translate it. He or she would ask Menzies if he knew the writer personally, because this would influence the nature of the reply. If writers just gave a name and initial without indicating their gender, the secretaries would look them up in the telephone directory, so that they would have the correct form of address on hand for their response. On occasions, Hazel Craig would draft a reply in shorthand in pencil on the verso of the letter received. The details of the mechanics of reception and response reveal that the letters were heavily mediated and that even if responses bore Menzies' name and were issued with his authority, they were a collective and a collaborative enterprise.

A few correspondents caused amusement in the office. Mrs Beniams of New Zealand, for example, raised eyebrows when she blamed Princess Elizabeth for marrying a descendant of the Battenbergs, the enemies of Great Britain, and for good measure she asserted she was Captain Cook's great-granddaughter. She was not the only person in the British Commonwealth to express misgivings about the royal marriage, but her extravagant genealogical claim did not convince anyone. Craig noted to Menzies: 'Although this is from an admirer of yours, I am afraid she is a bit barmy'.[25] She warned him against another correspondent as she forwarded her letter: 'Be careful here – she is as ga-ga as they are made – completely nuts'.[26] Ernest Cooper of Western Australia wrote a 23-page, double-spaced letter on the merits of peace and co-operation in preference to inter-party feuding, as well as on the telepathic messages which he had been receiving about this. He went on, 'I could write much more than all this, on that and allied subjects and may do soon'. William Heseltine, hitherto a patient reader, pencilled a marginal note: 'Not to me I hope'.[27]

There were serial offenders, whose repeated and lengthy correspondence seems to have been a symptom of either dire loneliness or a deep-rooted fixation. Joyce Atkinson wrote often and profusely from her home in Queensland. Her letters arrived every few days in the winter of 1958. Before the secretariat had time to acknowledge one of them, another would arrive, so that the secretaries resorted to responding to them in batches. She had been identified as a problem as early as 1955, as Hazel Craig explained at some length to Menzies in a typed comment:

This woman has a complex, but you are her 'hero'. As you can see she runs to pages and pages every week.

We have sent her some of your speeches and now she asks whether she can incorporate (in full) your speech to the Institute of Management in a book she intends to write. Personally I don't think it will ever see the light of day. I think perhaps I should tell her that this is now the property of the Institute of Management. Would this be correct? [*Menzies wrote 'Yes' in the margin.*]

I am quite positive she is on your side, and would not do anything to harm you, but is 'over eager' or a bit 'queer'.[28]

As the cases of George Hodge and Oswald Ziegler, mentioned below, will show, Hazel Craig's frustration with problem correspondents was not directed exclusively at women. But however trying the circumstances, the secretariat maintained its tolerance and composure.

At the same time, showing her public face, the secretary assured writers that they had every right to address the prime minister and that they would receive a fair hearing. Victoria Brown wrote a bitter and pessimistic letter which concluded 'I am told you will pass this to the waste paper basket as "Gutter Topic"'. But Hazel Craig assured her that this would not be her fate, since 'any citizen is always at liberty to write to the Prime Minister and, unless the letter is not signed, or has no address, attention is given to it'.[29] When Mrs Powell of Bendigo wrote, 'I suppose you will think I have an awful cheek writing to you', Craig told her it was her right as a citizen to do so, in these terms: 'It is the right of every citizen to write to the Prime Minister should they desire information, and he is only too happy to do his best for them'.[30] Mr B Cowling of Tasmania certainly appreciated this. 'Frankly, sir', he wrote, 'I even like having the knowledge of being able to write to my Prime Minister and state what I believe. Many countries cannot do this'.[31] Writing upwards was an essential democratic right.

Not everybody expected a reply from Menzies. Timothy Western of Camberwell (Victoria) wrote to attack the government's general incompetence and especially its failure to allow more Asian immigration, concluding: 'What will become of this letter, I am not sure. Will you, as Prime Minister see it? Will it be answered, or will it be treated with contempt? Be this a democracy, I will receive an answer. But is it?'[32] Western did receive a reply from secretary Les Moore, explaining that his previous letters had been ignored because they were abusive.

Expectations notwithstanding, Menzies was very assiduous in replying. Consider the sample of 3681 letters presented for statistical analysis in chapter 2. If we exclude from the tally all messages that clearly did not seek a reply, such as thanks-for-your-condolences and other goodwill cards, the net total remaining from the sample is 3408. Of these, the very high figure of 74.1 per cent received a reply from Menzies' secretariat. The secretariat's efficiency in this domain, however, was in decline. In 1949–50, the first year sampled, the reply rate was almost 80 per cent (79.95). In 1958, by which time the volume of incoming correspondence had considerably increased, it fell to under 73 per cent, and in 1964 the reply rate had declined further to 71.8 per cent. Even this figure represented an extraordinarily high rate of response. It is possible that there were fewer replies because more requests were being dealt with either in person or by telephone, but this is a guess because presumably such informal replies were not always recorded.

Delays were inevitable: secretaries constantly apologised to correspondents on Menzies' behalf because he was too busy, overseas or preparing to go overseas, so that he had neglected his personal correspondence. Papers were mislaid as Menzies travelled between Canberra, Melbourne and Sydney, as well as overseas, and the secretary had to apologise for finding them weeks later. Most writers got a reply eventually, even if it sometimes took months to arrive, waiting for a parliamentary session to end, or for Menzies to return

THE PERSONAL HOTLINE

from an overseas visit. Even when a writer specifically told Menzies not to reply, he or his secretariat still wrote a response. Sometimes where there is no written reply on file, instead there is a note to say that he had phoned the writer, or spoken to him or her in person, in the case of members of Parliament. Replies often enclosed a copy of a recent Menzies speech, or an extract from Hansard, and sometimes an autographed photograph, although the office was slow to prepare for this kind of fan-mail exchange and for several months in 1950 did not comply with requests for a photo.

Menzies' election win in December 1949 stimulated a deluge of congratulatory messages, which overwhelmed the newly installed secretariat. Profuse apologies were issued for the delay in replying to them all, in these terms:

> As you will realise, many thousands of messages were received by Mr Menzies, not only from within Australia, but from all over the world. It would have been a physical impossibility for him to reply personally to all of them, and it was for that reason 'acknowledgement' cards were sent out, with small typed notes from him which did not necessitate his signature.
>
> Necessarily, however, it will be a matter of courtesy for him to send personal letters to a number of prominent people.[33]

In other words, and quite counter-intuitively, the sender was reliably informed that if he or she had not received any response yet, it could well be a sign of their important rank.

There were a few favourite ways of replying, even if the responses were never completely uniform. Walter Henderson had written a supportive letter, which included a personal element and an invitation for Mr and Mrs Menzies to visit him, and he received this courteous reply which was typical of many:

Dear Mr Henderson,

Although with the pressure of Parliamentary duties the Prime Minister has not had an opportunity to reply personally to your letter of the 28th October he has asked that I will send a message to thank you for the encouraging way in which you have written.

He was interested, too, to know that your daughter is still absorbed in her work.

Mr Menzies sends his best wishes to her and to you and his thanks for your open invitation to him to bring Mrs Menzies to visit you.

Yours sincerely,
E.M. Wilkinson, Private Secretary.[34]

Although this was a typical response, it was not completely standardised, and there was plenty of scope for a tailored, personal reply.

Prime ministerial apologies might be phrased typically as follows: '[...] as you will doubtless realise, in the last couple of months he has been hard-pressed with parliamentary matters and, more recently, in preparation for this very hurried visit abroad, and more or less personal matters were neglected'.[35] Letters of support and congratulation were acknowledged in this courteous style: 'I am writing to thank you and your wife for the sentiments expressed in your letter of 17th August. It is very warming to receive such letters of congratulations from my friends and I am deeply appreciative of your thoughtfulness'.[36]

When a correspondent put forward a plan for reform or laid bare a grievance, the usual response was to thank them for their 'practical interest' in writing. This phrase was used repeatedly to acknowledge but at the same time deflect the inquiry, but there were very few standard, pre-prepared response formulae. If correspondents raised a thorny problem, the reply would ignore it and just convey good wishes.

Correspondents therefore only rarely succeeded in establishing the direct personal connection with Menzies which they expected would provide the answer to their troubles, but they could usually count on a personalised response which was not merely the equivalent of today's impersonal, pre-recorded message. Of course, there were always a few correspondents who would not be fobbed off by apologies for delays, and who resented the interference of officials whose obstruction they were trying to circumvent. These individuals had higher expectations of the correspondence and they appeared as troublemakers. Arthur Richardson of Adelaide was one of those who wanted Menzies to dismiss William McKell as Governor-General as soon as he became prime minister, arguing that McKell's appointment had been a party-political measure engineered by the Labor Party. When he failed to get a commitment from Menzies on this score, he exploded. Although Menzies had been ill as well as busy, Richardson wrote:

> I must protest strongly against your clear attempt – which in itself arouses suspicion – to avoid the issue until after the election [...] I do not expect Mr Menzies to have time for letter writing, but I do expect him to find time to dictate a plain and simple answer to this vitally important question. I expect my letter – incidentally a friendly one from a supporter—to be treated seriously.

Richardson was not apologetic and he was particularly impatient with the evasions he received from the prime ministerial secretariat. He added in a postscript: 'I and my friends are not interested in the "very many queries" Mr Menzies is dealing with "all over Australia"

– at any rate not to the point of having this particular query sidestepped'. Menzies was shown this letter and made a pencilled note: 'No – ignore'.[37]

Similarly, Edward Wright from the Blue Mountains (New South Wales) was provoked to anger when his attempt to secure a personal appointment did not receive the desired response from the government. He attacked both Menzies and the relevant minister thus:

> As the prime inspiration for Australia's most rapidly rising national enterprise – passing the buck – and chief Dalia Lama [sic] of Canberra, may I direct your attention to the fact that the word of your Repatriation Minister, Cooper, is worthless; or his health is no longer equal to his present position.[38]

William Heseltine pencilled in his understandable reaction to this outburst: 'I felt that this letter was couched in terms of much [such] rudeness as to require no acknowledgment – WH'.

There was little similarity here with letters to President Obama, who regarded letters from constituents as a vital connection with the electorate, a recall to the first principles of representative democracy. He even framed one letter on health insurance and hung it in the White House to remind him of the people he had promised to help.[39] Menzies' reaction to his correspondents was less idealistic. There is some evidence that in time his secretariat lost patience and became a little more privately cynical about individual correspondents. In 1964, George Hodge asked Menzies to donate a Bible to his local Presbyterian Church, but Hazel Craig rejected his pleadings with a note dismissing them as 'another try-on [...] Poor struggling little Presbos, I guess'. This time Craig had underestimated Menzies, who agreed to make the donation.[40] Considering Menzies' well-known Presbyterian sympathies, it is surprising that she failed to correctly anticipate his response on this occasion.

THE PERSONAL HOTLINE

She similarly lost patience with Oswald Ziegler of Ziegler Publications, who sent several letters asking Menzies to write a foreword to a coffee-table book on Australia, to authorise a reproduction of his portrait, and then to let him call it 'The House that Bob Built'. He got permission for the portrait but not for his other requests. Hazel Craig 'mistrusted him' and warned Menzies, 'The Lord forbid that you should fall for this', because 'he is an awful humbug really'.[41]

Perhaps the most telling sign of a new and less generous attitude was the creation in 1965 of a 'no-reply' file, which mainly includes letters from eccentrics and religious fanatics. Most of the contents of the 'no-reply' file was received during Menzies' retirement, but it nevertheless contains several items from 1965 and January 1966, including a few complaints about pensions and the means test. Unlike the treatment of the vast majority of correspondents in previous years, these correspondents received no answer. The discourse of the archive is eloquent here: grumbling pensioners were classified in the same category as cranks.[42] When, in late 1963, one Brisbane correspondent asked for a copy of Menzies' 1942 speech *The Forgotten People*, she was told that it was out of print – perhaps a symbolic reflection of the Forgotten People's reduced status towards the end of Menzies' term of office.[43]

Correspondents certainly were rude and they were often deferential, but they had a common goal. They hoped for a personal epistolary conversation with Menzies, whom they assumed could assist them with a range of problems, some political or administrative and others more personal. When they encountered a wall of secretaries across their path, they had several different reactions. Some were outraged that their message had not reached the prime minister in person and had failed to obtain the desired outcome. Some resorted to ruse to slip their letter through the protective net, sending it to Mrs Menzies or conspicuously labelling it 'Private and Confidential'. None of this worked. Some just accepted secretarial intervention and even embraced it as an opportunity to open up a conversation with a new correspondent. As noted in chapter 2, a growing number of letters was addressed directly to one of the secretaries. The initiatives shown by Menzies' secretarial staff even encouraged this. When a woman wrote from Texas offering advice on how to deal with the rabbit problem, which she had been reading about, Everil Wilkinson wrote her a long and spontaneous explanation of the particular problems faced in country Australia, especially the difficulty of constructing boundary fences in sparsely populated rural areas.[44] Her generous reply was far longer than the original letter, showing the willingness of secretaries to engage with individual correspondents, at least in these early years.

If we compare Menzies' secretariat with that of François Mitterrand in the 1980s, we find an enormous difference of scale, even allowing for the fact that France's population was five times the size of Australia's. Mitterrand might have received as many letters in a single day as Menzies received over a whole year, and the French president had a secretariat 50 times larger to deal with them.[45] In both cases, the same notion of a direct, personal exchange with the national leader inspired the correspondence. In the French case, however, the mere size of the corpus inevitably tended to make the exchange more distant and impersonal. Perhaps the continuing illusion of the personal hotline to the top only made sense in a smaller country with a slimmer apparatus of government.

5

*'Please don't think
I'm a crackpot'*

THE RHETORIC
OF APOLOGY

Weapons of the weak

'Please don't think I'm a crackpot', wrote Petty Officer Groves, 'and lay down this small epistle without reading what I have to say. It will only take a minute to read, and I am sure you can grant me that small indulgence'.[1] Menzies' correspondents were well practised in the art of humble apology. It was one of the rhetorical devices they employed to capture the reader's attention. Sometimes it reflected a genuine difficulty in drafting a letter; for those who wrote rarely, and for the elderly and infirm, manipulating writing implements did not come easily, and it required some experience to be fully expert in the social grammar of letter-writing. At other times, the opening apology was a standard tactic to overcome the recipient's presumed impatience and to invite him or her to consider the real purpose of the letter. As in Petty Officer Groves' 'small epistle', the humble apology was laced with an urgent demand on Menzies' time.

Such difficulties and hesitations were an inherent feature of writing upwards, whenever ordinary citizens searched for a convincing way to appeal in writing to powerful superiors. The deferential language of the Menzies letters echoes the expressions of loyalty and the calculated obsequiousness found in similar corpuses elsewhere, from the peasants of southeast Asia to humble petitioners in Tsarist Russia.[2] Australian letters had a distinctive character: writers often addressed Menzies with great familiarity and, as voters, they could not be entirely ignored. Nevertheless, whether correspondents were subjects under a dictatorship or citizens in a constitutional democracy, apology, personal flattery and vows of loyalty were all part of the armoury they raided in search of a favour or a small personal advantage. In the case of Menzies, this may have only involved a request for his autograph. Obsequiousness had an important preliminary function, preparing the way for reminding Menzies of what he and the writer had in common. Having done this, the petitioner finally presented his or her more or less urgent demand, wrapped up in the ritual language of self-abasement. Just like individual requests for help, complaints too were strategically sugar-coated in promises of devotion and fidelity to the Liberal cause. Insubordination and complaints were disguised by pledges of loyalty which did not challenge the symbols of power. Deferential language and an outward show of conformity were the everyday resources of humble petitioners, the 'weapons of the weak' which formed the conventional prelude to any self-interested claim.[3]

This chapter will review the ways in which correspondents expressed their strategic apologies, as well as the difficulties they encountered and the excuses they made for their lack of epistolary literacy. I will then survey the credentials that correspondents offered to justify their requests, and the networks – regional, ancestral, political or religious – which they considered bound Menzies to them. Claiming a prior connection with Menzies made their overtures to him legitimate and worthy of attention. This was a rhetoric of affinity, which justified the writer's approach on the basis that Menzies and the writer had something in common: a common affiliation with a church, for instance, or with Scotland or perhaps with Menzies' constituency of Kooyong. In the final two sections, I will investigate some of the special favours and requests in the supplicatory letters which Menzies received. Some asked for a simple letter of introduction, others were desperate for help to resolve problems in their personal lives. Their pleas ranged from the mundane to the bizarre. In many cases, their requests were accommodated.

The rhetoric of apology

Menzies' time was precious, and the writer could not presume to encroach on it without apologising for doing so. 'Of course', wrote one woman from Chatswood (New South Wales), 'I know that my thoughts are not of the least importance in your busy life'.[4] The unfortunately named Mrs Pain began with these words: 'Firstly I wish to say: "I apologise for this personal letter", as I just know how every minute of your valuable life is being taxed; but my request is so urgent and very sad'.[5] Such apologies were essential preludes to a plea for assistance or a demand for serious attention. 'This is no letter from a crank', protested Neville McDonald, before recommending that Menzies should read Napoleon Hill's self-improvement book, *Think and Grow Rich,* and he sent Menzies two copies in case one of them failed to reach him.[6] A Mrs Brown similarly offered the standard apology: 'I am reluctant', she wrote, 'to trespass on the limited time of Australia's busiest man'. She soon overcame her reluctance, however, and a two-page letter followed about the problems she encountered in installing a telephone line.[7] Writers apologised for pestering the prime minister or for their apparent impudence in writing to him. One writer took up his pencil and tried to by-pass the usual approach channel by addressing his letter to Heather Menzies, the prime minister's daughter, in these terms:

> Please forgive me for writing this letter, you probably get a lot of begging and in fact, unpleasant letters, so I won't blame you if you don't encourage me, I ask you to believe me, that I won't annoy you or pester you in any way, your word is law to me, so, if you choose to ignore this I'll simply know I'm not worthy of your help.[8]

This correspondent was so engrossed in his self-effacing apology that he failed to arrive at the real point of his letter. He received a reply inquiring what exactly it was that he wanted.

Many writers struggled to find the appropriate form of address, and perhaps 'Dear Mr Ming' is one symptom of their confusion. As we have seen in the samples analysed in chapter 2, 65 different forms of greeting were used in 1958, and another 64 in 1964 – another testimony to a general uncertainty. Occasionally a writer felt authorised to adopt a familiar tone, and 100 letters in 1958 opened with 'Dear Bob'. Sometimes the conventional apology was offered as if to a close acquaintance. Mrs Williams of Warrnambool (Victoria) wrote of her prayers for Menzies, the problem of loafers in the trade unions and the difficulty of living on a pension, and she signed off with, 'Well good night Dear Friend and thank you again I hope I have not given you a headache'.[9] Familiarity, however, could be a provocation, and this seemed to be the case with the angry correspondent who began 'Bro Menzie'.[10] If familiarity was not appropriate, the writer had to decide whether to address Menzies by his name (as in 'Dear Mr Menzies') or his title ('Dear Prime Minister'), or a combination of both, as in 'Dear Mr Minister'. As noted in chapter 2, deferential modes of address (including 'Dear Sir' and variations thereof) were popular. Gladys Spickett, writing from England, experienced a common dilemma: 'I am not sure if I am addressing you in the right manner but I can assure you that I am very sincere'.[11] She addressed him as 'Dear Mr Menzies' so she need not have worried. Mr Punjabi, on the other hand, had no problem when he wrote from Gujarat to ask for Menzies' autograph: 'My Dear Chacha, This little letter of mine may come to you as surprise [sic], but my dear Chacha how can I tell you that my hand, Can not be prevented to write something to you to achieve my long cherished desires'.[12] 'Chacha' in Hindi means paternal uncle. It was used to address independent India's first prime minister, Jawaharlal Nehru, for example, as 'Chacha Nehru'. Here it suggested affectionate respect and deference to a wise elder. Mr Punjabi had found the perfect solution to a common problem.

In apologising for writing to Menzies, authors expressed an exaggerated sense of their own insignificance. As one cricket fan put it, Menzies was 'higher up the batting order than I am'.[13] A young Indian correspondent defined himself in these self-deprecating terms:

> I am a teen-aged Indian boy [...] My hobby is to correspond with internationally important men, whom I consider would not disappoint or ignore me, irrespective of their exhaulted [sic] and busy jobs, since I know that I am nothing but a tiny drop in the human-ocean.[14]

José Barredo similarly introduced himself as a Filipino father of seven children, and asked Menzies for a second-hand transistor radio for Christmas, with the exaggerated modesty characteristic of supplicatory letters: 'At first', he wrote, 'I was too shy indeed writing this believing that you, being the greatest man of that great country in earth, wouldn't mind answering this futile missive from a humble and poor peasant'.[15] Elsewhere in the letter, he refers to living in a deprived 'barrio', suggesting an urban residence, so the 'peasant' reference might be a flourish, but the humility it expressed was part of the standard rhetoric of writing upwards.

Housewives were especially prone to insist on their own irrelevance, like Mary Stewart in London, who began 'Although a mere, insignificant English housewife [...]', before recommending that a royal residence be set up for Queen Elizabeth in Australia.[16]

Similarly Mrs McAuley of North Sydney emphasised her own ignorance of the world: 'I am nearly 66 years of age. I know very little about Politics, and nothing about "Communism". I have had my hands full rearing 12 children including two sets of twins and I want them to live in Peace'.[17] But she confidently sent Menzies some examples of her poetry. Recent immigrants, too, expressed a kind of false reluctance to address Menzies, as if they were butting in on a national conversation that was not yet entirely their own. Ed Vieglais, who was possibly of Latvian origin, wrote, 'At first I want to beg excuses for myself that I dare to annoy you with my letter about a matter what of course [sic], is not my task, especially, for I am just a migrant here'.[18] He wanted to complain about the number of crime stories reported in the Australian daily press.

Father Murphy SJ of Newman College, University of Melbourne, wrote at Easter asking Menzies to 'Forgive a person of no consequence breaking in on the Pascal Peace of a person of much consequence (destined, I hope, to be even more)'.[19] He was certainly of enough consequence for Menzies to arrange a lunch meeting with him to discuss university affairs, and Murphy later wrote a letter of thanks, assuring Menzies that he had a number of unsuspected well-wishers – unsuspected, perhaps, because they were to be found in rarefied Catholic circles. Menzies' own Presbyterianism was well advertised, but he always maintained many friendly contacts within the Catholic Church.

The unequal status of correspondents when writing upwards could be turned into an asset. It offered an opportunity to challenge the recipient. Edward Hampel addressed Menzies thus, as if he were spoiling for a fight: 'Are you big enough to listen to an ordinary working man? If not, you should throw this in the waste-paper basket now'.[20] Menzies was sometimes told that it was his duty to take an interest in what ordinary people were saying and thinking. It was to his advantage to hear from humble and insignificant writers, because he needed to keep in touch with the mood of voters. 'Probably', wrote

THE RHETORIC OF APOLOGY

AE Hyland, a retired Trade Commissioner, on the topic of revaluing the currency,

> you and those with whom you have been discussing the matter on which I am writing have covered all I am about to say, and yet as one of the ordinary people I feel there might be interest to you in a little, perhaps, of it.[21]

Not in spite of their anonymity, but rather *because* of it, some writers felt Menzies *needed* to be interested in what they had to say, because they were representative of those whose voices were rarely heard. Mr Kempe wrote about industrial unrest in 1955:

> I am writing this in the hope that you may find time to read a letter from an ordinary citizen, as I feel that in your position you may not come into contact with the man in the street as often as might be desirable, and therefore you may miss out to a certain degree on Public Opinion.[22]

In these cases the standard rhetoric of apology was turned inside out; the letters argued not that they intruded into the prime minister's valuable time but rather that, in his exalted but remote position, Menzies needed to make time to read them in order to keep in touch with ordinary Australians.

Writers offered many excuses for their poor handwriting and lack of epistolary expertise. Lack of education prevented Mrs Hurrell from writing as well as she might have wished. She was grateful for her pension and told Menzies so on one sheet of lined paper, writing in biro with no margins or punctuation. She concluded her letter: 'I had to learn myself Sir I never went to school hope you can understand this dreadful scribble'.[23] Mr Houghton of Canterbury (New South Wales) apologised because he felt weak after his accident, and E Campbell of Kootingal (New South Wales) simply wrote in telegrammese:

'Excuse scrawl badly crippled by disease'.[24] Writers were sick, or their sight was poor and this made their hand unsteady. 'I know the writing is a bit wobbly, but that's from the medicine I'm taking', was 64-year-old Margie Cantor's excuse, but she promised dutifully to vote Liberal at the next election if she was alive to see it, 'because I like to be governed by gentlemen not rogues'.[25] They pleaded they were in a hurry, like Edna Smith who apologised as she was rushing off to church.[26] She underlined the word 'church' as if to signal that this was a cast-iron excuse. They were rushing, perhaps to catch the mail, like Gordon McKillop, who wrote, 'Sorry, no typewriter or time to re-write in correct phrase'.[27] For Beryl Danahay, the mere thought of writing to the prime minister was enough in itself to bring on a nervous state which produced 'wobbly' writing.[28] The quality of the paper was also a potential cause of embarrassment, and writers begged forgiveness for running out of good quality notepaper; there was none to hand or it was too late at night to go out and buy some more.[29] Leonard Jones wrote to Menzies on the back of his own eviction notice and hoped he would understand his predicament because 'God is urging me to write to you'.[30]

The range of excuses offered for poor paper or wobbly writing indicated that, for many, letter-writing was an unfamiliar task, accomplished only through a considerable physical and mental effort. They wrote in pencil, on cheap, blue, lined notepaper or on whatever paper came to hand. They did not always have the best instruments with which to master writing technology. Once having determined to try, they came up against another handicap: writing to an eminent prime minister made the task doubly intimidating. There were many reasons for 'writer's block', but this fear informed all of them. Mrs McNaughton of Little River (Victoria) had sponsored an English family in the 'Bring out a Briton' campaign and wondered why they had not appeared. She wrote to Menzies in trepidation: 'Trembling, I approach the head of our government, yet confident that you will give me your earnest attention for one moment'.[31]

Writing to Menzies could bring on a fever and could be a health hazard. 'My heart is exceeding the speed limit (according to medical orders)', wrote another woman, adding 'my auld hand is rather shakey with nervousness!'[32] Margie Cantor, already mentioned, confessed that she had written three letters and destroyed them all before she finally overcame her inhibitions and communicated her suspicion that the Ministry of Health was being defrauded.[33] Writing to the prime minister could be an ordeal which led correspondents into very unfamiliar territory.

At least they were grateful for Menzies' accessibility, and they praised him for it. Joan Lewis, a would-be emigrant from Britain, was amazed to receive a reply from Menzies, and she wrote to Hazel Craig:

> Your letter from the Prime Minister Mr Menzies came as a complete surprise to me to-day. I never knew it was possible that such a person so high in the country, and with so much work and worry as well, that Mr Menzies has, could possibly take notice of a housewife. I don't really know how to start to thank you.[34]

British correspondents assumed that this unusual degree of friendliness was a national characteristic. E Porter, seeking to emigrate from England, sent a query about the Assisted Passage Migration Scheme, writing: 'It may seem a colossal nerve for anyone to write to the Prime Minister of Australia [...] but – nothing venture, nothing gain. Anyway, having visited Australia I know that even the highest ranking people are approachable'.[35] In fact, Menzies had a personal reputation for being available. Reminding him of this was a rhetorical strategy designed to make Menzies pay attention and, if necessary, take action.

The rhetoric of affiliation

Writers adopted subtle tactics to justify their personal approach to Menzies. Their letters developed narratives in which they had some previous contact with him. Perhaps they had met him or a member of his family in the past, although the writer realised that Menzies was unlikely to remember the encounter. Or perhaps their paths had crossed at some point because they had lived in the same area, or belonged to the same professional organisation or church congregation. The Scottish connection, as we shall see, was a favourite method of claiming a common interest which authorised them to write to Menzies with a small request. This was a powerful network which provided one of the anchoring rhetorics of the correspondence: it was based in a mutual experience, ancestry or connection which demonstrated the writer's affinity with Menzies and claimed they were both united in the same cause.

Stewart McInnes of Geelong College in Victoria had several claims to Menzies' attention, and he condensed them all in a few sentences. Firstly, as he told Menzies, he had once spotted the prime minister at a cricket Test chatting to Don Bradman, and then there was more, as he wrote:

> You knew my uncle years ago when you were practising law. I live in Camberwell Vic and You visited my parents one night when we used to live at Colac. I heard you speak at a Speech night at Strathmere Girls' School in Melbourne where my sister was boarder.[36]

McInnes evoked a shared enthusiasm for cricket, acquaintance with a relative, the legal profession, previous geographical proximity in the Melbourne suburbs and a school event to establish his right to be heard; all these mapped out a common territory where he and

Menzies shared an interest or where they had 'met' each other without Menzies realising it.

Schooldays were an important entrance point for CE Plummer, also of Camberwell (Victoria), who reminded Menzies of their days in the Lower Fourth at Wesley College, when he (Menzies) was a Prefect.[37] One British businessman wrote and even addressed Menzies as 'Dear Bob', on the strength of private conversations they had enjoyed on board the *Queen Elizabeth*, presumably on the long voyage to Southampton.[38] 'After all', wrote RJ McGarvie, 'we both went to the same church "Trinity" in Camberwell – years ago'.[39] It may have been years ago, but the reminder enabled Mrs McGarvie to establish an essential link which would give her privileged access to Menzies.

Mrs Muriel Webster of Hughesdale (Victoria) provides a final illustration of this kind of claim to personal affinity. She wrote to ask Menzies to help her pay a security bond for her two teenage sons who were in jail, and her letter began:

> It is some years since I knew you in Ballarat, but I attended St Andrew's Kirk and was a friend of your sister Belle and also my family by the name of McKillops were friends of your family and also your relations the Harry Adams. Perhaps you would remember my sister the pianist of Ballarat.[40]

She and Menzies were, she claimed, old acquaintances, former members of the same Presbyterian congregation, and furthermore she used to know Menzies' sister and, in case Menzies was still mystified, their two families had been good friends. She had established her personal credentials, which was an important way of justifying her request, even if it was an impossible one for Menzies to satisfy. On some occasions, Hazel Craig would first ask Menzies if he actually knew the correspondent, before drafting a reply to their letter. She needed to verify their claims to affinity, which would influence the tone of the response they received.

Correspondents cited the Scottish connection whenever possible to establish a link with Menzies, and they did so all the more readily because Menzies frequently advertised his Scottish ancestry. He visited Scotland on trips to Britain and he would turn up to Robert Burns commemorations in Melbourne wearing a kilt. He was a member of the Melbourne Scots Club and the Royal Caledonian Society, and fellow members of these clubs used this as a springboard from which to launch a greeting or a request. Sometimes the connection got him into trouble. When he was reported as telling a British audience that he thought Scottish Australians were the best Australians, he received complaints, both from a native-born Australian who felt slighted, and from another correspondent who asked in protest, 'What about the Irish? What about the Welsh?'[41] Apparently, neither the English nor those from other countries of origin carried much weight. Every time that Menzies visited the United Kingdom for a Commonwealth Prime Ministers' Conference, Scottish nationalist organisations tried to recruit him for the cause of Scottish independence.[42] He consistently ignored them.

Women knitted him clan tartan scarves.[43] Another sent him a gift of heather.[44] An Inverness art dealer sent him an original 1820 print of the Menzies clan, to congratulate him on his 1949 election victory.[45] One correspondent asked Menzies to get him some books on Scottish country dancing, and if possible autograph them, because he could not afford to buy any himself.[46] Correspondents knew that the ancestral home of his clan, Castle Menzies, still stood in Perthshire, and a few had been there. Helen Pepys was one – she fondly remembered picking snowdrops as a child in nearby Aberfeldy.[47] The vicar of St David's at nearby Weem, where Menzies' grandfather was born, asked for help with the restoration of his church, and Menzies responded with a donation of £10.[48] Mrs Gray offered Menzies a family heirloom, consisting of a bracelet made from the wood of

Stirling Castle, which burned down in 1855, threaded with gold. At the same time, she claimed to be a descendant of Mary Queen of Scots. This was a generous but extravagant gesture, and Menzies urged her to keep the bracelet in her family.[49]

Claims to affinity could be authenticated by inserting morsels of Scots verse or dialect in the letter, as when Sam McGregor sent a copy of Robert Burns' poetry and addressed Menzies as 'Dear Brither Scott'.[50] Burns was a regular reference point. CA Hood was brought up by a Scottish parson, and quoted Burns (but in his own English version):

> Bring a Scotsman from his hill
> Put in his cheek a whisky gill.
> Tell him tis Royal Georges will.
> And there's the foe.
> He'll think no more but how to Kill two at one blow.[51]

These anti-English sentiments probably fell wide of the mark as far as Menzies was concerned.

The Scottish network was also a Presbyterian connection, and Menzies' fellow religionists often played the Presbyterian card. As his followers well knew, Menzies had married Pattie Leckie in Kew Presbyterian Church, and this affiliation was often recalled.

Edith and Margaret Drummond of East Malvern (Victoria) asked Menzies to pay a visit to their namesake, a Presbyterian minister in Edinburgh. 'I am not writing to you as our Prime Minister', they wrote, 'but rather as a friend – a fellow Presbyterian – a fellow Scot and a loyal supporter of the cause of Liberalism'.[52] In their view, that made three good reasons why Menzies should oblige them. Presbyterian Church Elders regularly offered congratulations and prayers for Menzies' success.[53]

Besides all the correspondents who claimed Scottish ancestry, voters in Menzies' own constituency of Kooyong also had a strong basis for making a claim on the prime minister's time. Constituents appealed for his intervention either to install or improve a telephone line to their home or business, to cut through bureaucratic tangles and eliminate delays. Menzies always referred these cases to the Postmaster-General for a report, and his sponsorship of their inquiry produced results, or at the very least an explanation of why the petitioner should be patient a little longer. Camberwell Business Men's Club, for instance, wanted his intervention to secure better local post office facilities.[54] Father McNamara of East Kew asked for Menzies' assistance to persuade a local bank to give him a loan to build a new church. In support of his request, he reminded Menzies of the Catholic Church's role as a bulwark against communism.[55] Menzies received several dozen letters annually which can be clearly identified as either coming from his Kooyong constituency or else related to local constituency matters. In 1958, the number of Kooyong or Kooyong-related letters rose to 185, or 13.5 per cent of all Australian letters. The number fell away later as the demand for new telephone lines was satisfied. As a good constituency member, Menzies would respond to requests from individuals, local business and church organisations. At Christmas 1953, he obtained permission for the shopkeepers of Kew to erect an illuminated Christmas tree outside the Kew Post Office, to raise funds for the Children's Hospital and the Kew Mental Hospital. The electricity bill for the Christmas lights was covered by the Postmaster-General.[56]

Other ways of performing the rhetoric of affinity can be briefly summarised. Menzies had made many contacts in the legal profession before he had entered politics, and a few correspondents traded on this connection. Since Menzies was an honorary master of Gray's Inn in London, the law opened up another international network for him. Menzies was a member of several gentlemen's clubs, including the Savage Club of Melbourne, of which he became president. He received messages and requests from other 'Savages', as they called themselves, claiming affinity on this score. The Liberal

Party network across Australia, including Liberal parliamentarians, frequently claimed his attention.

Lastly, there was a network of ex-servicemen and their organisations which petitioned Menzies. Strictly speaking, this cannot be called a case of affinity, since Menzies had never served in the armed forces – something often held against him. This was ostensibly why the elitist Melbourne Club refused to admit him, although there may have been other underlying resentments at work here as well.[57] Army veterans and their relatives, however, wrote of their hardships and of sacrifices for the nation in wartime to which they presumed Menzies would be sympathetic. Victoria Brown, asking for a better deal for pensioners, wrote of 'We who gave our sons and brothers and husbands to fight for this "Wonderful" Country and who helped to make the country what it is today'.[58] A writer would frequently introduce himself as a veteran of one or both world wars, before further identifying himself as a Scot or as a voter in Kooyong. He or she might then go on to give their age, as if this too earned them an audience, and a mother or a war widow would stress how many children she had brought up. On this register Mrs Hardy pleaded for a pension for her 92-year-old mother, asking, 'My mother had three sons at the war, I wonder what they fought for?'.[59] Jean Guy wrote six pages about her struggles to find work and justified her letter in these terms:

> As an Australian citizen, a widow of Sergeant Thomas Francis Guy, M.M., wounded on the Somme and at the Battle of Amiens – gassed and nerves, but I didn't need a pension when he died in 1925 and never claimed it – my only son also did six years right through, also wounded Tobruk and Finchhafen [sic].[60]

Mrs Guy referred to the battle of Finschhafen, fought in Papua New Guinea in 1943. A personal narrative of family military sacrifice was a solid platform for a request or a complaint.

When Alexander MacClure wrote to Menzies from Roseville (New South Wales) about his war disability pension, he used several rhetorical ploys, but he began by identifying himself as a war veteran, prefacing his appeal with, 'As an ex-member of the 1st and 2nd A.I.F.' – in other words he had fought in both world wars. He now suffered from pulmonary tuberculosis as well as duodenal ulcers and stressed his history of patriotic sacrifice for the country. 'We did not fight for the Country', he added, 'as a prelude to selling out to the Communists', and he informed Menzies that he had always supported the Liberal Party ever since he first cast his vote as a front-line soldier in France.[61] Just to make sure he left no stone unturned in his appeal for help, he told Menzies that he also belonged to the clan McLeod.

Without sacrificing an ounce of sincerity, Menzies' correspondents were nevertheless artful writers. They adopted a variety of rhetorical ploys to establish their credentials. In order to justify their approach to the prime minister, they inserted themselves into the networks which they felt were most significant to him – the Scottish connection, the Presbyterian Church, the Kooyong constituency, the legal profession or the Savage Club. If possible, they played on several of these registers in the same letter, adding where appropriate the plea of the army veteran or the war widow to explain why they were especially worthy of consideration. These were some of what I have called the anchoring rhetorics on the basis of which requests were formulated. Having presented their *curriculum vitae*, what exactly did correspondents ask for in their letters of supplication? Their requests will be reviewed in the next two sections.

Businessmen bearing gifts

Requests or recommendations from businesses in Australia or overseas consistently made up a small proportion of the correspondence.

Businesses frequently requested a personal interview with the prime minister, which was rarely granted. Some companies simply wanted to send Menzies their annual report or present him with their annual calendar. From time to time, they advertised their product by sending him a personal gift. In 1955, the Australian Wine Producers Association sent him a case for Christmas.[62] Mount Pleasant and Reynella wineries would later follow suit, guaranteeing Menzies some well-lubricated Christmas seasons. Hotels invited him to stay with them, Prunier's of London offered him dinner, and he was cordially invited to visit the Casanova nightclub in Mayfair while he was in London – as far as we know, this was another invitation he did not take up.[63] Pressure of work was the usual excuse. Occasionally, however, he was very glad of a free ticket and would make time to take advantage of it. When JC Williamson theatres offered tickets to the Old Vic theatre, he gladly used them to enjoy a performance of *Macbeth*.

Chambers of Commerce and Manufactures sent along their annual reports, and invited Menzies to speak at an annual dinner. They asked him to provide a 'puff' for one of their publications. Individual companies often petitioned the prime minister for a licence to import essential goods and equipment. Textile mills needed to import more animal hair, and there were frequent pleas to allow the importation of medical goods from the US.[64] They recommended lower tariffs, encouraging more foreign investment, and they appealed like the Rhodes Motor Company in Melbourne to Menzies 'in your high position as Business Manager of Australia'.[65]

Companies needed government contracts, or else some assistance on facing their competitors. Thus Bristol Aviation Services begged Menzies to stop buying American aeroplanes, and promote Anglo-Australian co-operation instead.[66] The Graziers' Corporation stressed the importance of Japan as a wool market.[67] In 1957, Menzies visited Japan, and the Japanese prime minister reciprocated by visiting Australia, symbolising a thawing of Australian-Japanese relations still struggling to emerge from the shadow of the Second World War. A few companies were too important to ignore, and the prime minister sustained a continuing correspondence through 1955 with Fortescue Meredith over uranium mining in Queensland.[68]

Frank Packer was another frequent correspondent, and his Australian Consolidated Press was a consistent Menzies supporter. Together with Fairfax, owners of the *Sydney Morning Herald,* and other press publishers, he positioned himself to take full advantage of the opportunities offered when commercial television began in 1956. He and Menzies had a mutually supportive relationship. When Packer sent Menzies a telegram from London in 1950, referring to 'the magnificently impartial support you receive from the Australian press', he was presumably making a tongue-in-cheek comment on his own fulsome support for the Liberal Party.[69] Packer was well rewarded: he received a CBE in 1951, and Menzies was careful on this occasion to stress that he had recommended Packer for the honour not in recognition of his supportive work at the Sydney *Daily Telegraph*, but for his wartime service with the Allies Works Council.[70] Packer went on to receive a knighthood in 1959.

Menzies did not enjoy unanimous media support. He was often at loggerheads with the *Sydney Morning Herald*, especially over the Richardson Report of 1959, which controversially recommended salary increases for members of Parliament. Menzies accused the press in general, and the *Sydney Morning Herald* in particular, of whipping up public frenzy over this issue for no good reason. Approaching the federal election of December 1961, the Sydney press (except the ever-loyal *Daily Telegraph*) subjected Menzies to a barrage of criticism, which failed to dislodge him, although it may have helped the Labor Party retain control in New South Wales in the state elections.

Menzies' associations with Australian and overseas businesses should not be exaggerated. Overall, they produced less than ten per cent of the entire correspondence. Business correspondence absorbed 78 letters in 1949–50, or nine per cent of the total, and 168 letters in

1955, which has been sampled here, amounting to 8.3 per cent of the total number received.

Asking for a favour

In 1903, a 17-year-old American wrote to ask the king of Belgium to help him buy a new elephant, to replace one that had died, thus depriving the young man of the small income he made from giving elephant rides.[71] Requests to Menzies half a century later tended to be less exotic but perhaps they were sometimes more practical. As we have already seen, requests from Kooyong constituents to have a telephone line installed produced results, even if, as one supplicant admitted, asking the prime minister to get a telephone installed seemed like taking a sledgehammer to crack a nut.[72] Schoolchildren overseas who asked Menzies to send some Australian stamps also received a favourable response. Menzies received many pleas for help from those who considered themselves eligible for a War Service Pension, a Widows' Pension or an Ex-Serviceman's Home Loan. These were diverted to the appropriate public service department. The flood of requests for help with the aged pension are considered in chapter 6; requests for a photograph or an autograph were covered in chapter 3 on Menzies' fan mail.

There were constant demands for Menzies to grant an audience, receive a delegation or arrange a personal interview. Writers always hoped for direct access to the highest political level, which was why they wrote in the first place, but they were rarely accommodated. Menzies' time was too valuable, unless a very influential person or business interest was involved. To protect his time, he made it a rule never to give personal interviews while Parliament was in session.

Correspondents asked Menzies to write them a letter of introduction, especially if they were travelling to Britain and hoping to facilitate a few key meetings. He often obliged, although sometimes this was impossible. Walter King, for example, a former mayor of Concord (New South Wales), asked for a letter of introduction to Winston Churchill. Hazel Craig replied, apologising for the fact that 'the Prime Minister of Great Britain is not as accessible as our Prime Minister is and Mr Menzies is unable to do as you ask'.[73]

Visits to England spawned a multitude of requests for access to the Queen or a royal event. There were requests to organise an invitation to a royal garden party for the writer, an invitation to the Royal Enclosure at Ascot racecourse, or to the Trooping of the Colour ceremony. All such requests were channelled through Australia House in London. One Londoner asked Menzies to procure an autographed photograph of the Queen herself.[74] The chance of seeing the Queen during her visit to Australia in 1954 was another reason to write to Menzies for privileged access. One thing Menzies could sometimes achieve for supplicants was to get them tickets to a London cricket Test, which he did for a couple who wanted to see Australia play at The Oval in 1953.[75]

Individuals wrote to recommend a person for a decoration, and they asked Menzies to send a personal message to a relative who was celebrating a notable birthday. This was persuasive if the family were Liberal supporters and the recipient was very elderly. Mrs Lowe asked Menzies to send a congratulatory greeting to her parents on their 70th wedding anniversary, and he had his private secretary Geoff Yeend send them a telegram.[76]

On many occasions, however, Menzies could not satisfy a correspondent's request because the law could not be subverted on their behalf. When one Englishwoman asked for help in getting her Pekinese puppy out of quarantine, there was little that could be done.[77] Similarly, another Englishwoman wanted to take three pet cockatoos to Tasmania, but again, Menzies would not circumvent quarantine regulations.[78] Several correspondents expected Menzies to help them in conflicts with the tax office or another government department. One was AHA Macquart, a qualified accountant and former Liberal candidate for the New South Wales Legislative Assembly, but now unemployed. Social Security had asked him to take a job as a labourer, which he interpreted as an attempt by government officials to 'shame the intelligentsia'. When problems like this arose, Menzies referred the letter to the relevant department.[79]

Letters sought an entry into Menzies' family and domestic life. Wendy Solling wanted permission to paint his daughter Heather's portrait, which was also declined, although the artist had by then had several successful exhibitions of her work.[80] Madge Lyons, former cook at the King's Head pub in Sydney, sought a job at the Lodge as housekeeper or assistant cook. This was referred to Pattie Menzies, who brushed it aside dismissively with a pencilled note: 'Nobody need be out of a cook's job today'.[81]

The supplicatory letters received by Menzies included several from writers seeking a solution to personal problems ranging from the irritating to the desperate. Mrs Herbert of North Carlton (Victoria) was among the irritating category when she asked Menzies to do something about her troublesome Italian neighbours who were allegedly mistreating their lovely pet dog.[82] Others hoped the prime minister would answer more serious physical and emotional needs. They asked, for instance, for any old clothes which the Menzies family had to spare. This was typical of the extreme hardship expressed by aged pensioners, discussed in more detail in chapter 6. Others needed a loan, like an Austrian immigrant who asked Menzies for £50. He was out of work, ineligible for a pension because he was only 59 years old, and he faced eviction from his residence in Mount Gravatt (Queensland). He begged Menzies 'don't, don't let me down' several times, underlined in red.[83] He was refused and was told that the prime minister received many requests for loans, but that he would only respond to residents of his own electorate or charities like the Red Cross. Mr Thomson was in a similar situation, facing eviction although he was an invalid. He despaired of the state government (of New South Wales) and petitioned Menzies to find him a block of land somewhere. 'I sometimes wish the Japs had got here and killed me', he wrote, 'perhaps the Commos will be more successful'.[84] Menzies, however, was impervious to death wishes.

Menzies' intervention was required on occasion to resolve marital disputes. One divorcee in London, for example, wanted Menzies to compel her husband in Victoria to pay her maintenance.[85] A Ballarat man wanted Menzies' help in a child custody dispute with his former wife, who had taken their nine-year-old son to live in New South Wales.[86] Menzies sensibly told him to take his solicitor's advice, but it is notable that such requests received a reply at all. More harrowing was a letter from a Croatian woman who sent in an example of her needlework and asked in vain for a job. She was suffering from extreme anxiety and perhaps great loneliness, when she wrote in German: 'I am not happy in my marriage, for my son is very badly treated and I cry every day and endure my lot with daily weeping'.[87]

Supplicatory letters had exaggerated expectations of Menzies' powers. They might be useful in obtaining a telephone connection or a letter of introduction and, very rarely, they secured a small donation, as the vicar of Weem could testify. At the same time, writers assumed that Menzies possessed the ability to smooth their access to high places (especially when royalty was going to be present), to secure them employment and even resolve conjugal discord. Obiba Forson, from the Gold Coast in West Africa, wanted plenty: he sent a wish list for books, papers, two Bibles, 'your own team photo', and a bandage to cover his leg. 'If you sent all them to me', he assured Menzies, 'I will send you some monkey skin and some interesting things'.[88] But Menzies apparently had little use for a monkey skin.

6

*'I am sir [sure] you will
act as human bean'*

THE CRY OF THE DISTRESSED PENSIONER

Forgotten People

Several substantial issues occupied Menzies' correspondents over a number of years: among them were the communist threat, the nefarious influence of the Catholic Church, and the health and welfare of the British royal family. One theme, however, stands out for its longevity and its ability to spur people on to write to Menzies: pensions and their insufficiency. Political history has its own interpretation of the key problems of the Menzies era, but it largely presents a view from above, which does not necessarily correspond with the way ordinary people experienced life at the time. The view from the grass roots looked different. For ordinary writers, pensions were the single most consistently cited issue in the Menzies letters. In 1958, not normally identified as a year of hardship, Menzies received 62 letters about pensions, outnumbering the 45 explicitly anti-communist letters in his correspondence for that year. Pensioners' letters were still arriving in 1965, by which time the anti-communist frenzy of earlier years was no more than a distant echo.

I include different kinds of pensions within this broad category:

Age Pensions, Widows' Pensions, Invalid Pensions. Correspondence on the inadequacy of all kinds of pension provision revealed undercurrents of hardship and suffering among old people to which the government appeared insensitive. The letters told stories of hardship and near starvation. They reacted in a seasonal way, their agitation growing in intensity as the date of the annual budget approached. Even after the budget offered some relief to pensioners, they continued to write of their disappointment. There were plenty of reasons for writers to vote against Menzies on the pension issue, but in practice many correspondents protested their loyalty to the Liberal Party at the same time as they castigated the government for its inertia. In fact, they saw their support for Menzies as a compelling reason why he should listen to them.

Pensioners had a better claim than anyone to the title 'Forgotten People', although they were not forgotten in quite the same way as Menzies envisaged in his radio talk of 1942. Menzies referred to those whose interests were ignored both by large business corporations and by trade unions. In their correspondence, however, pensioners felt forgotten by everybody – including Menzies himself. In 1956, Sydney Moss of Beverly Hills in Sydney's south-western suburbs described old age pensioners as 'the forgotten people' and challenged Menzies to do something for them since they were praying for death. One year later, he repeated the reproach, adding 'I tell you one thing now, I am never going to vote for your party'.[1] Suffering was especially acute in periods of high inflation, and the government's failure to respond adequately to pensioners' cries of distress provoked letters like Henry Muller's desolate appeal to Menzies to act as a 'human bean', which heads this chapter.[2] The purchasing power of the age pension fell in the early years of Menzies' government, and it only recovered its 1949 value in 1954–55. Its real value fluctuated over the next decade, and only started to climb consistently after 1960.[3] The individual testimonies of the Menzies letters introduce us to the human dimension of these statistical trends.

THE CRY OF THE DISTRESSED PENSIONER

The government was not completely inactive on the pension front. The level of the age pension was increased eleven times in Menzies' period of office.[4] The maximum payment available was £2/10/- per week in 1951, and doubled over the next decade to £5 in 1961. At the same time, the means test on both income and property was progressively relaxed, and in 1958, the government awarded pensioners an additional 'supplementary assistance' of 10s per week if they lived in rented accommodation. After 1951, a pharmaceutical benefits scheme was also available to age pensioners.

Widows' pensions, which were also means-tested, were improved in the same piecemeal fashion. Property and income qualifications were relaxed, and by 1964, widows who maintained a dependent child were entitled to a maximum weekly payment of £8.[5] But civilian widows lacked the political influence of war widows and the aged, and their benefits remained inferior to what other groups received. They remained the most deprived group of all. The government's measures were never enough to rescue some correspondents from destitution.

The Liberal government tinkered with welfare benefits in other ways, too. Child Endowment, for instance, had first been introduced under Menzies himself in 1941, but was extended to include the first child for the first time in 1950. This was entirely consistent with Menzies' ideology of assisting the aspirations of middle-class families, although income tax deductions for spouses and dependent children did even more than Child Endowment to reinforce the traditional middle-class family and the status of the sole male breadwinner, without ruffling as many feathers.[6] Families with children thus drew on a double benefit, consisting of Child Endowment as well as a tax deduction, which looked like killing one bird with two stones.[7] The real value of Child Endowment was allowed to run down, but beneficiaries were not means-tested, and this was a cause of irritation to those on pensions who *were* subjected to a means test.

Pensioners' rhetoric

Pensioners' correspondence was sometimes bitter but often deferential. It could simultaneously express both loyalty and resentment. Pensioners travelled down several rhetorical avenues to present their discontents, and one of the most eloquent was the rhetoric of pioneer values. Pensioners constructed a heroic narrative of hardworking pioneer generations betrayed by an ungrateful nation. 'The generations gone by', claimed WM McGee, 'including we living aged, with daylight-till-dark hours, grinding, unrewarded toil and rough conditions, built the foundations of today's prosperity'.[8] 'The old man of yesterday', wrote J Leslie of Sydney in the same vein,

> took this virgin Australia in his bare hands and with sweat, hardship and low wages fashioned it into a haven for the self-seeker, the shirker and the loud-mouthed commo of today [...] The old man of yesterday travelled to Walgett, Burke, Cobar and Hay for a few weeks work in a shearing shed as a shed hand at 25s per week and his keep, and if he was not a fast worker and got the sack, it was just too bad.[9]

His letter implied a criticism of the over-indulged workers (or 'shirkers') of today, as well as of the government's reluctance to assist age pensioners. He assured Menzies, nevertheless, that his letter was intended to be helpful, and that he did not expect a reply. He received one regardless, thanking him for 'the practical interest [shown] in putting your views', which was a favourite response formula addressed to difficult or hostile correspondents.

J Leslie's heroic narrative was a way to legitimise the pensioner's claims, but evoking pioneer sacrifices was not a male monopoly. Mrs Beggs opposed the pension means test by recalling how she helped her parents to clear the land and burn trees and scrub in the evening, before getting up early in the morning and walking four miles to school the next day. 'We children of years ago', she told Menzies, 'had to cart water from dams, cut Thistles with [illegible word] hoes all the Xmas holidays, drive cattle to water', among other physically demanding tasks.[10] Pensioners cast themselves as 'we the pioneers', claiming responsibility for the foundation and eventual prosperity of the country, and therefore meriting fairer treatment.[11]

The rhetoric of wartime sacrifice was a further strategy employed to claim a better deal for pensioners. This applied particularly to invalid veterans and war widows' pensions, and assumptions about the value of wartime service were implicit in the complaints telegrammed to the prime minister by the Returned and Services League (RSL). In angry reaction to the meagre provisions of the 1953 budget, for example, the federal executive of the RSL considered the budget offered inadequate relief to war widows and others incapacitated in the service of the nation.[12]

The social prestige enjoyed by ex-servicemen guaranteed that war pensions carried none of the stigma sometimes impressed on recipients of other forms of welfare payments. Correspondents nevertheless felt that the patriotic sacrifices of soldiers and their families were not adequately rewarded. Mothers of soldiers who had died in action and veterans' relatives generally were seriously aggrieved. 'My mother had three sons at the war, I wonder what they fought for?' asked Mrs Hardy, the sole carer for her 92-year-old mother who could not obtain a pension.[13] Violet Hancocks, whose only son was killed in the war, protested: 'A hero's mother is surely worthy of a little better than this. I gave my all for Australia; surely Australia can now do a little for me'.[14] Veterans themselves were less prone to dramatise their situation. Mr A Dennis was an artilleryman from 1914 and appealed for a pension rise simply to 'let us old soldiers expire in comfort'.[15] His letter was appropriately dated Anzac Day 1955.

High price inflation aggravated the sufferings of the elderly. In 1951–52, price inflation was running at 20 per cent per annum, and rose to a peak of 22.5 per cent, partly as a result of the government's defence spending and over-rapid investment in economic development.[16] Arthur Fadden, as Treasurer, tried to limit the damage with his so-called 'horror budget' of 1952, which increased income and company taxes and foreshadowed a tightening of import controls. Fadden would subsequently take pride in this budget as one of his best, but it lodged in the popular memory for the pain it inflicted and the mistakes of economic management which made it necessary.[17] Menzies had promised the electorate that he would 'put the value back in the pound', but price inflation undermined this objective as far as the Australian consumer was concerned. Opinion polls conducted between 1951 and 1953 showed that only 15 per cent of respondents thought they were better off than 12 months previously.[18] Mr Horner from Melbourne, whose letters never achieved complete literacy, told Menzies in his own idiosyncratic spelling that

> this peace of papper is supposed to represent the Australian Royal pound and the Queen's money, with the pound at its present value you will be able to take it down and use it for lavatory papper as it will only be good for that perpuss sir.[19]

Inflation eased in 1955, but stable and continuous economic growth proved elusive, as commodity prices fluctuated wildly and the economy stuttered its way into the stop-go rhythm characteristic of the Menzies decades.[20] In spite of minor changes to the regime of the means test, civilian widows remained a particularly impoverished group.[21]

The value of fixed incomes was falling fast, with adverse consequences for small property-owners who rented accommodation to a tenant but were prevented from raising rents by state government controls which persisted into the mid-1950s. Mrs Kerley complained that she was not entitled to welfare concessions because she had to let two rooms in her home to pay for home maintenance, council rates and property insurance.[22] She had a small income, but nevertheless felt that without any assistance her situation was precarious. Holders of government bonds and those who had subscribed to war loans were equally vulnerable as inflation eroded the value of their investment. Mrs Morgan of North Bondi (New South Wales) was just such a property-owner, aged 76 and finding it difficult to make ends meet in a time of 'H.C.L.' (High Cost of Living). She signed her letter 'Mrs M.J. Morgan, widow very sick'.[23] Menzies wished her a speedy recovery. In Melbourne, Fred Skues appealed for the abolition of the pension means test, and found his fixed income from Commonwealth bonds could not cover the 'ever increasing cost of food such as meat, vegetables, groceries, etc., rates, repairs and general maintenance of our home, domestic help (a necessity to us) we are faced with a certain anxiety for the remainder of our lives'.[24] He perhaps belonged to one of the Liberal Party's classic constituencies of support: a lower middle-class couple who owned their own home, and had some investments and enough money to employ a domestic help. In the circumstances of the early 1950s, however, their future looked bleak.

The correspondence suggests that government inertia on pensions hurt some members of the middle class who normally formed a bedrock of support for Menzies and the Liberal Party. Lloyd Burgess argued that a relaxation of the means test

> would indeed provide for very many people in Australia, particularly for the vast middle section of the community made up principally of home builders and small business people and give them a sense of security and just reward for their efforts.[25]

Edward Hampel of Mundaring (Western Australia) provides an even better example of this social group of natural Liberal voters who objected to the means-tested pension. He first announced himself by attacking Labor Party leader Evatt and socialism in general. Then he identified himself as a semi-skilled worker who owned a small property and was in the process of building himself a house. He proceeded to locate himself sociologically, thus: 'I belong to that category described by Labour as "petty capitalists". Small property and farm owners, small storekeepers and garage men, etc. Financially not much better off than the pure wages man, but possessing a little more initiative'.[26] He found social welfare schemes demeaning: 'We have our pride', he wrote. 'We much prefer to pay our way [...] to licking the boots of petty officials and pleading poverty to get "free benefits".' He felt the same way about the aged pension, which encouraged applicants to plead their own poverty. 'Instead of making the applicant prove poverty', he advised, 'make him prove sobriety, financial responsibility and industry'. Hampel valued his independence and self-reliance. In social and cultural terms he represented a core Liberal constituency and shared the party's fundamental values. But the pensions means test undermined them.

Correspondents appealed to Menzies' Christian soul. They called him to account to practise what he preached. 'In your virtues as a Christian and your happiness as a father and grandfather', pleaded the desperate Violet Hancocks, 'please realise my deprived fate and help me'.[27] George Young of Bankstown (New South Wales) deplored Menzies' parsimonious attitude and protested against the inadequacy of the 2/6d rise awarded to age pensioners in the 1953 budget. He felt that 'old people today had less notice and care taken of them than stray dogs', and asked, 'Is this part of our Christian way of life that we have so often heard you preach and speak about?'[28] He looked forward to the 'political funeral' of Menzies and his government, and predicted that there would be few mourners.

Menzies was regularly reminded of his duty of humanitarian care for the vulnerable, framed in terms of a New Testament concept of Christian charity. Mrs Lampard had worked for 14 years as a nurse to the Sydney poor, and appealed to Menzies as a professing Christian. She referred him to verses of Matthew's gospel on ministering to the hungry, the thirsty, the naked and the sick, and followed up with an extract from James' Epistle including, 'Go to now, ye rich men, weep and howl for your miseries that shall come upon you'.[29] Christian references formed another important rhetorical landmark in pensioners' letters of distress.

On 2 September 1953, Menzies gave a radio talk in the 'Man to Man' series much appreciated by Liberal devotees. He tried to minimise, or at least relativise, the disastrous impact of inflation by comparing Australia's level of prosperity with that of other advanced countries. Arguing from an American survey, he told listeners that Americans, Canadians, Frenchmen and Russians would have to work longer hours to achieve the equivalent of the Australian standard of living. He was referring essentially to the basic price of foodstuffs in the countries mentioned. On the following day, the Institute of Public Affairs took issue with him in a letter which exposed the flaws in the rosy scenario he had described. The American survey outlined the situation as it existed in 1950, now made obsolete by steep price rises. In fact, Australians were paying much more than Americans for clothing, white goods and cars.[30] Menzies' over-optimistic broadcast cannot have cut much ice with struggling pensioners.

Poverty and pride

Minor adjustments to welfare services, and *ad hoc* measures to relax aspects of the means test, failed to mitigate the depth of persistent poverty in Australian society. Although the 1950s and 1960s are vaunted as a time of increasing prosperity, hardship and even starvation lay just below the surface. Thirty years ago, Stephen Garton's research unearthed some telling indications of this situation: in 1950, an inquiry by the Victorian state government and the Brotherhood of St Lawrence found that 15 000 Melbourne pensioners were unable to buy sufficient food and clothing.[31] In 1966, John Stubbs, author of *The Hidden People*, estimated that 25 per cent of all old age pensioners lived below a notional subsistence level, some of them without electricity or running water and reduced to eating dog meat.[32] In the same year, Professor Ronald Henderson invented the concept of the poverty line, linking it to the level of the minimum wage, and found that one in eight Melbourne families were living either below it or else dangerously close to it.[33]

Their dire predicament was amply illustrated in pensioners' letters to Menzies, in which the rhetoric of hardship articulated its own indictment of government neglect. The Pensioners' Amenities Society focused on the plight of the homeless, warning that the pension was a pittance and that 'an ever growing army of aged on receiving their pension must decide whether they will spend it on a room in a residential [hostel?] costing about £3 per week or whether they will sleep out and eat for they cannot do both'.[34] Mrs Howard in Sydney's eastern suburbs complained at the level of the widow's pension (then five guineas per week) and challenged Menzies to draw up a budget on which she and her three children could survive.[35] In Menzies' own constituency of Kooyong, Mrs Hume found it difficult to afford a hot bath fired by a coke heater and dared not call a doctor because of the expense. A recent rise in telephone charges left her little choice but to sacrifice her telephone.[36] Menzies' response to her frustration was to send her a copy of his speech for the Defence Preparations Bill – a staggeringly inappropriate gesture in the circumstances but one which clearly indicated the government's spending priorities.

Correspondents were often living in sub-standard accommodation, which they and their supporters vividly described. In Warrnambool (Victoria), Mrs Williams could not afford to re-roof her house and negotiated a minefield of buckets and dishes in her bedroom and kitchen laid out to catch the leaks.[37] In Jindabyne (New South Wales), Marie Irwin simply had nowhere to live and told Menzies that the local Catholic priest was putting her up. She begged him in vain: 'Could you please lend me £10 I will try to give it back to you if I win a prize I am not too well'.[38] Jean Thornley

THE CRY OF THE DISTRESSED PENSIONER

knew at first hand the problems of elderly people in Sydney's western suburbs and reported that:

> Some of the old people are living under shocking conditions. One old lady we took wood out to yesterday hasn't even got a decent bed to sleep on and the rats made us very welcome. Poked their noses out from everywhere. They had gnawed all through her cupboard [...] We are visiting over 40 just in the outskirts of Penrith alone.[39]

The new prosperity of the late 1950s had left many people far behind.

Lack of clothes and footwear was a recurrent problem in the correspondence. In the otherwise well-heeled Sydney suburb of Woollahra, one pensioner wrote to Menzies to bemoan her lack of 'warm undies' and the impossibility of affording to have a pair of worn shoes mended.[40] JW Heggarty had trouble keeping warm in winter. He asked for a donation of blankets and flannel shirts. To forestall accusations of waste and profligacy, he insisted that he did not smoke or drink and had not bought any clothes for 17 years. 'All the clothes', he wrote, 'are dead men's clothes'.[41] His appeal for a clothes donation was declined.

Food and drink had to be severely rationed. In Sydney, Mrs Clarke, who incidentally was a strong supporter of Menzies, remembered collecting 'throw out' fruit and vegetables discarded in the daily markets. She claimed that she had dislocated her shoulder by carrying heavy loads and deformed her feet by wearing second-hand shoes.[42] One correspondent suggested distributing leftover school milk to pensioners so that they could add it to their tea.[43] Alice Morgan, who clearly lived alone in inner-city Melbourne and struggled to keep her head above water, told a poignant story in conversational style. It began, 'I did a silly thing this week'.[44] Her 'silliness' consisted of craving a little steak for dinner. She hoped to buy a piece which would last for two meals, but the butcher charged her 6s. and it only provided one. Morgan felt guilty about the expense and needed to chastise herself. 'I suppose I was extravagant', she wrote, 'but tonight all I had was tea and raisin bread. I have a soup cube as well. It's a good thing tomorrow is pension day because there's only a little bit of butter left and a dessertspoon of tea'. This tale of relative deprivation exposed the hand-to-mouth existence of the elderly poor in stark detail. No doubt tales of hardship were sometimes prone to exaggeration, but this one, in its intimate honesty and detail, does not appear fictional. Morgan ended her letter in surprising fashion by effectively undermining the force of her own grievances: 'Don't worry about people being cross', she wrote as if to spare Menzies any grief. 'It will all come right.' A few correspondents were ashamed to complain about their lot, or else refused to admit that poverty made them miserable.

Sometimes the suffering of correspondents is overshadowed by their breath-taking optimism and hope in a better future. There were always consolations in life as Mrs Williams explained: 'I thank you for all the pension but when one is in Debt on account of grand children there is nothing left all I have is the sunshine of "God" that shines in my heart'.[45] And if God did not always provide much sustenance beyond sunshine, correspondents could always dream of another, happier life. Mrs Flamank of Rowland Flat (South Australia), for example, pleaded for a loan to cover her debts and promised to repay it from her Child Endowment payments (she had seven children under the age of 11). 'Oh Mr Menzies', she begged,

> I often Romance thinking what it would be like to have a home of our bery own [*sic*] big shady trees and lawns so we could have swings and playground for the kiddies fruit trees etc [...] Its now we need the necessities [...] everything seems so futile.[46]

THE CRY OF THE DISTRESSED PENSIONER

For correspondents like Mary Flamank, the Australian suburban dream would remain pure fantasy.

Whatever hardship they endured, pensioner correspondents maintained their pride. Rhetorical signposts in their letters pointed to the need to uphold their dignity and self-respect, even if these qualities were potentially compromised by the act of writing a supplicatory letter itself. 'We don't want charity', Victoria Brown protested, 'we wan't [sic] what is rightfully ours'.[47] One Queensland woman was seeking relief (in vain) from heavy death duties owed on the sudden death of her husband, and was forced for the first time to contemplate drawing the age pension. She wrote, unhappy at the prospect: 'I am not enjoying the idea of having to surrender my independence, nor to accept help. Call it "dirty pride" if you will. Wonder if you and your colleagues have forgotten there are still some proud people in the world?'[48] Pensioners anxious to preserve some personal self-esteem had great difficulty under the regime of the means test which, as Menzies himself had put it in 1943, forced the applicant to 'prove his poverty' in order to qualify for the benefit.[49] The careless or light-hearted attitude of parliamentarians to the pensioners' predicament compounded their discontent. Mr Raymond wrote to complain about a speech by a Labor member referring to pensioners as 'These wretched half-starved desperate people', not because it distorted the truth but because the extremity of the phrase seemed to deprive the pensioner of any dignity.[50] Whatever his situation, Mr Raymond refused to be considered 'wretched'. Another indignant Liberal supporter asked 'Could you advise government members not to indulge in jeering laughter whenever the matter of the pensioner's plight is mentioned in the house?'[51] Not only, she complained, did this create a very bad impression on radio listeners, but it was extremely hurtful to struggling old people who were reluctantly compelled to apply for a pension.

'Rebellious widows'

The pension issue generated rage and rebellion. Much of it centred around the debate on the means test, and the benefits or disadvantages of introducing a universal National Insurance scheme. Such a scheme, never implemented, would have drawn on contributions from all citizens, who would all then have been eligible to receive benefits without having to pass a means test. It would have created a welfare state in Australia in the sense that the term was understood in Britain and the Nordic countries. In the past, Menzies himself had advocated such a broad contributory scheme, believing it would keep welfare funds solvent and avoid the embarrassment sometimes caused to individuals by the means test. In the 1940s, however, the Labor Party had objected that flat-rate universal contributions would be unrelated to the contributor's real ability to pay, and that a graduated tax was a more equitable funding resource. The debate continued into the 1950s, but the means test was not replaced. Menzies was reminded of his 1949 promise to consider a National Insurance scheme, and pensioners cited the British example as a successful model, but to no avail.

For correspondents, the problem with the means test was that it degraded the applicant. 'There is a very big crop of Old Boys', wrote a Country Party member, 'which are very disgruntled and even bitter at having to pauperise themselves before they can get the age pension'.[52] Relaxing the means test requirements did not change this; the means test on property and income created an incentive to sell assets and reduce savings. A pensioner with £200 in the bank risked a reduction in her pension. What was Mrs Kerley to do in such a situation, she asked, 'Are we to bury it in the back yard or hide it in the house and chance being robbed and bashed to death?'[53] Relaxing the upper limit on pensioners' income could not dispel the conviction that the government cared little for the pensioners' difficulties. It was pointless, according to one woman, to allow the elderly to earn more at an age when they were increasingly incapable of any sustained work at all.

THE CRY OF THE DISTRESSED PENSIONER

'Ones strength does not permit one to do it', she wrote. 'Also no one will employ you as they want full work for full pay. So please do not humiliate us any longer by a mere pittance to exist.'[54] 'Nobody [...] likes to employ an old person', wrote another pensioner. 'We are a blot on the landscape.'[55]

The means test was perceived as a punishment for hard work and thrift, precisely those middle-class virtues which Menzies had once promoted. Mrs Chapple felt there was no reward for hard work and saving for the future, adding a Scottish rebuke: 'Fair Play is Bonnie Play'.[56] Mr Hamilton was hurt and bewildered by his situation, asking what was the purpose of thrift for 'we "middle classes"'? 'Many of my friends', he added, 'spend every "razoo" they get because "we can have a whale of a time now, and get the pension later?" "Why should we save?"'[57] James Fitton had built his own home but suffered from arthritis and depended on drugs, although he did not qualify for pharmaceutical benefits. He threatened to vote Labor, protesting: 'I have been saving all my life, never gambled or drank. I have never seen England which I left 34 years [ago] [...] I could have got a pension long ago if I had not been honest. An honest man gets nowhere'.[58] Fitton asked for the complete abolition of the means test. In deciding to modify the means test rather than abolish it, Menzies appeared to pensioners to be undermining one of his own heartfelt objectives: supporting the thrifty middle classes.

Labor Party leader Herbert Evatt made the means test an important issue in the 1954 election. Evatt had succeeded Chifley as Labor leader in 1951 after a distinguished international career which brought him to the presidency of the United Nations General Assembly (1948–49). He had successfully campaigned for the defeat of the 1951 referendum to dissolve the Australian Communist Party. In 1955, however, he failed to prevent the departure from his party of its Victorian Catholic faction, and he became determined to prove that the sensational defection of Soviet agent Petrov had been deliberately managed by the government to deliver victory to the Liberal Party in the 1954 election, when Menzies secured a majority of seven. Until then, prospects for a Labor win in 1954 had looked promising.

Before the 1954 election, Evatt promised that Labor would abolish the means test within the life of the next Parliament. This set off alarm bells in the Liberal Party branches where party faithfuls realised that Evatt had seized the initiative and that this could give Labor a decisive electoral advantage. Their anxious letters warned Menzies that a response was advisable or else voters would be alienated. They understood the importance of the issue. Menzies took the high ground and refused to enter a bidding auction. Instead he warned of the dangers of inflation – a familiar conservative response to left-wing social reform projects.[59] He now argued that Australia already had a universal scheme of welfare contributions, and that this was embodied in revenue from a progressive income tax. In 1954, however, many more correspondents were agitated or disappointed by the government's failure to abolish the means test than were moved to write about the Petrov Affair.

The means test tended to disadvantage women. Married women wrote resenting the fact that their husband's income was taken into account when they themselves were of pensionable age (60 or over). Meanwhile single women asked for a more generous ceiling for their permissible income. Lifting this ceiling, according to Miss Morrissey, would be 'an Elizabethan gesture', and she reminded Menzies that allowing women over 60 to work could not possibly have a detrimental effect on Australia's birth rate.[60] Women formed the vast majority of pensioners, because they were eligible for it five years earlier than men and because they tended to live longer. Demographic and statistical probabilities ensured that most of those who wrote to Menzies to complain about pensions were women.

The Australian model of social welfare thus prevailed, in spite of resistance from many of its beneficiaries. Based on the principles of means testing, refusing to adopt a universal contributions scheme and giving large scope to private health insurers, it would fall short of a welfare state as it was conceived in northern Europe. Writing in 1965, historian Thomas Kewley called it a welfare 'system' with 'coherence and consistency', which seems open to debate, given the long and indecisive discussions during the 1940s and 1950s about its fundamental nature and purpose.[61] The age pension, for instance, never explicitly decided whether it was a supplement to income or a substitute for one. A contributory scheme was considered, debated, but ultimately rejected. There was a very pragmatic reason for this – it was too expensive. In 1954, Menzies argued that the abolition of the means test would cost the Commonwealth £100 million per annum. In 1961, the argument remained identical, but the stakes were higher: it would now cost about £140 million to remove the means test.[62] After Labor failed to win the 1954 election, abolition was a very remote outcome, and it became more and more improbable as time passed.

The problems and hardships of age pensioners were strong arguments for the introduction of a compulsory superannuation scheme, but this did not arrive until 1991. Until then, only temporary and *ad hoc* measures could be expected. 'Giving paltry, humiliating concessions, medical benefits, and scholarships here and there, is only fooling with the whole problem', Joy Muir of Mosman (New South Wales) realised. 'But people were not born in sunny Australia to live in poverty and misery – it isn't necessary any more!'[63] This critique of the government's piecemeal approach is worth quoting because it was written only a year before Menzies retired when, according to a commonly held view, Australia had already reached the promised land of wealth and security. Frustration and hardship, however, were ever-present companions for the aged.

The rhetoric of resentment in the correspondence aimed at several different targets. The first in line were the nation's wasteful youth, whose inconsiderate behaviour contrasted poorly with the more responsible and far-sighted older generations. The elderly vented their wrath against shirkers and bludgers. A Little of Gympie

(Queensland) argued that the means test was 'creating a nation of loafers'.[64] Mrs Hume perceived that less work was being done every day and it was being done less effectively. 'People are just being taught to be dishonest', she wrote, 'it's the only way of keeping up'.[65] Recent immigrants were another obvious target for disgruntled pensioners, since once naturalised they were eligible for Child Endowment, which was not means tested. Since they had made no sacrifices for the country, this was deemed unfair.[66] Australians as a whole, some thought, were becoming more selfish.[67] Arthur Walker wrote six foolscap pages in purple ink on very poor paper, a combination of materials which eloquently expressed both his poverty and his outburst of rage against the government's failure to increase war pensions in 1953. He demanded the indexation of pensions against the cost of living. He denounced the rich and powerful, the politicians, judges and divers snobs whose indifference was unfairly neglecting the poorer classes.[68]

These grumblings provoked Liberal supporters to threaten to withhold their vote at the next election. J Leslie warned Menzies that he had been elected in the first place largely by virtue of the old age pensioner's vote.[69] George Young, incensed by Menzies' failure to attend a pensioners' meeting in Sydney Town Hall, which he attributed to cowardice, also threatened a voter backlash against the Liberals.[70] 'Like myself', Mrs Missing warned five years later, 'there are many rebellious widows in a quandary, as to how they will vote on November 22nd?'[71]

Almost every small rise in pension provision was greeted with disappointment, if not derision. After the budget, a few letters asked for their pension rise to be backdated. This was the case in 1953, when the maximum age pension rose by 2/6d to £3/10/-. A Queensland correspondent facetiously told Menzies that he was expecting a cheque from Treasurer Arthur Fadden for his raise, backdated to 1 July, the beginning of the fiscal year.[72] Another anonymous pensioner was so disgusted that he sent a 2/6d postal order to Menzies with a

THE CRY OF THE DISTRESSED PENSIONER

sarcastic note: 'Noble Sir, Please accept my 2/6 Rise a fitting reward for your generosity to the Pioneers of Australia'.[73] Menzies was condemned as a callous monster. Miss Donald from outer Melbourne had received a reply to a query about pensions and protested about the response, which 'had the usual political evasions we are so used to over the air when Parliament is in session'. She was now convinced that 'you, as a man, have not very much heart, a rather ruthless spirit, interested mainly in fat agricultural cheques. With very little interest in human beings'.[74]

Mrs J Shaile, an invalid and partially sighted pensioner with diabetes from inner-city Sydney, agreed. 'I wonder if your brother would have done a better job for the pensioners', she told Menzies. She had not been able to find a home, and real estate agents, she wrote, 'look at me as though I was mad'. Then she rounded on Menzies:

> Sir, I have never heard of you doing a good turn for any body
> in your life, and I suppose you know you are not liked, but
> I know you don't care about us we don't even exist in your eyes,
> I wrote to you once before, and I got the same as I'll get this time (nothing).

She concluded sourly: 'I have had my say, and it will cost me a stamp, but that's life, it always costs'.[75] At least Mrs Shaile was right about one thing: she would not receive a reply. Once, pensioners' complaints had received a polite response from the secretariat explaining the government's limited financial resources. By 1965, however, their letters of complaint were being shuffled into the 'no-reply' tray.

In the long run, the population was ageing, although the implications of this for the welfare budget of the future were hardly appreciated in the 1950s. Government spending on age and invalid pensions doubled between 1949 and 1954 to over £81 million per annum. It rose again by 146 per cent between 1954 and 1964 to almost £200 million.[76] This was by far the largest item of expenditure on the social welfare budget, with Child Endowment running second. In 1955, Mrs Julia Hosking of Melbourne sounded a lonely prophetic voice, looking ahead to more apartment buildings constructed by State Housing Commissions to provide affordable accommodation for the elderly, and warning Menzies of a new situation in welfare provision because life expectancy was sure to rise.[77]

In the meantime, Menzies would continue to receive resentful letters from the disaffected pensioner, mobilising his or her rhetorical resources to appeal for a Christian gesture in recognition of wartime service and past sacrifice. Self-designated 'rebellious widows' wrote angry and distraught letters in response to government inaction. They sometimes outlined lives of extreme deprivation which belie the common association of this period with rising affluence and material comfort. They negotiated a welfare environment which remained underdeveloped and which, if the correspondence is to be believed, failed to eliminate a bedrock of poverty which persisted in spite of growing prosperity.

7

*'Much as I love our little Queen,
I think she needs a spanking'*

BRITAIN AND THE EMPIRE

A schizophrenic nationalism

In the Menzies years, being British was an integral part of Australian identity. 'It is our great privilege', wrote Mrs Brown of Kyneton (Victoria), 'to live under the British Crown. We are British and you never forget it. Don't allow Australia to forget it either'.[1] As historian Neville Meaney put it, 'Britishness was the dominant cultural myth in Australia', up to at least the 1960s.[2] The British connection was cemented by financial and commercial links and the common memory of wartime struggles, protected by the policy of restricted immigration, and celebrated at key points in the calendar, including Empire Day and Anzac Day. And yet it was more than just a friendly connection for, instinctively, Australians did not even think of Britain as a foreign country. In 1948, Menzies himself had proclaimed that 'the boundaries of Great Britain are not on the Kentish coast, but at Cape York and Invercargill [on the South Island of New Zealand]'.[3] The Australian 'way of life', which correspondents referred to as though it was an endangered species, was no different from the British 'way of life', although exactly what it consisted of remained unclear.[4] Australia's values were British values and its culture was

British culture, even though 'British' has always been a problematic concept in the United Kingdom itself. Technically, Australians were still British citizens. It was therefore assumed that British immigrants would merge seamlessly with Australian society, so that the idea of assimilation did not even apply to them. Pro-British sentiments were an expression of the schizophrenic Australian nationalism of the post-war age; only later did Australian nationalism conceive of itself as independent from, and sometimes antagonistic towards, Great Britain.

Britain's dominant position in Australia's cultural imaginary weakened during the 1960s. In 1956, the Suez crisis exposed the limits of British military power beyond the Middle East. The White Australia Policy, which privileged British immigration, was coming under fire both at home and abroad. The solidarity of the British Empire, or the Commonwealth as Menzies was now forced to call it, was starkly challenged by the international campaign against apartheid in South Africa. These developments and their repercussions in the Menzies correspondence will be discussed in the following chapter.

Australia, then, was changing but it was perhaps even more significant that Britain, too, was entering a stage of post-colonial adjustment. These developments would transform the close relationship between Britain and Australia which was taken for granted by Menzies and cherished by many of his correspondents. For one thing, the arrival of migrants from the Caribbean and the Indian sub-continent was literally altering the complexion of British society. For another, the notion of a European free trade area offered Britain better prospects for economic growth than the old imperial trade preferences. Menzies and many of his correspondents belonged to an old and disappearing world in which the British Empire was still an influential embodiment of global whiteness. His world view, however, was approaching its natural expiry date.

This chapter considers the correspondence in the light of strong popular attachment to Britain, the monarchy and the Empire. The letters testify to the profound reality of loyalty to the monarchy, as evidenced during the royal tour of 1954, as well as to the residual desire to cling to the Britishness of Australia even as changing circumstances inexorably diluted its significance. They show, at the same time, how much the writers identified Menzies himself with British-Australian nationalism. Furthermore, Menzies had many correspondents in Britain itself, and they too looked to him for leadership in Commonwealth affairs.

British loyalties and 'British justice'

Memories of wartime solidarity underpinned the rhetoric of Empire. 'At heart', wrote Captain Rhodes of Rockhampton (Queensland), 'under the inspiration of leadership, the people of Australia are no less British than were the men and women of Dunkirk'.[5] No doubt he was recalling the spontaneous civilian armada which crossed the English Channel in May and June 1940, in whatever small craft were available, to evacuate the remnants of the British army cut off at Dunkirk. Australia, too, he implied, was ready to make similar efforts and similar sacrifices. Amateur poets supplied Menzies with their efforts in celebration of Britain's wartime role, and this sample from a correspondent in Minnesota provides a brief idea of its flavour:

> The British peoples bravery,
> So grim, tenacious, bold,
> Has saved the world from slavery
> In Hitler's strangling hold.
> Democracy is well entrenched
> On England's rugged coast,
> Where men, with hand on rifles clenched,
> Of freedom still can boast.[6]

In a slightly patronising tone, the Young Conservatives of the City of London congratulated Menzies on his electoral victory in 1949, noting that

> We are ever mindful of the great help Australia has given us during the years of war and since and for which we in this Country are truly grateful, working and hoping that one day in the not too distant future we shall once again be at the giving end.[7]

In this letter, the Chairman also 'remembered with pride' Menzies' personal role in Churchill's War Cabinet during the Second World War. This was one reason for Menzies' high profile and popularity in Britain.

Prevailing economic and geopolitical realities further strengthened the relationship, as correspondents continually reminded the prime minister. Mrs Sweeney of Moonee Ponds (Victoria) berated Menzies for an election speech in which he referred to £600 million of foreign investment in Australia, without specifying that the greatest part of this investment came from Britain.[8] Australia remained part of the sterling currency bloc, and regularly suffered a shortage of dollar reserves, which is what had prompted petrol rationing in 1949. Sterling eventually became fully convertible in 1958. Australia imported British goods at preferential rates. Britain, in turn, was a good market for wool and food products and took most of Australia's exports until Japan overtook it as Australia's leading customer in the 1960s.[9] In other words, this was not merely a sentimental relationship. When Menzies committed troops to the British Commonwealth's military effort in the Malayan Emergency in 1950, few correspondents objected, suggesting widespread backing for imperial solidarity.

The same can be said for British atomic testing after 1952 at Maralinga in South Australia. Gladys Spickett saw Menzies on British television and wrote:

> I felt proud and grateful to hear you say you were British and
> the fact that in the event of war we are still one big family.
> The thought of war, ever present in the back of our minds and
> H bomb and all the other terrors seemed not quite so fearful.[10]

Uranium mining in South Australia further implicated Australia in British atomic weapons development.[11]

In the eyes of his followers, Menzies personified the organic tie with Britain. He himself identified with Britain's parliamentary institutions and with his own Scottish heritage. The fact that he had often felt frustrated by Churchill's authoritarian style during the war did not diminish his devotion to the Crown and the defence of the Empire.[12] When the Garbett family wrote a three-page letter to congratulate Menzies on his election victory in 1949, and to wish him a Happy Christmas, they said:

> It is such a relief and joy to know that now we have for our
> Prime Minister a man 'who is British to the bootheels'. We stand
> with you all the way [...]
>
> In the last five years it has seemed as if our beloved empire was
> falling to bits – members breaking away, internal dissension,
> tradition and customs thrown to the winds.
>
> Would it be possible for us to use again the title – 'British
> Commonwealth of Nations'? 'British' meant and stood for so
> much to those within and without the Empire. And it will again
> – with you to help and work and guide.[13]

Lillian Iles in Melbourne felt a similarly renewed confidence, writing: 'I am 100% British and [...] believe much of the real worth of the British at home, both personnel and means will transfer to a nationalist Australia. It will strengthen and cement both us and the Old Country by this integration'.[14] With Menzies at the Lodge, 'It will be more like Canberra with someone holding functions in the true British way', predicted another correspondent.[15] Exactly what she understood by the British mode of hospitality is unclear, but as far as these correspondents were concerned Menzies' election had restored the rightful balance of the world. Planet Australia and Planet Britain were once again in proper alignment.

Just as Menzies represented allegiance to Britain, so too did the Liberal Party itself. A 16-year-old correspondent from Fort Street High School in Sydney made this absolutely clear, writing, 'The Liberal Party is everything that I believe in more or less. Firstly because [it] is the British party, secondly its defence policy is more than all to be desired – it makes us a strong Australia to be proud of, thirdly it is a free enterprise party'.[16] EW Vernon from Harbord (New South Wales) suggested that the Liberal-Country Party coalition should be renamed 'The British Australian Party'.[17] He wanted to distinguish it from the Australian Labor Party, which he thought had been captured by a foreign power, by which he meant the Pope. A 'British Australian Party' was clearly not regarded as subject to foreign influence.

Britishness involved more than commercial preferences and a groundswell of popular monarchism. It also represented shared values of fairness and equality. Grumblers in the Menzies correspondence very rarely asked for an Australian 'fair go'; instead, they appealed to a sense of 'British justice', which was assumed to be fair, impartial and accessible to all. The Loyal Orange Institution of Victoria congratulated Menzies on his handling of the Petrov Affair, which exposed the activities of Soviet spies in Australia, and which is discussed further in chapter 9. On this occasion its members affirmed that 'we trust that the high standards of British justice will ever be maintained in Australia'.[18] Mrs Elizabeth Jackson was an invalid pensioner in Brisbane suffering from diabetes. She was convinced that the recent death of her husband had been caused by a firm of solicitors which had been harassing him over his bankruptcy case. 'Mr Menzie [sic]', she pleaded, 'why do you as Prime Minister of this fair land allow such cruelty to go on surely there is British justices [sic]'.[19] She went on, 'I will put the matter before the Queen Mother and ask her to tell our Dear Queen Elizabeth about this matter'.

Both supporters and opponents demanded 'British justice' when they felt they had a complaint. Rachel Hindle sent a series of letters and telegrams protesting against a wide variety of social injustices. They included the deployment of troops to Malaya without the people's consent, and she also referred to the parliamentary privilege case which led to the imprisonment of Frank Browne and Ray Fitzpatrick in 1955.[20] Browne and Fitzpatrick, respectively editor and owner of the *Bankstown Observer*, had been judged guilty of violating parliamentary privilege in attacking Charles Morgan, Member for Reid in Sydney. Their case was heard by Parliament, but they were denied legal counsel and imprisoned for 90 days. Rachel Hindle was not the only correspondent who felt that the due processes of law had not been observed in this case, nor was she the only one who appealed to British values and attacked the apparent denial in this case of 'the ethics of British justice'. Maurice Ashkanasy, on the other hand, believed that justice certainly *had* been done when the Commonwealth government declined to collect income tax from compensation payments received by Jewish victims of Nazi oppression. This decision was 'in line with the best traditions of British and Australian political life'.[21] The ideal of British justice acted as a kind of court of last resort, providing theoretical protection to the weak and a benchmark by which public administration could be judged by every citizen.

Symbols of monarchy and Empire

Australians remained attached to the symbols of Britishness – the flag, the anthem, the pound sterling, at least until decimal currency was introduced in 1966. For WR McFerran, Chair of the Australia Day Committee in 1959, flying the flag on the national holiday was a reminder that 'we live under the Union Jack, that Great Britain is our Mother Country and her flag is also embodied in our flag'.[22] The idea that Australia should develop and publicise its own 'National Song' interested many correspondents but it appeared to annoy Menzies. He insisted that a national song was all very well, but could not replace 'God Save the Queen' as Australia's National Anthem.[23] Menzies' own fondness for the ceremonial of monarchy is well known. In historian Judith Brett's assessment, he suffered from a narcissistic craving for acceptance by the Mother Country, soothed by his being made a Knight of the Order of the Thistle in 1963, and by succeeding Churchill as Lord Warden of the Cinque Ports in 1966, a sinecure he held until 1978.[24] The Lord Wardenship was a purely ceremonial position which had once involved guarding England's channel ports in the southeastern counties. It came with a distinctive uniform, which Menzies proudly wore.

When Australia planned to adopt decimal currency, Menzies hoped the new currency would be named the 'royal'. The idea had insufficient public support and Australia was dollarised. The image of the monarch, however, was retained on the coinage. Several correspondents wanted to introduce a Commonwealth flag. Wing Commander Malet even sent Menzies a flag of his own design, featuring a central sun ('which never sets on the Commonwealth'), and sections radiating from it in black and white, brown and yellow, representing the Commonwealth's many-coloured races. Malet had been proudly flying the flag at his Hampshire home.[25] Menzies returned the flag, so I was unable to appreciate its qualities at first hand. A New Zealand correspondent had a slightly different perspective:

he wanted to make the British Union Jack a compulsory and integral part of the flag of every Commonwealth country, demonstrating that Britain was the common link that united them.[26]

The most powerful symbol of all was the monarchy itself. Correspondents plied Menzies with requests for tickets and invitations to royal events in England. They were usually referred to Australia House in London, which managed requests to attend royal garden parties, held ballots for tickets to the Royal Enclosure during the Royal Ascot race meeting, not to mention the Trooping of the Colour ceremony.[27] In 1953, Menzies received many coronation tributes and celebratory poems. In fact, a good proportion of the poetry offered to Menzies throughout his term of office related to the British royal family. Poems were patriotic and pro-British, in a triumphant 'Rule Britannia' register, often praising the royals, from Wallace Simpson to Elizabeth II herself. Gertrude Hart wished Menzies 'a lovely time' at the coronation in 1953, where he joined the distinguished procession, adding of the young monarch, 'she's a beautiful creature – and as brave as she's bonny!'[28] Not all correspondents expressed whole-hearted approval. Edna Smith in East Melbourne, for example, deplored the British government's decision to cancel its allowance to the Duke of Windsor (formerly the uncrowned Edward VIII), writing, 'Much as I admire and love our little Queen, I think she needs a spanking – what would her Grandfather think. He would pass out'.[29]

There was little opportunity to spank the monarch during Queen Elizabeth's enormously successful royal tour of Australia in 1954, although many correspondents were desperate to get close to her. Some writers wanted a personal introduction to the Queen, others wanted Menzies to pass on their good wishes, and another wanted an autographed copy of the banquet menu as a souvenir of the visit.[30] Many found themselves inevitably excluded from royal functions, although they felt they were entitled to be present if they were ex-servicemen, representatives of charitable organisations or staunch Liberal Party supporters.[31] Mrs Brown asked for tickets to the ball at

Melbourne's Exhibition Hall, on behalf of her two daughters, 'as they are young refined ladies like your own daughter' and because the family had always voted Liberal.[32] Occasionally resentment boiled over when members of this social and military elite were rebuffed. Vernon Davies, an ex-soldier with a decoration for distinguished service, experienced an attack of royal function rage when he could not pay personal homage to the Queen, 'other than standing in the fourth row of the crowd in the street'.[33]

As historian Jane Connors has convincingly argued, there was no doubt about the widespread popularity of the 1954 royal visit.[34] The tour lasted eight weeks and the Queen travelled to every capital city except Darwin. Probably over six million people lined up to catch a glimpse of her, which goes some way to explaining why Vernon Davies had to stand in the fourth row of spectators. On one hot evening in Sydney, 2000 people fainted in the crush while waiting for a fleeting royal appearance. There was no mistaking the strength of popular royalism, which cut across party political boundaries and was by no means an exclusively female addiction. JJ Cahill, Labor premier of New South Wales, was reportedly presented to the Queen more than 30 times during the royal visit, and a newspaper poll showed that 68 per cent of Labor voters were pro-monarchist.[35] This was a celebration of national and imperial unity. Sir Garfield Barwick (then a constitutional lawyer but a future Chief Justice) wrote to Menzies that he judged the visit a success: 'I felt the Queen's visit has done us all good, made us feel more of a community, increased and strengthened our coherence as a people, and closed our ranks against alien ideologies'.[36] The Empire remained a world bastion against communism.

Popular monarchism also expressed a fascination with ritual and tradition. This was no time for spanking, but one for savouring the mystique of monarchy and the emotional pull of the monarch's presence. 'Magic filled the air', according to George McKinnon writing about Menzies' speech at the royal banquet, 'you proceeded slowly and majestically to the glorious climax' and the royal toast. 'We are yours', Menzies assured the Queen. 'Surely', felt McKinnon, 'there is nothing more a man could hope to attain [...] I felt like shouting at its close [i.e. of the speech]'.[37] The moment demanded grand gestures and expressions of chivalry, and this was a domain in which Menzies would always outscore his political rivals. When Premier Joe Cahill refused to invite Menzies to a dinner held in honour of the Queen, he was denounced for his pettiness and lack of chivalry. For Ada Dawson of Leichhardt (New South Wales), this was a 'gross indecent studied [...] unpardonable insult', from 'the great unwashed and unkempt Labour [sic] party with all its corruption and vindictive spite'.[38] The royal presence was a powerful agent which could bring class prejudice into stark relief.

There were further royal visits in the Menzies years after 1954, although the royal personages involved all ensured that there was no repeat of Queen Elizabeth and Prince Philip's exhausting agenda of 1954. In 1958, the Queen Mother arrived to open a conference of the British Empire Service League. In 1959, Princess Alexandra of Kent made a very popular visit for the Queensland Centenary. In 1963, Queen Elizabeth and Prince Philip returned, and in 1964 Princess Marina (daughter-in-law of King George V) came to Sydney for the British Exhibition, to be followed in 1965 by Henry, Duke of Gloucester. Menzies recognised the popularity of such visits, but feared Australia was approaching royalty saturation. When a visit by the Princess Royal (Mary, daughter of King George V) to the Adelaide Festival was under discussion (it did not eventuate), he wrote a revealing message to Sir Eric Harrison at the Australian High Commission in London:

> The visit of Princess Alexandra to Australia has been a most notable success. There is, as usual, a constant press clamour for more Royal visits. I do not yield to this clamour, for two reasons. The first is that I would not wish to have a

Royal visit every year, since I believe that such visits can be overdone. The Crown should not become too familiar or commonplace [...] My own devotion to the Throne leads me constantly to the idea that formal Royal visits to Australia should be relatively rare and therefore on all occasions significant and stirring.[39]

Menzies' capitalisation of the words Royal, Crown and Throne here is notable. Perhaps he was right that remoteness was essential for preserving the monarchy's mystique. Perhaps, equally, the Australian obsession with royalty had its limits. For historian Mark McKenna, 1954 was the last hurrah of Australian monarchism. Future royal tours generated only muted fanfares and thinner crowds.[40] When, in 1960, the Queen's sister Princess Margaret married Anthony Armstrong Jones, it hardly caused a ripple in the Menzies correspondence.

Empire solidarity

In 1950, 15-year-old Linda Murphy wrote to suggest adding a Commonwealth Remembrance Day to the commemorative calendar, a reminder of the strength of the imperial bond with which many Australians closely identified.[41] The decolonisation process was gradually transforming the Empire into the Commonwealth. In 1958, the Royal Empire Society informed Menzies that it had changed its name to 'Royal Commonwealth Society', and Menzies reluctantly replied, 'I suppose we must recognise the realities!'[42] Whatever its title, the Commonwealth still shaped the way Australians viewed their place in the world. It could be exploited as a means of better assimilating non-British immigrants, and its influence was a potential antidote to creeping Americanisation.[43]

For Menzies himself, the British Commonwealth and its leaders formed a top-level epistolary network. The prime minister of Ceylon sent him mangosteens from his own estate, while the South Africans plied him with sherry – gifts denoting a close personal association and the bond which united all Commonwealth administrators.[44] He hosted visits from both Canadian prime minister John Diefenbaker and New Zealand prime minister Walter Nash in 1958, and corresponded with Southern Rhodesian governments. British members of Parliament with an interest in promoting imperial trade, like Leo Amery, were also regular correspondents. The correspondence situates Menzies within a Commonwealth ruling elite whose members maintained regular contact with each other. Menzies made regular trips to attend Commonwealth Prime Ministers' Conferences in London. Biographer Allan Martin chronicled 14 such journeys to Britain while he was prime minister, apart from unscheduled visits like the one for Churchill's funeral.[45] Liberal backbenchers may have felt uneasy about his repeated and occasionally prolonged absences, but ordinary correspondents never complained. On the contrary, they wished him *bon voyage,* and they presumably agreed with Enid Campbell when she wrote that seeing Menzies playing a part in world affairs made Australians feel proud.[46]

Menzies had a leading role within this network of Commonwealth politicians. When he won the 1949 election, some saw his success as a defeat for 'socialism' which the rest of Empire should and would follow. New Zealand did so but, in Britain, the Tories failed to defeat Clement Attlee, and had to wait until 1951 for the victory which would give them 13 continuous years in power. As far as conservatives were concerned, Menzies, rather than Britain, offered true imperial leadership. Sir Louis Hamilton wrote from London that 'the time has come to tie up the Empire into a close and firm alliance, otherwise the British race will cease to exist as an entity. What's more we feel you are the man to bring it about'.[47] I will return to the racial underpinnings of Menzies' Commonwealth network to which Hamilton alluded, but here the emphasis is on correspondents' view of Menzies as one leader, if not *the* leader of the

British Commonwealth. Another British correspondent envisaged the Commonwealth as a body exerting a strong collective influence in the world. 'The time has come', he wrote, 'for you in Australia, Canada and New Zealand to add your council [sic] to the affairs of the Commonwealth as equals'.[48]

Correspondents cast Menzies as the protector of the Empire against the spread of communism, and envisaged the Commonwealth as a primary target of Soviet conspiracies. Miss Gladys Jones wrote indignantly, 'I am fiercely British although Australian born and have long since been incensed and hostile towards those who are plotting the downfall of Britain at the instigation of the rabble "Tsar" of Russia, by endeavouring to disintegrate her Empire'.[49] Mrs Duff wrote in similar vein in the aftermath of the Petrov Affair: 'as a citizen of the British Empire, I would beg you to stop Dr Evatt in his efforts to make the Royal Commission on Espionage null and void'.[50] Protesting loyalty to the Commonwealth or Empire was a regular theme in the rhetoric of the correspondence; it made it clear that Menzies' battle against communists was not just a domestic Australian affair, but that it also had a Commonwealth context. As far as Fredrick Findlay was concerned, communists were traitors to our British way of life, and firmer action as well as 'intestinal fortitude' were needed to preserve it.[51]

What held the Commonwealth together? There were several ways of expressing Commonwealth solidarity: one lay in the implementation of the Colombo Plan, launched in 1951 by a group of nations to finance infrastructure projects in Asian countries and to welcome Asian students to Australian universities. Menzies repeatedly cited the Plan when he wanted to argue for Australia's imperial role and her good intentions towards Asian countries.[52] Another bond was the Assisted Passage scheme for British immigrants, discussed below. Cricket was a third confirmation of imperial friendships. Menzies kept in touch by correspondence with several high-profile English cricketers, including Alec Bedser and Herbert Sutcliffe.[53]

He corresponded with Douglas Jardine, captain of England in the notorious bodyline Ashes series of 1932–33, in his capacity as manager of the Scottish Australian Company, and was sad to hear of Jardine's death from lung cancer in 1958.[54] He joined the 'Forty Club', an English cricket club for players over 40 years old.[55] Perhaps most striking of all was his reaction to the illness of Molly Cowdrey, mother of English batsman Colin. He sent her a personal telegram and put in a personal telephone call to her Surrey home to wish her well.[56] Cricket for Menzies expressed the imperial bond with Britain, and the connection could have a very personal dimension.

The Commonwealth, as imagined by Menzies' correspondents, was overwhelmingly white. With the exception of Ceylon, where Menzies retained epistolary friendships, it linked the white-dominated dominions and territories of Canada, New Zealand, South Africa and Rhodesia with Australia. White supremacism was the cement which held it together. When one English correspondent outlined his ideal agenda for the Commonwealth Prime Ministers' Conference of 1957, he included an item on the 'treachery of Asian African and Dagoes of South American Republics', and looked forward to solid Canadian and Australian leadership.[57] If Australia under Menzies was the head of the Commonwealth family, then Indian prime minister Nehru was its black sheep, regularly accused of treachery, presumably because of his sympathy for anti-colonial struggles and his championing of the Non-Aligned Movement, which undermined the Commonwealth's role as an anti-communist bastion. The same English correspondent just mentioned labelled Nehru a 'mischiefmaker'.[58] Supporters of the ruling white minorities in South Africa and Rhodesia were very keen to enlist Menzies' support, as a correspondent from Transvaal made clear, writing:

> Australia and the Union of South Africa, and let us say
> Southern Rhodesia as well [...] are the only White Countries of
> the southern hemisphere. We two – Australia and South Africa

need an unbreakable link of friendship, of strength to keep up White Supremacy! If we fall, one of us – all will be lost.[59]

A London correspondent suggested buying the island of Madagascar from France and resettling southern Africa's problem Indians and 'half whites' there. He added: 'We don't want to see protestant whites smashed again as in the Boer war'.[60]

Decolonisation transformed the Commonwealth Prime Ministers' conferences where Menzies was a regular and very influential participant. Menzies' secretary Hazel Craig recalled that once the Commonwealth Prime Ministers' Conference had been a small and intimate event before many former colonies became independent.[61] It had once been a white man's club, but it increasingly welcomed leaders from newly independent countries in Africa and Asia. Several correspondents resented the intrusion of black politicians. MF Chamberlayne called it a 'Black Man's Club', urging Menzies to control 'that arrogant rabble, led by Nakrumah [sic] of Ghana, the self-styled Hitler of Africa'.[62] The old pattern of Commonwealth governance was also changing in another sense: the presence of Mrs Sirimavo Bandaranaike, appointed prime minister of Ceylon in 1960, ensured that the Commonwealth was no longer run exclusively by men.

'Ten Pound Poms'

In 1955, the millionth post-war immigrant arrived in Australia. She was Mrs Barbara Porritt from Yorkshire, a choice contrived and publicised to project Australia's British identity and boost a sense of Anglo-Australian unity.[63] The Assisted Passage scheme, inaugurated in 1947 and reaching its peak in the 1960s, provided selected British immigrants with transport to Australia for a mere £10. The 'Ten Pound Poms' were living embodiments of the British connection. Between 1945 and 1982, about 1.5 million emigrants arrived in Australia from

Great Britain and Ireland. The vast majority of them (84 per cent) were English, destined to provide the skilled and semi-skilled workers required by a rapidly expanding economy.[64] They had to undergo a health test, and ideally they would be under 45 years old.

Most importantly, they were white. Mixed-race British applicants found it hard to gain selection, like the Barnes family, whose father was an unskilled worker in receipt of a disability pension. The biggest stumbling block to emigration, however, was his daughter Velma, born in Britain but the illegitimate child of a black American father, whose whereabouts were unknown. The Australian High Commission reported that 'she has very dark skin with short black fuzzy hair, broad flat nose and thick lips'.[65] In this case colour trumped Britishness, and the Barneses were not admitted.

British immigrants left behind a memory of economic depression, austerity and post-war food rationing. They were 'invisible' in the sense that it was assumed that they had no assimilation problems. Without a distinct status of their own, their collective voice was effectively silenced. Their difficulties, their sense of disorientation and their 'narratives of dislocation' and 'identity tensions' were only slowly recognised.[66] Menzies' correspondents valued their presence. A former British emigrant to Australia who was seeking employment as a recruitment officer felt that 'Australia needs good pommy workers, to help balance the Southern Europeans [...] Good workers, resolute and plenty of guts, are the qualities I look for, plus perseverence [sic] and patience'.[67]

As this letter indicated, Britain alone could not provide all the labour Australia required, and an influx of workers from the region bureaucrats called 'Southern Europe' increasingly diluted the Britishness of the intake. By 1958, Menzies was receiving an increasing number of letters either from or about recent immigrants, from Greece, southern Italy, Malta or Eastern Europe. Sometimes immigrants pledged their support for the fight against communism, sometimes they communicated their difficulties in finding employment. 'This is another America', thought one British immigrant who asked that all new arrivals be treated equally.[68]

Correspondents feared that Australia's pro-immigration policy would dilute the British character of Australian society. The British Immigration League, based in Sydney, urged Menzies to preserve British Australia and to ensure that the British made up the majority of immigrants.[69] There was a danger that Australia would be 'inudated [sic] with foreigners', according to another correspondent, if more was not done to transport assisted migrants from England, who were waiting several months for an available ship.[70] In fact, of those who emigrated to Australia between 1945 and 1973, over 11 per cent came from Italy, seven per cent came from Greece and Cyprus and just over five per cent from Yugoslavia.[71] These 'New Australians' (i.e. non-British immigrants), as they were known, were a problem for another writer, because they introduced tuberculosis, and Australia required 'British protestants, not Dutch or knifing Italians and Nazi Germans. These are all here in thousands, and all of them hate our Royal Family'.[72]

National stereotypes, together with a visceral anti-Catholicism, fuelled Australian xenophobia. Major Riley of Surrey Hills (Victoria) assured Menzies that Italians, Maltese and 'Southern Europeans' would not assimilate and urged Menzies to 'keep the heart of the empire strong' by securing a faster rate of British immigration.[73] Assimilation policies created tensions which just did not arise in the case of newcomers from Britain. Mrs Hedge complained that 'we were told to show the migrants our Australian way of life (which of course is the British way of life) only to find they are trying to force us into their way of life'.[74] Italian immigrants were a particular target, because they allegedly had a poor military record and belonged to a race of criminals. 'Did you ever have a look over the type of dagoes that are coming here Crist [sic] help us if we ever have to depend on them to defend this country', agonised one correspondent, adding in his own spelling style, 'I am suprised at the number of migrants thate are comeing here that are Roman Catho surley you can get Prodestants'.[75] There was a pervasive fear that New Australians would vote overwhelmingly for Labor and furthermore swell the ranks of Roman Catholics. The Protestant Council of New South Wales was alarmed because an unbalanced immigration policy was 'upsetting the denominational balance of the population'.[76] In a few years, according to one Liberal Party supporter, Catholics 'will swamp our vote and then with their customary underground engineering Protestants will be shouldered out of jobs (high + low)'.[77]

The British connection thus had a strong denominational dimension. When historian Linda Colley analysed the formative period of a homogeneous British identity in the 18th century, she underlined Protestantism as a vital element gluing together the disparate elements of the United Kingdom.[78] The same could be said of Protestantism as the cement of imperial identity. Thus the need to keep Australia British not only inspired racially based xenophobia against Italians, Greeks and Maltese, but also resurrected sectarian hostility against Catholics. Irish immigrants are 'just scum', declared one Sydney woman, while a correspondent in North Queensland wanted 'our Kith and Kin' to populate and develop northern Australia.[79] They, and only they, were the 'Right Type'.

After the British, the Dutch, Germans and Scandinavians stood at the top of the hierarchy of preferred immigrants, and Asians at the bottom. In between were Italians and Greeks, who arrived in great numbers during the 1940s and 1950s, the so-called 'Southern Europeans', who made up about a quarter of immigrants between 1947 and 1961.[80] 'Southern Europeans' were of course 'white' immigrants, although a few correspondents thought otherwise. GE Bagot from London, for example, considered that the admission into Australia of Maltese and Sicilians had 'broken' the White Australia Policy.[81] 'Italians', wrote Joyce Atkinson, 'are quite dark-skinned enought [*sic*] to destroy a white Aus. policy'.[82]

In denial over Suez

The vigour of pro-British sentiment gradually faded, not so much because of any cultural transformation within Australia, but rather because Britain's role in the world was itself in question, in a phase of post-imperial adjustment. On the whole, Menzies' correspondents were reluctant to accept that their world view was out of date. Mrs McLay, for instance, wrote from Sydney to object to a BBC broadcast in which Menzies had referred to the USA and Russia as 'the two greatest nations of the world'. She interpreted this as an insult against Britain, and she wrote:

> During your years as Prime Minister you have made many pompous statements which have riled many more people than myself [...]
>
> Why relegate Britain to the background [...] After all Britian [sic] has done for the whole of the world, over the last long terrible years I feel that statement of yours is unforgiveable.[83]

She wrote three years after the Suez crisis of 1956 had demonstrated to many that Britain was no longer capable of playing an independent role as a global power. The nationalisation of the Suez Canal by Egyptian leader Colonel Gamal Abdel Nasser announced a surge of pro-Arab nationalism and potentially threatened oil supplies to Europe. Menzies knew nothing of Egypt, but in September 1956 he led a diplomatic mission to present Nasser with a compromise on behalf of the Western powers (the Dulles Plan): Egypt would retain nominal sovereignty, but the Canal would be placed under international management. Unsurprisingly, Nasser refused to accept the plan. 'These Gyppos', Menzies wrote privately, 'are a dangerous lot of backward adolescents, mouthing the slogans of democracy, full of self-importance and basic ignorance'.[84]

BRITAIN AND THE EMPIRE

Menzies' vocabulary on this occasion revealed a leader fully in tune with his correspondents, who were failing to adjust to the realities of the post-colonial world. The abortive French and British military intervention which followed was co-ordinated with Israel in the secret Protocol of Sèvres, in which the Israelis agreed to contrive a pretext for war. Menzies was kept in the dark about this manoeuvre and about collusion with Israel. When he did become aware of the deception, he nevertheless continued to defend the British position. The United Nations condemned Britain and France and demanded a troop withdrawal. The USA did not defend the invasion of Egypt, leaving Britain and France isolated.

Correspondents congratulated Menzies over his pro-British position, many of them British, like Enid Morgan from London who thanked Menzies for his stand over Suez. 'I know', she wrote:

> I am only one of many quiet British people who thought you were right and were so happy to have our innermost convictions voiced so well by you.
>
> I only hope the authentic British point of view, which you in Australia have voiced so well, will make of our Commonwealth Conferences, a real creative force for good in the world. That is what people miss, the creative common-sense that is, as I see it, so typically British.[85]

Beatrix Mustill was another Londoner who acclaimed Menzies as the leader Britain needed:

> How I and many others, she wrote, wish you were Prime Minister of Gt. Britain and the Commonwealth. All English-speaking peoples must keep together now [...] we still have guts, without being bullies, as our service men showed when sent to open fire in Egypt [...] But our politicians should never have sent them.[86]

She continued to discuss the pusillanimity of British political leaders and their lack of war experience, concluding, 'I wish you were a few years younger, Mr Menzies, even so, I'm sure you are the only level-headed man to tackle the job'. For these correspondents, paradoxically, Menzies's position as the maestro of the Commonwealth emerged from the Suez debacle not just unscathed, but even enhanced.

Oswald Groser, a Scottish schoolmaster, seemed to be defying logic when he congratulated Menzies over the Suez crisis and judged that 'the real deep unity of the Commonwealth and Empire and the USA is reappearing'.[87] In fact, Western solidarity had been severely strained by the American refusal to endorse military intervention in Egypt, and the Commonwealth itself was split, since Canada and South Africa also refused to support it. A few writers, on the other hand, did recognise the underlying divisions within the Commonwealth and the Western powers as a whole. Squadron Leader Hughes wrote to explain that although Menzies had solidified the Anglo-Australian bond within the Royal Air Force, the crisis had caused a rift between the USA and the Empire.[88] Others recognised that a more diplomatic approach would be necessary in future to keep Middle Eastern oil out of Russian hands, and recommended a rapprochement with Saudi Arabia.[89]

The imperial tie with Britain was further undermined by British interest in, and eventually membership of, customs unions in Europe. In 1961, Prime Minister Harold Macmillan applied for British membership of the European Economic Community (the 'Common Market'), which provoked Menzies into repeating his defence of Commonwealth trade preferences. This gave ammunition to France's President de Gaulle, who vetoed Britain's entry in 1963 on the grounds that Britain was still too tied to its global Empire to be fully committed in Europe. One Sydney correspondent denounced Menzies for undermining Britain on this issue, writing, 'You have done your dirty work to cripple England, along with that Traitor and Dictator De-Gaule [sic]'.[90] Britain's membership of the far less ambitious European Free Trade Organisation (EFTA), founded in 1960, also frightened correspondents.[91] Mary Gray wrote from Scotland to denounce EFTA as a sinister attack on national sovereignty, and also as an attempt to drive a wedge between Britain and the Dominions.[92]

Australians had comparatively little to say in the correspondence about Britain's attempt to join the European Economic Community, even though Leslie Bury, Minister for Air, was forced to resign from cabinet in 1962 after suggesting that the potential damage to Australia of Britain's application had been exaggerated. Most letters on this subject came from Britain itself, from writers keen to preserve connections with the Commonwealth and asking Menzies to help their cause. 'I hope that you can keep us out of the Common Market', wrote HS Featherstone in Kent, with exaggerated expectations of Menzies' power over British politicians.[93]

Dissenting voices

Not all correspondents subscribed to the selective xenophobia of the majority; nor did all correspondents share the majority's respect for British royalty. A few dissenting voices should be recognised, like that of the Anglican vicar who interpreted Australian intervention in Malaya not as a gesture of imperial solidarity, but as colonial subservience to British capital and Australian rubber investors.[94] British nuclear testing on Australian soil also provoked complaints. Mrs Joy Sundfors complained that Australians had not been consulted about the tests and their views had been taken for granted. She was extremely sceptical about scientific reports that the explosions were not producing harmful radiation. 'Let the people know the truth', she demanded, 'let them know what you are up to – and then you will learn what "Australia's Views" really are'.[95]

The royal tour had allowed Australians to feel a part of an

'imagined community' of a united nation. The widespread sense of belonging under the monarchy, however, depended on a myth of unity which disguised the fissures within Australian society. According to this myth, as Australian Studies scholar Ewan Morris has pointed out, Australia was free of class conflict, the Indigenous population revered the monarch and 'New Australians', successfully assimilated, came together as loyal Commonwealth citizens.[96] There was undoubtedly some dissent under the surface. Isolated voices told Menzies he was out of touch with popular views of the British monarchy and its relevance. They questioned why taxpayers should have to underwrite the cost of expensive royal visits, which served no purpose except to give politicians more excuses for lavish banquets.[97] In a different tone altogether, one South African correspondent launched a vituperative attack on the royals, denouncing them as insipid and brainless. In her view, Princess Margaret was a prostitute and a home-breaker, and 'that bloody bitch the Queen' was little better. This correspondent invited Queen Elizabeth to abdicate immediately in her favour. The writer had spent time both in prison and in a mental hospital, but what triggered this extraordinary tirade is unclear.[98]

Mr Jones in Melbourne thought detachment from Britain was inevitable and desirable. He wrote without regret about the decline of Empire: 'Australia today [*in 1950*] is so vastly different from 10 years ago and to see English politicians trying to preserve an Empire departed, by clinging like a dying man to a straw to Dominion status as a substitute is appauling [*sic*] and even foolish'.[99] He foresaw that Britain would eventually need to find new markets beyond the old Commonwealth. 'Better cut the cord', he advised, 'and stand on her own footing. England needs Adult-hood and let the offsprings shift for themselves'. Jones turned the conventional centre-and-periphery model of the British Empire on its head. It was England, not Australia, who should learn to stand on her own two feet, and fend for herself without relying on the Empire.

These correspondents belonged to a small minority of disbelievers. The majority of writers continued to subscribe to an ideal of a white, Protestant Australia with a close cultural affinity with Britain. They frequently introduced themselves to Menzies by writing, 'I am a hundred per cent British', or 'As a proud Australian and a Britisher', identifying their patriotic loyalties in order to legitimise their approach to Menzies. The discourse of Britishness and imperial unity provided one of the anchoring rhetorics of the correspondence, constituting essential foundations on which a claim on Menzies' attention, a criticism or a comment could be formulated.

For the most part, the correspondence invites us to take more seriously the profundity of monarchist loyalism in 1950s Australia, and to acknowledge the vigour of popular xenophobia. Sentimental monarchism is still with us, even if it is easily ridiculed by intellectuals. The racial assumptions which structured ideas about Britain, Europeans and Asians are with us too, even if xenophobic targets have evolved and even if some previous victims have themselves turned xenophobic. It is a paradox of successful social integration that immigrant groups themselves support policies of exclusion. Australian nationalism has certainly changed but these deep-rooted prejudices have not. The discourse of White Australia never died, it just went underground, temporarily obscured by a superficial multiculturalism, until One Nation brought it to the surface once more.

8

'A Commonwealth Citizen in every woodpile'

IMMIGRATION AND THE WHITE AUSTRALIA POLICY

Asian phobias

The White Australia Policy or, to be more accurate, the *Immigration Restriction Act* of 1901, had regulated the immigration of 'alien races' since Federation. In order to maintain a homogeneous and white Australian society, it excluded coloured immigrants. Yet this policy of institutionalised racial discrimination was evolving. In the postwar era, exceptions and exemptions gradually allowed the entry of more migrants of Asian origin, including wartime refugees, Asian students and Asian spouses of white Australians.[1] A series of high-profile deportation cases suggested that upholding the racialist assumptions of the policy in general did not prohibit individual exceptions.[2] After 1956, non-Europeans could become Australian citizens, if they could show 15 years' residence and a willingness to assimilate. A dictation test had been used to exclude unwanted immigrants, by demanding that they write a text of 50 words, in a European language to be selected by customs officials. The infamous dictation test was abolished in 1958 and, in fact, it had only been used a handful of times since the end of the Second World War.[3]

IMMIGRATION AND THE WHITE AUSTRALIA POLICY

By 1961, between 800 and 900 students came to Australia under the Colombo Plan, and there were already over 20 000 Chinese in the country.[4] The opposition to racially based exclusion mounted, led by the churches, universities and others sensitive to the damage that the policy was causing to Australia's reputation in the region. The policy was changing, but it was only under Menzies' successor Harold Holt that citizenship was opened up to Europeans and non-Europeans on an equal basis.

Historian David Walker's two magisterial books on Australian attitudes towards Asia – *Anxious Nation* and *Stranded Nation* – are sensitive to the underlying fears and anxieties which shaped the policy of exclusion, and which surface regularly in the Menzies correspondence.[5] He appreciates, too, the ways in which Australian characterisations of Asians reflected their own identity problems. Frequent assertions that the 'Asian mind' was irrational, emotionally over-sensitive and effeminate expressed Australia's self-image as rational, phlegmatic and boldly masculine. Walker emphasised the keen interest in the workings of 'the Asian mind', a phrase illustrating the idea that all Asians displayed the same psychological features, disregarding the cultural differences which separated, for example, the Pakistani from the Filipino. At the same time, Walker does not neglect the dissenting voices – of those who recommended a more tolerant, less condescending and above all less racialised approach. The dominant story, as he puts it, of fear and exclusion must be balanced against the counter-narratives which looked forward to a more pluralistic Australian society. But these dissenting voices were drowned out in the Menzies correspondence.

Bearing in mind Australia's enduring Asian phobias, this chapter registers the erosion of Australia's restrictive immigration policy. First, however, it will discuss the repercussions in the Menzies correspondence of the crisis of southern Africa which shattered the unity of the Commonwealth so prized by correspondents in the previous chapter.

The Commonwealth in disarray

The Suez crisis, as noted in the previous chapter, tested Commonwealth unity; but what shook it to its foundations was the international outcry against the apartheid regime in South Africa. Apartheid, which South Africa officially translated into the euphemism 'separate development', effectively signified racial segregation and discrimination against the black population. After 1960, the regime was subjected to intense scrutiny. This, more than anything, shattered Menzies' conception of the Empire as a union of white, English-speaking peoples promoting global stability.

On 21 March 1960, 69 black South Africans were shot dead in a demonstration against the pass laws in the Transvaal township of Sharpeville. International outrage was deafening, and the Commonwealth Prime Ministers' Conference now had to face the very real possibility of Commonwealth disintegration (South Africa effectively left the Commonwealth in March 1961). From Essex, the Barking Young Liberal Association told Menzies that 'there is no place in the commonwealth family for a Nation which pursues such odious and Neo Nazis doctorine [sic]'.[6] Christian responses rammed home the message, as when one of Menzies' constituents linked apartheid with Australia's own version of racial discrimination, referring to the White Australia Policy. 'No land that calls itself Christian', she wrote, 'should keep a man out because of the colour of his skin'.[7] Another constituent fired off a telegram to denounce the 'Hitlerite reign of terror' in South Africa, comparing it to the Soviet invasion of Hungary and the Chinese treatment of Tibet, and warning that the Commonwealth could dissolve unless it made an unequivocal stand against brutality.[8] A correspondent from Tanganyika (soon to become independent Tanzania) with first-hand knowledge of South Africa told Menzies that the white ruling minority there had fatally insulated itself from world events and lived in a world of unreality, which 'almost had an Alice in Wonderland content'.[9]

IMMIGRATION AND THE WHITE AUSTRALIA POLICY

These examples could be multiplied threefold. South Africa's racial policies now appeared deeply corrosive of Menzies' triumphalist claims for the Empire and its unity. Correspondents readily drew parallels with Australia's own racially exclusive immigration laws. Calls for universal male suffrage in southern Africa would also have implications for the status of Indigenous peoples in Australia. Demands for racial equality in Africa would inevitably rebound on Australia itself.

A few writers made the comparison between the treatment of blacks in South Africa and the historic fate of Australia's Indigenous inhabitants. 'If Africans are all to have votes in S. Africa, you will soon have to be giving votes to your aborigines in Australia', warned EN Neville from London, in a letter generally very supportive of Menzies.[10] The situation in Australia, however, was vastly different. In South Africa, a stable black labour force was essential to the profits of the mining companies; in Australia, the Indigenous work force was, for the most part, marginal to the economy. Furthermore, the black population was in a majority in South Africa. Giving the vote to Australian Aboriginal people would not, as in South Africa, lead to the end of white rule.

More frequently, writers saw implications for the White Australia Policy. There was a groundswell of international opinion against any legislation based on racial discrimination; this could sweep away Australia's racially based immigration bans just as it might foretell the doom of apartheid in South Africa. One London correspondent painted a grim picture of the consequences of relaxing immigration controls. Consider, he proposed, what happened in the United Kingdom:

> the trickle of blacks became a flood; West Kensington and Paddington became negro slums almost overnight and then we had the gory battles of Notting Hill, Nottingham and the rest [...] give citizenship to just one negro and the Trojan Horse is in.

> It only needs one negro to get his foot in the door and next thing there will be a Commonwealth Citizen in every woodpile. They breed like rabbits.[11]

Australia, in his view, would do well to heed the warning, restrict citizenship qualifications and keep its borders closed.

Not all correspondents were hostile to the South African regime. According to one Menzies supporter in London, the problem had been exaggerated because, after all, everyone had riots from time to time, and Sharpeville was nothing exceptional in the overall context of white settler colonialism.[12] Others registered the changes brought about by decolonisation, and protested against the new domination of the Commonwealth by independent African and Asian nations, where communist influence appeared strong. Thus one Surrey correspondent deplored 'the deterioration in good fellowship among Commonwealth States, which has occurred since the elevation of petty coloured states to commonwealth status. [...] White supremacy in some parts of Africa must be maintained at all costs in order to prevent the communisation of the whole continent'.[13] She went on to recommend a two-tier membership system within the Commonwealth. Another English writer had a more hard-headed view of the importance of South Africa's mineral wealth. He wrote: 'With a smug superiority the/we English revile their fellow humans in South Africa whose conduct to the natives is neither more nor less cruel than was our own to our own poor a hundred years ago'. But mining depended on cheap black labour and this was maintained by the system of apartheid. If anyone was to blame for the crisis, this correspondent argued, it was international investors and shareholders.[14] E Samson announced from Wales that the Commonwealth was approaching obsolescence since it was now dominated by the 'coloured races'. He remained strongly in favour of some form of racial segregation.[15] According to a Sydney correspondent, 'ignorant black savages' had been permitted to dominate the debate. 'African negroes', he added, are 'totally unfit to take over any serious responsibility'.[16]

In February 1960, British Conservative prime minister Harold Macmillan had famously declared before the South African Parliament that 'a wind of change' was blowing over Africa. Menzies later responded with his own 'wind of change' speech, delivered on television on 11 September 1960, in which he argued that only South Africans could solve South African problems and condemned Soviet and Chinese meddling in African affairs – a speech which inspired an immediate congratulatory message from author Frank Clune, among others.[17] Menzies steadfastly refused to condemn apartheid and insisted that the problem was a domestic South African matter. Reactions were violent, but extremely mixed. Some condemned Menzies for effectively condoning racial oppression; others denounced Macmillan as a traitor to the Commonwealth. The question of race segregation was much more than a question of domestic policy, urged Reverend Denne from Lancashire, and it could hardly be equated with issues like the nationalisation of the coal mines. Australia ought to be on the side of human rights and freedoms.[18]

Two entire folders of letters are devoted to welcome home messages sent to Menzies in April 1961.[19] They include both appreciations and condemnations of his stand on South Africa at the Commonwealth Prime Ministers' Conference in London. Correspondents from South Africa hailed Menzies as a hero. A few (a minority) continued to condemn South African racial oppression. On his return, many hailed Menzies' speech of 11 April to the House of Representatives as 'glorious – and I mean glorious'.[20] In this speech, Menzies now felt free enough from international constraints to declare his opposition to apartheid, while at the same time deploring South Africa's exit from the Commonwealth.

In April 1960, the Kew (Victoria) branch of the Communist Party sent a resolution condemning Menzies as the sole champion of reactionary racism, and this was followed by several other anti-apartheid motions, sent in by both Communist and Labor Party branches.[21] This was the first time the correspondence registered such interventions on the left since the attempt to dissolve the Communist Party in 1951. An African correspondent in London judged Menzies' policy of non-interference as 'a refusal to serve the Commonwealth'.[22]

On the other hand, correspondents condemned Macmillan and the British in general for abandoning traditional Commonwealth values. 'The Mother Country is rapidly losing its grip on issues of political significance', according to G Phillips in Suffolk, and he noted 'a disturbing deterioration of traditional British character'. British leaders were lacking in patriotism and the country had become fatally 'cosmopolitan', which was probably a veiled expression of his distaste for the recent influx of immigrants. Decolonisation, in his view, was a failure, since Ghana (Britain's former colony of the Gold Coast until 1957) had, in his view, turned into a totalitarian state under Kwame Nkrumah, a world leader of the Non-Aligned Movement.[23] The theme of British betrayal was underscored by several correspondents. Another English correspondent appealed to Menzies for help because British politicians were 'boneheads' in face of 'the coloured invasion that is taking place on this small island'.[24] Macmillan's attitude deeply distressed some and was hard to explain because, after all, the British prime minister had sound Scottish ancestry. 'The English people have gone Black minded', according to one disaffected Londoner, who feared that 'the White people in the British Empire are to be sacrificed for the nigers [*sic*]'.[25] Anglo-Australian solidarity was under threat. The challenge sometimes came from unexpected sources – not just from Christians, liberals and socialists who opposed white racism, but also from diehard imperialists who condemned British attacks on racial intolerance in South Africa.

The crisis in Southern Rhodesia extended and prolonged the intense debate about race and majority rule in southern Africa. The Federation of Rhodesia and Nyasaland was in the process of dissolution into its component parts: Nyasaland (which became independent

Malawi), Northern Rhodesia (which became independent Zambia) and Southern Rhodesia. The British government remained unwilling to sanction independence in Southern Rhodesia unless majority rule was introduced, which infuriated the white ruling minority. In 1964, the British Conservative government, pressured by independent African states, refused to invite Southern Rhodesia to the Commonwealth Prime Ministers' Conference. After Labour leader Harold Wilson took power in Britain in 1964, the conflict between London and Salisbury intensified. Southern Rhodesia's prime minister Ian Smith rejected Wilson's demand for 'one man, one vote' and, in 1965, Southern Rhodesia adopted UDI, a unilateral declaration of independence.

As in the South African case, correspondents from Rhodesia looked to Menzies to save them both from their own black majority and from British politicians who, as they saw it, had become the puppets of the black African lobby and the United Nations. One female writer from Southern Rhodesia accused Britain of only listening 'to agitators with black skins', and told Menzies that many European settlers 'regard you as their only hope'.[26] Peter Lincoln, an Australian in Northern Rhodesia, sent a very sober letter about British decline, ingrained sentiments of white supremacy and the white settlers' fear that a violent revolt might erupt. He now found 'it is so damned hard to be both British and Australian at the same time!'[27] This letter showed that the organic tie between Britain and Australia discussed in the previous chapter was now being stretched to the limit.

A writer from Salisbury (Southern Rhodesia) defended his country's political system, and warned that 'it would be suicidal now to hand over control to a mass of illiterate and irresponsible half savages who [...] would set up an autocratic government and create a state of chaos as is evidenced in the Congo and elsewhere'.[28] As he interpreted the situation, the British government had abandoned the white settlers in southern and eastern Africa, who now faced possible genocide and annihilation. Correspondents cited the precedents of Kenya and the Congo: in Kenya, the British had defeated the anti-colonial Mau-Mau rebellion, but the country had won independence in 1963; the independence of the Congo from Belgium in 1960 provoked civil conflict and attacks on white settlers, and opened up the possibility of Soviet intervention – a nightmare scenario for white Rhodesians.

Correspondents from southern Africa appealed to Menzies to argue their case to the intransigent and misguided British who now seemed to be betraying them and the white Commonwealth. From Salisbury, Guy Sears begged Menzies for support, since 'you will probably be the only friend we have at the Prime Ministers conference'. Menzies was summoned to defend the interests of the English-speaking world against England itself, poisoned as it was by 'the terrible lunacy of Macmillanism'.[29] For many, the Commonwealth itself was a lost cause, and its disintegration of minor consequence. Austen Brooks, Deputy Chairman of the League of Empire Loyalists, was so disgusted by the refusal to invite Southern Rhodesia to the Commonwealth Prime Ministers' Conference that he wrote to recommend the dissolution of the Commonwealth and its replacement by a new association of 'British nations', presumably including Rhodesia.[30] 'This collection of coloured parasites', wrote one British correspondent referring to the conference, 'are attempting to dominate the commonwealth. It would be better that the white countries separated from the coloured rabble and wreck the conference'.[31] Menzies' ideal of a united Commonwealth, working for world peace and against world communism, was now dead, disfigured by racial conflict. Even its traditional supporters were clamouring for a quick burial.

IMMIGRATION AND THE WHITE AUSTRALIA POLICY

'History is calling, and others are answering'

The White Australia Policy, consistently defended by Menzies, was gradually eroded by a series of ministerial actions and decisions not to act. In 1949, the government dropped its attempt to ban an Indonesian woman married to an Australian and resident in Australia for five years (the O'Keefe case).[32] In 1950, Harold Holt, as Minister for Immigration, rescinded the deportation of Gamboa, a Filipino-American serviceman who had an Australian wife and children. In 1965, the government deported a six-year-old Indian Fijian girl, Nancy Prasad, born in Australia, but in doing so it defied a wave of humanitarian public sympathy for the Prasad family.[33] Concessions were made to long-term residents and to Japanese war brides, and ministerial discretion was decisive in such cases.[34]

Restricted immigration still had bipartisan support, until the Labor Party officially removed it from its policy platform in 1965.[35] Most correspondents vigorously defended the White Australia Policy, even though it came under attack from India and other Asian countries. In Australia, a group of professionals and Melbourne University academics formed the Immigration Reform Group (IRG) and began campaigning for the regulated admission of non-European immigrants.[36] The IRG, however, was extremely cautious: it recommended an annual intake of 1500 non-European immigrants. This was a limited number, and the proposal did not challenge the racial criteria underlying government policy.[37] Traditionalist correspondents urged Menzies to maintain the policy and resist growing demands to introduce limited quotas of immigrants from Asian countries. 'We can remain a European people if we keep our present laws', thought one Melbourne woman, 'otherwise we commit racial suicide, apart from the larger numbers of the mongoloid and negroid peoples, their chromosomes are more dominant and we would be bred out of existence'.[38] She feared that the Colombo Plan, of which Menzies was proud, encouraged mixed-race marriages and 'brought heartache to mothers in the community'. As we have seen, apart from facilitating trade with Asian countries, the Colombo Plan also introduced several hundred students of Asian origin to Australian universities every year. Australia's colour bar was condemned by the foreign press and by Christians and liberals at home. In spite of this, a crude social Darwinism, 1960s-style, continued to inform Australian prejudices in favour of Britain.

In the age of decolonisation, David Walker argues, the newly independent nations of Asia treated Australia as a pariah.[39] In Indonesia, Australia favoured continuing Dutch control and thus supported white colonialism. The White Australia Policy marked Australia out as a hostile neighbour, while the controversial deportation cases already mentioned advertised the government's determination to exclude all coloured immigrants and apply what Babette Francis called the 'laundry detergent test' of whiteness.[40] Australians thought of themselves as an egalitarian society, but whites were more equal than others. The policy of exclusion was justified by its protagonists for economic reasons, in that it prevented an influx of cheap labour and thus maintained a high standard of living; and for social reasons, in that it preserved the homogeneity of Australian society. In the 1960s, however, dissent was growing. For one thing, Australia's Asian neighbours were increasingly seen as potential markets for foodstuffs and commodities rather than as a threat. Meanwhile, liberals and humanitarians were uncomfortably aware of the damage that racial exclusion was doing to Australia's reputation overseas. They urged reform, and the introduction of quotas to allow controlled immigration from Asian countries.

Menzies had a standard answer to critics who accused his government of souring relations with Asian powers. He routinely cited the Colombo Plan as evidence of Australia's neighbourly goodwill and readiness to assist Asian development. The Colombo Plan embraced support for development projects in Asia, and brought Asian students to Australian universities every year.[41] As soon as they graduated, however, they were expected to leave Australia. On this thin basis, Menzies believed that Australia had earned its credentials as a friend and benefactor in Asia. Not all correspondents were convinced by his response. KH Bell asked Menzies what he was going to do about feeding the starving masses of southeast Asia? The Colombo Plan was an inadequate response, he added, it was no more than a drop in the ocean.[42]

Correspondents still harboured deep-seated fears about Asia's enormous population and the rising influence of communism. This above all made Norman Nicolson anxious about 'the Asiatic influx'.[43] Nevertheless the Japanese were good customers for Australian wool, and in 1952 Australia overcame traumatic wartime memories and resumed diplomatic relations with Tokyo. In 1957, a trade agreement was signed between the two countries. Perhaps, after all, the best way to counteract Chinese communism was to make allies in Asia.[44]

Australia's best ally in Asia, however, was the USA, and Australia's first significant contribution to the Vietnam War in 1965, at America's side, provoked a howl of protest in the correspondence.[45] Several thousand Australian combat troops now joined the USA and South Vietnam in their fight against the communist regime of North Vietnam. One English correspondent predicted more damage to Australia's overseas reputation, since supporting America would only 'prolong the present agony in Vietnam'.[46] Mrs Reilly represented the Christian critique of military intervention, condemning the use of chemical weapons. She played the Presbyterian card: 'God', she wrote, 'as preached to me in the Presbyterian Church, is not on your side. If He is, he has descended into Hell. For it is hell your American friends are producing in Vietnam'.[47] The Menzies years ended with a reaffirmation of post-war hostility to Asia and the spread of communism. This time, however, his policies were vigorously contested.

The push for a change to immigration policy came from universities and the churches. In the 1950s, both the Australian National

University and Sydney University introduced the teaching of Asian languages, and in 1956 Melbourne University set up an Indonesian department.[48] In 1959, as already mentioned, the Immigration Reform Group was established at Melbourne University, to promote the reform of the White Australia Policy. When the IRG produced its influential pamphlet 'Control or Colour Bar?' in 1960, its print-run of 8000 copies quickly sold out. In 1964, a Gallup Poll found that 78 per cent of respondents wanted a change of policy.[49]

The government nevertheless resisted demands for quotas on immigration from Asian countries. This was a mistake, wrote Lance Oldmeadow, adding, 'I cannot bear to think that you really do not understand what educated Indians are thinking of our colour bar [...] Even Colombo Plan students cannot endure it'.[50] Australia needed to drop its attitude of racial superiority, urged Timothy Western. 'Australians', he wrote,

> may be good, they may be tough, but 10–15 million are not quite good enough to handle 100's of millions, even though they may be black, or brown, or yellow. But still the government keeps deporting Malays, handing out insults and face slaps to Asia, as if it were here by divine right.[51]

In London, Nigel Drury gave up his Australian citizenship in protest against the White Australia Policy. He recalled prime minister Billy Hughes' successful but 'shabby and equivocating' attempt to keep a clause about racial equality out of the League of Nations covenant in 1919. 'History is calling', he told Menzies, 'and others are answering'.[52]

The erosion of White Australia was also the erosion of British Australia. The Suez crisis had undermined Britain's global prestige, while apartheid discredited and splintered the Commonwealth and raised uncomfortable questions about Australia's domestic policies. The earlier consensus in support of a united British Commonwealth was no longer sustainable. As soon as the Commonwealth ceased to express the authority of the white settler populations of the dominions, and instead reflected the new diversity of a post-colonial world, correspondents were prepared to abandon it. Their fears of a black conspiracy against white power surfaced. Harry Alderman in South Australia made a great effort to come to terms with a changed world:

> I do not see, he wrote, why a black should be regarded as inferior because of his colour but, likewise, I do not see why he should get all his own way just because he is black and, generally, ignorant [...] I will try to think of the blacks as equals. I would be distressed to believe that they could ever be our masters.[53]

In spite of his limited effort to readjust to a new reality, old patterns of thought were not easily discarded.

Britain itself commanded little respect in correspondents' eyes. Macmillan had begun the steep decline with his 'wind of change' speech, his successor Harold Wilson had confirmed Britain's desertion of traditional imperial values with his opposition to white minority rule in Southern Rhodesia. Britain itself, wrote one British correspondent, had become fatally open to coloured immigration. The Mother Country was giving us 'the degrading exhibition of gratuitous servility in Her efforts to maintain a measure of ascendancy against communist infiltration in Her abandoned colonies'.[54] A significant feature of the correspondence was the crescendo of voices from Britain, South Africa and Rhodesia pleading for Menzies' support, and praising him as the only friend of white rule. At the same time, they warned him not to relax the White Australia Policy. 'The lifting of your immigration restrictions will spell death for Australia', predicted Mrs Gadd in Salisbury, Southern Rhodesia.[55]

The Menzies letters brought to the surface a vocabulary of racial invective and prejudice. We would like to think, perhaps naively, that the sheer nastiness that it expressed belongs to a past era. White racism, however, was not the only register on which the letters played. Menzies may have missed his rendezvous with history, as Nigel Drury suggested, but many writers added their critical voices to the correspondence. They criticised intervention in Vietnam, opposed the evils of apartheid, and urged a more open policy of immigration. But these voices always remained in a minority. Although the Menzies letters registered dissent and protest, the majority nevertheless upheld the fading dreams of white supremacy and imperial solidarity.

9

'Mr Khrushchev is planning something big'

THE CHANGING FACE OF ANTI-COMMUNISM

Three phases of anti-communism

Anxieties about communist subversion were all-pervasive in post-war Australia, before, during and after Menzies' failed attempt in 1951 to legislate the dissolution of the Communist Party. Whether communism was perceived as an internal or a foreign threat, its ideology of public ownership challenged Australian democracy's roots in private-enterprise capitalism and individual home ownership. Anti-communism further reinforced Australia's ties with that world bastion of anti-communism, the British Empire. In these ways, anti-communism became synonymous with the defence of Australian identity itself. Attacks on communism also had a moral dimension. The threat perceived in the correspondence sent to Menzies was underpinned by a sense that a spiritual crusade was being engaged with the forces of evil.

In the Cold War years, suspicion of communist subversion could be invoked in almost any cause. E Keates wrote from Newcastle (New South Wales), on the occasion of Menzies' visit there in October 1953, warning that the failure to provide his home town with an airport and a university was playing into the hands of the communists.[1] When Bruce Graham wanted Menzies to launch the first in a series of exhibition basketball matches being played by the visiting American teams, the Harlem Globetrotters and the Boston Whirlwinds, he did not fail to play the anti-communist card. Such sporting tours, he told Menzies, 'tend to offset the Communist propaganda, to the effect that the American Negro is a subjugated, servile and neglected individual'.[2] Correspondents persisted in seeing the most sinister motives behind trivial events. They were worried, for example, by the presence of the waterside workers on floats in the parade marking the centenary of the Eureka Stockade.[3] One woman even complained about a trade union picnic held at Manuka Oval in March 1954.[4] On this occasion the prime minister's secretary, Geoffrey Yeend, rebuked her, pointing out that unionists were perfectly entitled to hold a picnic, and reminding her that many Liberal Party supporters were trade union members. This was a rare flash of lucidity in an otherwise murky world of fear and suspicion. Normally, the rhetoric of anti-communism found writer and addressee in complete harmony with each other.

Following the Nazi-Soviet Non-Aggression Pact of 1939, Menzies had banned the Communist Party of Australia in the interests of national security. The ban was lifted by the Curtin government in 1943, when the USSR had become a vital ally in the war against Hitler. At the end of the war, Menzies was reluctant to restore the ban, regarding such a move in peacetime as undemocratic, and fearing that it would simply drive communism underground.[5] In 1948, at the time of the Berlin Blockade and the accession to power of the communists in Czechoslovakia, he seems to have reconsidered. By 1949, he had changed his mind. The Chinese Revolution had brought the communists to power; Labor's plans for tighter government control of the banking sector (commonly labelled 'nationalisation') seemed like a dangerous excess of central economic planning; and a series of strikes prepared fertile ground for an attack on socialism in the 1949 election.

For Menzies and for his correspondents, anti-communism was both a useful political instrument and the expression of a genuine fear of another possible world war. It provided a common linguistic register, which resonated with all conservative sympathisers and helped them discredit their political opponents. Anti-communism, however, was not a monolithic idea, and its mutations deserve to be dissected. This chapter suggests that it had three main aspects, roughly corresponding to three successive phases. Firstly, to oppose communism was to oppose militant trade unionism. The primary significance of anti-communism was its domestic dimension, and lay in its confrontation with trade union radicalism. A second phase was inaugurated by the Petrov Affair of 1954, which focused attention much more sharply on the hostile activities of the Soviet Union and their global reach. Opposition to union radicalism did not disappear, but now it acquired a new layer in which the target was a world conspiracy orchestrated by the Kremlin. A third layer of anti-communism solidified later, when the external threat appeared much closer to home, in Asia itself. In this later phase, the activities of 'Red China' and Indonesia captured the attention of Menzies' correspondents. All these faces of anti-communism were simultaneously present in the correspondence but, in each phase of the phenomenon, one of them dominated the rest.

Anti-communism and the fight against the trade unions

With the wartime emergency over, workers started to activate a backlog of wage claims. In 1946, strikes broke out in several industries – in transport, on the waterfront, in the collieries. This strike wave had hostile repercussions. In early 1949, an opinion poll showed that

70 per cent of respondents were already in favour of banning the Australian Communist Party, and 61 per cent of Labor Party voters supported the exclusion of communists from trade union office.[6] Then, in the winter of 1949, the coalminers of New South Wales went on strike for seven weeks. The coal industry ground to a halt and gas and electricity supplies were temporarily rationed. Labor prime minister Chifley sent in troops to get the mines working, and jailed union officials. This industrial action highlighted the possibility of communist-inspired disruption and provoked a conservative reaction which helped to bring Menzies to power in December 1949. In spite of Chifley's action, Labor was accused of being 'soft on communism', and Menzies promised to make the Communist Party illegal. 'For the Australian labour movement', wrote historian Meredith Burgmann, 'the Cold War was a domestic issue'.[7]

Several correspondents were frustrated by disruptions caused by industrial action. Doreen Gard wrote from near Millicent (South Australia): 'Out here on the land, Communism is only something we hear about, but rarely [sic] see. But every time I visit Melbourne I feel it with coal and tram strikes, and everything decent thrown into confusion.'[8] A Sydney woman, looking back from 1954, remembered

> the last Labor government and the misery we endured constant strikes, meat, coal, bread, milk, then every week or two no electric light Xmas time and the big department stores lit up with lamps and candles because the miners were always going on strike. I remember the black markets and continued food rationing long after the war was over [...].[9]

Others interpreted such events as evidence of an organised conspiracy, in which the communist-inspired Waterside Workers' Federation was deeply implicated. A Presbyterian minister confided that 'I am told that a communist plot to bring down your ministry "within twelve months" has been formulated and that it has begun operations by a series of apparently unrelated strikes or "stoppages" on the water fronts of Australia'.[10] There was support within the Liberal Party to introduce secret ballots in elections of trade union officials, in order to counteract what was seen as communist manipulation. Mrs Dougan of the anti-communist Bureau of Public Relations in Sydney even warned of communist influence in pensioners' associations, on the grounds that trade unions provided pensioners' delegations to Canberra with bus transport. Mrs Dougan threatened to come to Canberra to underline the problem, and Menzies' secretary William Heseltine pencilled a comment: 'Mrs Dougan didn't show up – thank God!'[11]

In Sydney, the People's Union of New South Wales bombarded Menzies with a series of long letters densely typed on foolscap paper, which were intended to open his eyes to communist conspiracies.[12] The People's Union was angered by a number of issues, both domestic and external. It opposed any idea of giving official recognition to communist China. It opposed compulsory union membership, and pointed out the communist infiltration of union leadership. The People's Union, through its indefatigable administrator AG Hebblewhite, warned Menzies that communism had completely infiltrated the Labor Party and urged him to expose this collusion.[13] A compulsory ballot before strike action, Hebblewhite argued, would neutralise communist influence.[14] The People's Union held meetings in factories and contributed a column to the *Daily Telegraph* until 1965. It was one of Menzies' most consistent and strident correspondents.

The People's Union aimed to keep Menzies up to date on the machinations of the communist world conspiracy. Its arguments were variations on a constant narrative, which ran roughly as follows: there is a world conspiracy to destroy democracy, emanating from Moscow; it has many supporters but their work is cleverly disguised so that innocent people are duped by it; the People's Union, however, knows the 'true facts' and has information which will expose the real nature of the 'Red Conspiracy'.[15] The organisation was very active in support of the 1951 referendum on the dissolution of the Communist Party, but the failure of the referendum did not in any way deflect it from its obsessive pursuit of anti-communism. Menzies, for his part, needed little prompting on this theme.

In September 1950, Menzies warned the country that a Third World War was likely to break out soon, and a few months later he predicted that it might occur within three years. Australia needed to prepare its defences. This was the pretext for both the introduction of national service and the attack on the Australian Communist Party (CPA). The story of Menzies' abortive attempt to ban the CPA has been often examined and need only be briefly summarised here. The Bill for the Dissolution of the Communist Party would have banned the party and other institutions found to be communist and seized their assets, and it would have prohibited communists from holding any office in trade unions or the public service. When, in March 1951, the High Court threw out the legislation as an unconstitutional violation of states' rights, Menzies decided to put the issue to a referendum, which, if passed, would have given his government the power to proceed with the ban.

At first the Bill for the Dissolution of the CPA stimulated enthusiastic support among correspondents. The Secretary of the New South Wales' Quarrymen's Union praised Menzies' stand against industrial chaos in these words, clearly interpreting anti-communism as a domestic issue: 'Australia salutes you, and the rest of the democratic world will follow suit [...] PS Not because they are communists but because they are out to sabotage the industrial economy of Australia, is, I think, the gist of the bill'.[16] Mrs McEneroe of Paddington in Sydney echoed these sentiments in a fairly representative hero-worshipping style:

> pardon me taking the liberty to write you these few lines. God Bless you. You are a tower of strenght [sic] a straight, good gentleman. You are doing a wonderful job a saver of Australia.

THE CHANGING FACE OF ANTI-COMMUNISM

> Long may you live to continue doing a great job you have saved Australia by crushing the Communist party [...] God Bless you and keep your lovd ones.[17]

Communism was denounced as an alien ideology, which operated in illegitimate ways to undermine peace and democracy. It preyed on gullible followers who included many Australian workers. Only very rarely did a correspondent express reservations about the government's offensive, like this wife of a South Australian Presbyterian minister who doubted the effectiveness of trying to dissolve the CPA. She predicted that the party would endure persecution as a clandestine organisation:

> I view with apprehension the proposed Bill to down the Communist party. I have just received today a letter from the Secty. of the Com Party (S.A.) in which he definitely states that the party WILL go on in spite of any opposition it receives. This resolution is no light one I feel sure and it seems to me that the opposition it receives will only drive it underground, making it a strong feater [*i.e. feature*] In the community. Compare the resistance movements in other countries.
>
> It seems to me that your method of fighting the Commos is purely negative and non-constructive.[18]

Even here, the correspondent shared the anti-communist assumptions of the Dissolution Bill, although she cast doubt on the best means of advancing the anti-communist struggle.

Menzies addressed rowdy meetings in defence of the referendum, at which he was frequently booed and heckled and provoked into at least one reference to 'communist scum'.[19] The referendum was narrowly lost – an unexpected result, considering that in May 1950, opinion polls had showed that 82 per cent of respondents supported the dissolution of the Communist Party.[20] Clearly a number of pro-government voters had defected, and possibly some had voted 'No' to express their dissatisfaction on issues which had nothing to do with communism.[21]

Evatt, as the new Labor leader, successfully attacked the legislation on an important issue: anyone officially 'declared' to be a communist would be presumed guilty unless they proved their innocence. The government preferred to put the onus of proof on the accused because this would make it unnecessary for ASIO to reveal its confidential sources in court. This reversal of normal judicial procedure, Evatt successfully argued, was a violation of legal rights. His message went down especially well in his home state of New South Wales, which returned a solid 'No' majority in the referendum.[22] Many pro-Liberal correspondents clearly agreed, questioning the suspension of the presumption of innocence. They continued to regard this as a fundamental principle of 'British justice' whose standards they were keen to maintain. Menzies' constituents did not hate communism any the less, but some of them refused to adopt illiberal means to suppress it. For this group of Liberal voters, the legal traditions of Westminster were sacrosanct. Evatt scored a rare victory over his rival Menzies in the 1951 referendum campaign, but it would be his last. In the coming years the deep personal animosity between the two party leaders would increasingly poison political debate.

The Soviet world conspiracy

In its second phase, anti-communism looked outwards, and focused more consistently on the threats to democracy posed by the aggressive ambitions of the USSR. This anti-Soviet face of anti-communism became more dominant after the Petrov Affair in 1954, but it had a longer history than this. Already in 1953, John Vardy of Lane

THE CHANGING FACE OF ANTI-COMMUNISM

Cove saw compulsory unionism and wage arbitration as signs that communism was taking over his home state of New South Wales. He wrote: 'if ever there was a time in the history of politics in N.S.W. when power initiated by Russia is getting the upper hand it is now'.[23] A Melbourne correspondent saw the hand of the Comintern in industrial 'go-slows'.[24] Florence Cardell-Oliver, member of the Western Australian Legislative Assembly, identified the same enemy when she condemned Housing Commission plans to build new apartments in her Subiaco constituency. She denounced this as a scheme to flood the area with Labor Party voters, but there was more about the apartment block that offended her: 'It is to be on the Russian plan including a crèche for children, a baby-sitter, a very small garden, a shop, etc., so that women may go out to work!'[25] The horrified exclamation mark which concluded her outburst seemed to suggest that Russia was now held responsible for sending women out to work and upsetting traditional gender relations. Menzies tersely replied that it was a state matter and that the proposed accommodation would not be funded by the Commonwealth.

In the same year, Josef Stalin died. H Reisman of Sydney wrote to offer his services as an observer of Russian affairs to the Australian Legation in Moscow, and noted, 'The Best of Kremlin is dead, but what of the future?'[26] This, however, was one of only two references to the death of Stalin in the entire Menzies correspondence. At this point, communists were being accused of controlling the trade unions and using the Labor Party as a front to undermine the Australian Commonwealth, but hardly any writers, before 1954 at least, accused them of being the puppets of Moscow, which was a charge they continually faced in Europe. Sometimes the silences in the correspondence are as eloquent as their polemical content. The absent Stalin was not directly relevant to anti-communist sentiment.

Although Stalin's name was hardly mentioned, his successor Khrushchev loomed very large. Mrs Zymantis, a recent immigrant and a very grateful one, was afraid that the Soviet Union was exploiting conflict in the Middle East, and her wrath against Khrushchev exploded. He was

> the biggest murderer and the greatest lier [sic] in this whole world, whose not one word is true [...] He sheds the blood of countless thousands, and still is not satisfied [...] He is Satan himself [...] He swallowed all our Baltic countrys [sic], he swallowed all friends and relations, and there are millions of slaves whose rights are much smaller those of our pets in our backyards.[27]

Khrushchev's speech to the Congress of the Soviet Communist Party in 1966 is conventionally seen as the tentative beginning of a 'thaw' which ushered in a phase of de-Stalinisation. Menzies' correspondents never perceived Khrushchev in this light. For them he was the architect of a sinister world conspiracy. 'Mr Khrushchev is planning something big', wrote Thelma Saunders, 'I do not know what it is but will find out soon and let you know'.[28] The events of 1954 were the turning point between the relative neglect of Stalin and the elevation of Khrushchev to demonic status.

The face of anti-communism changed because the Petrov Affair accentuated its Soviet profile. On 13 April 1954, Menzies announced the defection of Vladimir Petrov, a colonel in the Soviet intelligence service serving in the Soviet embassy, Canberra. A Royal Commission on Espionage was set up to investigate Soviet connections in Australia. A week after Menzies' announcement, Petrov's wife Evdokia was sensationally 'rescued' at Darwin airport from the hands of Russian operatives who intended to escort her back to the Soviet Union. The dramatic scene on the tarmac, as Soviet guards were prevented from taking off with the distraught Mrs Petrov, was widely broadcast throughout the world's news media. Mrs Petrov had been saved from the clutches of brutal Soviet thugs. The story put Australia on the map as the champion of freedom against cruel communist oppression.

THE CHANGING FACE OF ANTI-COMMUNISM

Menzies capitalised fully on the event, although his election victory in 1954 probably owed as much to an improving economic situation as it did to the windfall of votes he gathered from the Petrov Affair. The Royal Commission would later implicate members of Evatt's staff, and in 1955 the Labor Party suffered a fatal split, as supporters of BA Santamaria's Catholic-inspired, anti-communist movement seceded to form their own Democratic Labor Party. The schism affected different states unevenly: but it was particularly devastating in Victoria.[29] Since the new party gave most of its electoral preferences to the Liberals, Menzies' position immediately became more comfortable. Evatt accused Menzies of manipulating Petrov's defection for electoral purposes, but the current historical consensus agrees that Menzies did not control the timing of Petrov's defection, and that neither he nor ASIO manufactured documents to discredit the Labor Party.[30] Menzies had simply seized the moment and squeezed maximum propaganda value from it. Even though Petrov was an ineffective agent and had in fact been recalled to the USSR, Menzies intended to make the reality of Soviet espionage plain to all.[31]

Menzies received effusive letters of congratulations. In 1954, there were 66 letters specifically congratulating him on the outcome of the Petrov Affair, or deploring Labor's accusation that he had concocted the entire scenario. They included one from Kim Beazley Snr, a future Labor minister, and another from future Liberal prime minister John Gorton.[32] Although 66 letters of approval may not seem an enormous number, there can be no doubt about the intensity of anti-communist feeling in general. Some correspondents included evidence of 'distortions' in Labor Party propaganda or in the press in communist countries. Many congratulations arrived from North America, including some from the world's media, like the *Reader's Digest*, seeking an interview with the Petrovs. The Petrov case further reignited demands for another referendum to ban the Communist Party.

The ordinary writers who addressed Menzies on the affair had a slightly different perspective from that of the international press. One woman, for example, wrote including a letter to be passed on to Mrs Petrov (whose whereabouts were secret), and for many the Petrov Affair was very much a '*Mrs* Petrov Affair'. Their attention centred far more on the rescue of Evdokia Petrov, and on expressing sympathy for her ordeal, than on the defection of a Soviet spy. Nellie Harding of Milsons Point (New South Wales) made Menzies a hero and a saviour, writing:

> One feels it is an honour to be a British subject, and better still, an Australian born one – to be associated with a Leader such as you have proved yourself to be many times but this last experience has surpassed anything I have ever known at the age of 68 years.
>
> I do congratulate you heartily Mr Menzies on the Christian and Humane way you have handled the case of dear Mrs Petrov […] it was so calmly and genuinely fixed up by you, and now she enjoys the liberty of all Australians old and new.[33]

It is not absolutely clear that Evdokia Petrov sincerely desired to remain in Australia. Her husband's defection, however, had placed her in an impossible situation: if she returned to the USSR, she presumably faced an uncertain future as a traitor's wife. But this was not the issue for many correspondents, who saw only the heroic rescue of 'dear Mrs Petrov', a woman in distress. When *Woman's Day* magazine chose its Ten Women of the Year for 1954, it included Evdokia Petrov as well as Queen Elizabeth II.[34] Josephine Mitchell of Llanelly (Victoria) saw an article about Evdokia Petrov in *Woman's Day* and took pity on her. So she sent Menzies a book on the life of Christ to pass on to her, because as a subject of a communist regime,

Mitchell assumed, Mrs Petrov would know nothing about the love of the Christian God.³⁵

The Petrov Affair intensified the pervasive culture of fear and suspicion. The government fostered this poisonous atmosphere by continuing to denounce the peace movement of the 1950s, led mainly by Christian pacifists, as an unwitting tool of communist propaganda.³⁶ ASIO pressured individual sponsors and academics to withdraw their support for the Melbourne Peace Congress of 1959.³⁷ After 1956, Hungarian immigrants fleeing the Soviet crackdown in their country lent their support to anti-communism in Australia. Passports were blocked, university academics suspected of communist leanings were banned from travelling overseas, and individuals barred on political grounds from getting assisted passages to Australia.

Writers and artists had already been targeted as communist sympathisers, as anti-communist enthusiasts like WC (Billy) Wentworth attacked authors Katharine Susannah Prichard and Kylie Tennant, and accused the Commonwealth Literary Fund of giving grants to communists. In 1952, Menzies was informed that communist novelist Judah Waten had been awarded a grant from the fund. He consequently ordered all recipients to be screened by ASIO.³⁸ These attacks forced the resignation of writer Vance Palmer from the fund's advisory board in 1953.³⁹

Neighbours informed on each other, and the intelligentsia was a prime target. In 1955, Menzies received a denunciation of the ageing Dame Mary Gilmore from a woman who had briefly served as her housekeeper and companion:

> I thought you should be aware of her desperately anti-British feelings, and her pro-Communist associations. I understand she writes for the Tribune sometimes, and I should not be surprised if she is in touch with the Southern Irish Club in Sydney [...]

> I can't understand why Dame Mary Gilmore should want the British title of 'Dame', she dislikes Royalty and refers to 'William the Conqueror' 1066 as 'William the Bastard'.
>
> At 90 years her brains are working as well as ever.
>
> A lot of telephoning goes on at Dame Gilmore's. She does not go out but receives people at her flat.
>
> PS Dame Mary Gilmore is not an R.C. but likes anyone who is anti-British from what I could see.[40]

Letters like this can be attributed to the climate of suspicion and denunciation exacerbated by the Petrov Affair. Here the rhetoric of anti-communism merges with support for Britain, and attempts to damage Gilmore's reputation further by potential association with Irish Catholics. Most of the content of this letter is hearsay, and the author seems quite unaware of the fact that insulting the Norman Conquest could be seen as a truly Anglo-Saxon trait. Gilmore certainly did write for the *Tribune*, promoting her pacifist beliefs, but this was hardly a secret. Apparently no action was taken on this denunciation.

Communists were invisible but correspondents imagined conspiracies everywhere. One Sydney correspondent, who was a founding member of the Parramatta Art Society and the National Gallery Society, believed that one or other of these organisations was sheltering a communist cell.[41] He was not exactly sure which one. Artists, like writers and other intellectuals, were especially vulnerable. Graham Thorley, who was contemplating curating an exhibition of Australian art in the USSR, branded Picasso as a communist conspirator:

THE CHANGING FACE OF ANTI-COMMUNISM

I rather suspect that that wily old communist Picasso has been churning out his trash all these years in a deliberate effort to destroy the cultural standards of the democracies and the bait has been swallowed hook, line and sinker by a large and stupid intelligentsia in France, England and America.[42]

Patricia Heggarty of Brisbane wrote in the wake of the Petrov revelations to accuse the Australian National University of sheltering communists.[43]

Menzies received several individual denunciations just before and after Petrov's defection, which were directly referred to the security services. This was the case when one Victorian woman in 1954 denounced her former neighbour, who allegedly said 'he wouldn't fight for Menzies and that Menzies ought to be shot, that Russia and China have the right form of government'. 'He had Chinese friends visiting him frequently', she added, providing a car registration number, 'he is a potential communist and he is not honest. My impression and experience of him is that he is mental at times'.[44] Jeff Bate, a Liberal Party member of Parliament, was alarmed by gatherings of youths in uniform speaking a foreign language near the George's River in Sydney. ASIO reported that this was a false alarm; Bate had spotted a meeting of Plast, an anti-communist Ukrainian organisation which wore similar uniforms to those of the Boy Scouts.[45] In their zeal to expose the enemy within, correspondents were recreating the sinister environment which they so deplored in Stalinist Eastern Europe. WC Wentworth named Morgan's Bookshop in Sydney as a communist hotbed.[46] ASIO found that the bookshop sold a wide range of literature, some pro-communist and some not, and that no further action was appropriate.

In the May 1954 election, the Liberal-Country Party coalition was returned with a reduced majority of seven seats, although it failed to collect more than 50 per cent of the two-party preferred vote. Besides the Labor schism, which was fatal to the opposition's chances of victory in the short and medium term, there was another important casualty of the Petrov Affair. The Labor leader, HV ('Doc') Evatt, was severely discredited. In February 1955, Evatt wrote to Molotov, the Soviet Foreign Minister, to ask for the truth about the Affair. In October Evatt told Parliament that Molotov had assured him that the Petrov accusations had been fabricated. His astonishing naivety left him open to ridicule, and Menzies' correspondence accordingly reflected very negative views of his performance.

In response to Evatt's letter and his speech against the Royal Commission on Espionage, PP Buckland called him 'lower than a snake's ladder', perhaps reflecting a confused interpretation of the popular board game.[47] The Molotov letter was a trump card which Evatt handed to Menzies. In Sydney, Louis Conney, who aspired to a Senate seat, condemned Evatt in shaky English:

> This megalomaniac ispiring to become the next aspirant for the 10 000 pounds Stalin Price, ha become the greatest menace [...] [*sic*]

> It might comfort you dear Sir, to know, that nearly 300 000 New Australians victims of communistic persecution are on your side and it might be of comfort to you that several great forces are endeavouring your Victory – that Australia may for ever continue to remain White Australia – ruled under Christian and democratic principles.[48]

Mr Conney thoughtfully included a photograph of himself, brandishing a crucifix in one hand and hammer and sickle in the other, inviting the viewer to choose between them. The message that the fight against communism was a Christian crusade could not have been made any clearer. He was a recent immigrant, who identified with 'the victims of 13 nations behind the Iron Curtain' and swore loyalty to his new homeland.[49] Miss Crowley of Holbrook (New South Wales), on the other hand, was a Catholic and a disillusioned Labor supporter who admired Menzies for his broad-minded attitude on religious questions. She heaped scorn on Evatt thus: 'I admire you for the way you fight the comes [*i.e. commies*] (the Monsters). I used to vote Labour but Dr Evatt has shown his hipocery [*sic*]. no more for me [...] he is nothing but the commoe's agent'.[50]

The duel between Menzies and communist infiltration was seen as a test of virility, which Menzies passed with distinction. Marie Dahrencourt assured him: 'You can strangle them as you have got what it takes'.[51] Syd Hudson echoed these sentiments, though in uncertain spelling, writing 'it takes men of Guts – I mean as men at war and you have shown you true colours and attacked them with fury and you have a hug majority withe you [...] Excuse mistakes in writing but it is Honest and I am in a hurry'.[52] 'The people await a virile fight with the gloves off', added Jas Farrer, licking his lips at the prospect.[53] Correspondents revered Menzies as Australia's new strong man.

In 1971, journalist Alan Reid described anti-communism as an issue 'in many garbs but when the clothes were removed the naked figure invariably carried a hammer in one hand and a sickle in the other'.[54] As this chapter has argued, this was not always the case, but in the mid-1950s, fear of communist-inspired industrial sabotage increasingly saw the hand of the USSR behind the disruption. 'Im a British subject', wrote E Campbell, 'and as such I ask you not to back down in your attitude to the commo mob or to put it better Russia'.[55] Mrs Duff of Drummoyne (New South Wales) speculated on Evatt's allegiances, writing: 'Probably Dr Evatt has his eyes on favours from Moscow, and thinks if he can bring Australia under the Soviet he is assured of a high position'.[56] Mrs Hannan was even more explicit in identifying communist subversion with the Soviet Union:

> After many a decade of Soviet treachery and deceit, where is the decency of our statesmen, when they become collaborationists of the most evil forces which ever swept the earth.
>
> As the gluttonous Soviet Beast moves forward – ever forward – we throw our friends and allies and helpless humans to the oncoming marauding Russian Bear.[57]

Several recent immigrants from Eastern Europe had direct experience of Soviet-style regimes. The Federation of Ukrainian Associations, for example, invited Menzies to commemorate the Ukrainian famine of 1932–33, allegedly organised by their Russian Soviet oppressors, in which they claimed seven million died.[58] Frank Opeltz, a Hungarian who had been a prisoner-of-war in Russia during the First World War, showed an exceptionally broad knowledge of current world politics, and praised Senator McCarthy's attempts to root out communist subversion in the USA. He wrote to Menzies to warn him that 'In the witches' cauldron of the Kremlin Mephistopheles is brewing the hellish potions for the unsuspecting world'.[59] Eastern Europeans knew (quite literally) where the bodies were buried. AN Bendas wrote in Russian:

> It is not wise to keep silence over the doings of the bandits.
> There were not hundreds but thousands of bodies found buried.
> It would be a good idea to speak about it on the radio. [...]
>
> Why don't you trust me? I am not your enymy [sic] or your Government's – I only hate the communists. They killed my father in 1919 and took everything from us; my father was a very wealthy farmer.[60]

It was typical of the hybrid nature of the letters that, having established his credentials, Bendas concluded by asking Menzies for a loan.

THE CHANGING FACE OF ANTI-COMMUNISM

Anti-communism and the 'Asiatic influx'

When the Victorian informer mentioned above denounced her ex-neighbour in 1954, one of the things that aroused her suspicion was the fact that he had frequent Chinese visitors. The association of communism with Asian expansion was a third face of anti-communism in Australia, reinforcing the fears which had sustained the White Australia Policy for decades.

Contrary to expectations, the Korean War caused very few reverberations in the Menzies correspondence, perhaps because intervention there was relatively uncontroversial. According to opinion polls, 71 per cent of those questioned approved of Australian military involvement.[61] There was a slightly louder echo when Menzies sent troops to Malaya in 1955, but the real threat, as correspondents perceived it, was from China. Veronica Murphy of East Malvern (Victoria), for instance, insisted that the Australian government should not recognise 'Red China'.[62] Similarly, Hugo Morrisson sent a long, typed foolscap letter from Ireland, with much of it in red for greater emphasis, deploring the absorption of China into the communist bloc led by 'Red Russia', and denouncing the British Labour leader Aneurin Bevan as a communist in disguise. He followed it with another, this time in green ink, in the same vein, that is to say anti-Stalinist and anti-Bevanite.[63] Norman Nicolson of Melbourne warned that in Australia, communism signifies 'the open door to the Asiatic influx'.[64] Communism represented the latest version of the 'Yellow Peril'.

A turning point in correspondents' attitudes came in the Taiwan Strait crisis of January 1955, in which the Chinese People's Liberation Army defeated Nationalist forces to take possession of disputed islands off the mainland. This focused attention on what was then known as Formosa (now Taiwan), and on 'Red China'. The danger of war briefly reappeared and Australian trade unions appealed to the USA not to make any aggressive move.

In 1953, the Korean War ended and Stalin died. The Soviet Union promoted a policy of 'Peaceful Co-existence' with the West. Anti-communist attention turned towards southeast Asia. The rise of communism in Indonesia, in particular, became a grave cause for concern for correspondents. The People's Union warned in 1958 of the consequences of increased Soviet economic aid for southeast Asian countries. It would mean they would be able to undercut Australian products. Furthermore, the People's Union wrote, Indonesia was now part of the USSR's master strategy for the global expansion of communism and the encirclement of Australia.[65] In 1959, Chris Hallam took Menzies' previous prediction of a new world war in mock-serious vein, asking 'Dear Sir, Would you please tell me when there will be a next world war if any? As I think there is a very eminent [sic] danger that communism will advance on Australia through the North from Indonesia etc.'.[66]

The People's Union continued to bombard Menzies on the same theme. In January, Australian waterside workers were holding up the movement of Dutch ships in sympathy with Indonesia's confrontation with the colonial authorities in western New Guinea. Hebblewhite denounced this as communist economic sabotage, which was evidence of the Kremlin's designs on southeast Asia.[67] He followed this with many letters on the same theme, exposing the communist plan for southeast Asia and arguing that the People's Union was obliged to 'lift the veil' to uncover the Soviet Union's many devious disguises. 'The methods', Menzies was informed, 'by which a comparatively small group of gangsters working to Lenin's plans hold in subjection a thousand million of people have all been elucidated'.[68]

There was a subtle shift, however, in the emphasis of the People's Union's propaganda messages. Hebblewhite referred not merely to 'Lenin's plans', but also to a 'Stalin-Mao Tse Tung project', a notion which clearly signalled the growing Asian dimension of anti-communism. Indonesian aggression in West New Guinea, he wrote, revealed 'The existence of a long-term plan, known as the Stalin-Mao Tse Tung project, [which] provides for forcible induction of surplus Asian population into Australia'.[69] The discourse was the same, but the targets were moving. Sukarno, President of Indonesia, was one of them. Indonesian claims on West New Guinea brought the problem of communism dangerously close to home and could lead to the communist penetration of northern Australia, argued Hebblewhite.[70] Sukarno was a Soviet ally, and he urged forestalling the emergence of 'an Australian Cuba'. The aim of the so-called Stalin-Mao Tse Tung Plan was, after all, the military subjugation of Australia.[71] The People's Union was not alone in its fears of the spread of Asian communism. 'If we don't fix Indonesia soon', wrote a Victorian correspondent, 'the communists will be in Darwin within a decade'.[72] It was a short step from 'fixing Indonesia' to 'fixing Vietnam' and shortly after this letter was sent, the first Australian combat units arrived in South Vietnam.

A moral and spiritual battle

Menzies and his writing public shared a common understanding of the communist threat. Menzies' anti-communist rhetoric drew sympathetic responses from letter-writers which reinforced their common determination. When Menzies spoke of fighting a spiritual battle, writers readily replied in appropriate language, urging the defeat of the 'forces of evil'. When Menzies referred to the diabolical strategies of communist powers and their followers, writers reproduced the same rhetoric of demonisation on their letters. 'You must be a man of iron', wrote DG McDonald of Maitland (New South Wales), 'to stand up to their devilry and cunning'.[73]

Menzies himself was cast in the role of a hero or a saint in combat against the Devil. For Nance Smith of Moonee Ponds (Victoria):

you evidently have fulfilled my exalted ideal for you (brave, strong and true) I do not think there is another of our Parliamentarians who would stand up to our enemy the Communists, and expose their devilish aims as you have done! And to me you are the 'Bravest of the Brave'.[74]

At the House of Commons in Westminster, Waldron Smith heard Menzies speak on BBC radio about conducting 'a spiritual war against diabolical subtlety', and wrote to advise him to consult Ephesians, chapter 6, verse 12, which reads, 'For we wrestle not against flesh and blood, but against principalities, against powers, against the rulers of the darkness of this world, against spiritual wickedness in high places'.[75] Quoting from the Bible was a common method of endorsing and reinforcing Menzies' message, and of expressing the writer's solidarity with the Christian cause. Another Englishman, Robert Hadden, congratulated Menzies on his management of the Petrov Affair in language that was almost a self-parody: 'The cunning villainy of their hired assassins has been frustrated and Moscow must be very enraged. Communism was spawned in hell; and is the greatest curse the world has ever known'.[76]

The decline of anti-communism

Greater prosperity after 1955 dulled the edge of social antagonisms. The influence of the Australian Communist Party itself was in decline, and its membership had been contracting since the end of the Second World War.[77] Anti-communism accordingly lost its virulence, and in the 1960s, even the People's Union's diatribes became more irregular. None were sent in 1960, but the organisation briefly revived in 1961. There were again no letters from this source in 1962, and the stream died away completely in 1963. The usually indefatigable

THE CHANGING FACE OF ANTI-COMMUNISM

AG Hebblewhite had started to doubt the effectiveness of his own messages, writing rather enigmatically:

> It is always a difficult matter for us to assess the degree of seriousness with which you accept our representations. The writer is fully conscious of a relatively weak background on this question [*whose background?*] and the many difficulties in finding anyone who is in a position to evaluate our work to the point of treating our conclusions seriously. There are, unfortunately, very few people in the world to-day who can substantiate claims to expert knowledge on this subject.
>
> Our credentials therefore rest entirely on events and the fact that we accurately forecast them as relating to the Soviet plan of operations as we understand it.[78]

Hebblewhite seems to suggest here that Menzies himself has a 'weak background' in the field of anti-communism and is no longer taking the People's Union's letters seriously. This particular letter was provoked by plans to establish a Soviet embassy in Canberra. The upgrading of diplomatic relations between Australia and the USSR looked like weakness on Menzies' part and a betrayal of the anti-communist crusade.

In early 1959, British prime minister Harold Macmillan made an official visit to the USSR, which some writers found distressing for the same reason. Macmillan, however, presented his Soviet counterparts with some woollen products, which drew a positive response in Australia, perhaps opening up the enticing commercial prospect of the entire Red Army protected against the Russian winter by Australian wool overcoats. No doubt Macmillan had the future of the Yorkshire woollen industry foremost in his mind, but this was a signal that relations with the USSR were thawing, much to the chagrin of the People's Union and their supporters. They included the Victorian League of Rights, which wrote to express its dismay at Menzies' policy towards communist countries, which it predicted would lead to disaster. Menzies replied that we have to find a way of living with the communist powers because the alternative would be war.[79]

The anti-communist reflex which afflicted both Menzies and his correspondents blinded them to important global realities. They ultimately failed to understand the legitimate aspirations of Asian and African peoples to self-determination; instead, they only saw what they imagined was inspiring their struggles – a communist push for global domination. In the same way, they were insensitive to the Soviet Union's security fears and to the eastern bloc's anxieties about the real purpose of the NATO alliance. In their allegiance to the British Empire, correspondents implicitly identified with colonialism and tended to see all decolonisation struggles as a danger to stability.

The antagonism which correspondents expressed towards all forms of communism, whether domestic or foreign, became part of their sense of Australian identity. Their notion of Australianness was as yet only vaguely articulated, but they felt very deeply that communism was not a part of 'the Australian way of life'. Loyalty to Britain, on the other hand, certainly was a part of their identity, and it is remarkable how often letters to Menzies about communism evoked the British connection. As we have already seen, Nellie Harding prefaced her congratulations on the Petrov case with the phrase, 'One feels it is an honour to be a British subject, and better still, an Australian born one'.[80] 'Im a British subject', wrote E Campbell, 'and as such I ask you not to back down in your attitude to the commo mob'.[81] The Petrov Affair spawned effusive declarations of British loyalty.

The correspondents thus shared with Menzies a hatred of the evils of communism, defined as anti-Christian, Satanic and anti-British. On at least two occasions, however, letter-writers refused to follow

THE CHANGING FACE OF ANTI-COMMUNISM

Menzies, and for a moment disagreement weakened the common platform on which their dialogue was normally conducted. The first of these occasions arose from the referendum of 1951, when many writers refused to ignore judicial safeguards, such as the presumption of innocence, which they considered fundamental. These were part of their British heritage, which Menzies, in his zeal to persecute communists, seemed about to betray. The second occasion, as we shall see in the next chapter, was Menzies' own enmity against Evatt in 1955, which many writers found unnecessarily vindictive. Menzies was taken to task for allowing a personal vendetta to damage the image of serene statesmanship which he had so carefully cultivated. These letter-writers, therefore, did not react like robots to Menzies' cues. Instead they reminded him of the values they shared, and called him to account when he appeared to forget them.

10

*'People will weep
tears of blood'*

ANGRY LETTERS AND POLITICAL PROTEST

Rage and resentment

Letters of anger and resentment are an inescapable aspect of writing upwards. Acrimonious letters, sometimes anonymous, provide an outlet for ordinary people to express their rage and aggression towards superior authorities. Thus, during the First World War, King Victor Emmanuel of Italy received furious letters from his subjects holding him responsible for his government's mismanagement of the war and the resulting carnage on the Austrian front.[1] Their epistolary outrage was inspired partly by Christian pacifism, but also by anarchism and socialism, and it was occasionally accompanied by threats of revolution. Letters to Menzies were never quite as vituperative as this and fortunately they did not have cause to be. Unlike the Italian letters they did not include any death threats. At worst, correspondents threatened never to vote Liberal again, which suggests that anger was generated by disillusioned supporters as much as by his outright enemies. Nevertheless, writers used letters to curse and insult him, to protest against his policies and to accuse him of arrogance or indifference.

ANGRY LETTERS AND POLITICAL PROTEST

Many subjects aroused the temper of his correspondents, as we have already seen. Communists, Roman Catholics, 'Doc' Evatt's speeches and the government's failure to abolish the pensions means test were among those topics most likely to instil some heat into the correspondence. But they were not the only ones. One English correspondent was aroused to protest to Menzies and presumably to Australia in general when she found maggots in a recently opened tin of Australian Ardmona peaches.[2] Valerie Yeats was driven to rage and despair by a newspaper article predicting a rise in dog licence fees. This, she was certain, would increase the number of stray and abandoned dogs, and for her it meant that 'Decency is now dead – & there is nothing worth fighting for – any more'.[3] In this chapter, however, I principally concentrate on letters whose anger was directed at Menzies himself, letters which were insulting, hostile or critical of his personal conduct. The personal hotline to the prime minister, as we have seen, was the best means available to correspondents seeking a favour; it could serve equally well to convey indignation and disgust. Writing to a newspaper was a traditional way to voice a complaint, but writing to Menzies was a little different from sending a 'letter to the editor'. For one thing, writers did not seek publication. Instead they wanted to insult the prime minister personally and in private.

Milder forms of political protest are also included in the discussion. A group of political letters will be briefly analysed, in which constituents issued warnings to Menzies about the shortcomings of Liberal policy and the subsequent vulnerability of the government at an imminent election. The spectrum of emotions ranges, therefore, from outright anger to impatience and moderate complaints.

Smugness and complacency

Early in his political career, Menzies' air of superiority had antagonised the public and some colleagues. Correspondents continued to indict

Menzies for his smug and condescending attitude towards the poor. In 1955, he was accused of refusing to answer pensioners' grievances at a meeting in Brisbane: 'You are so smug', wrote Elizabeth Refoy, 'so sure of getting back'. Then her resentment at Menzies broadened to embrace the political species more generally: 'It sickens one to even listen to parliamentary debates on the air. All you do is exchange insults and slurs on each other. Then you expect people to vote. Australia is a wonderful country mismanaged'.[4] That was to be Donald Horne's argument in *The Lucky Country* (1964) in a nutshell.

When Menzies declined to attend another pensioners' meeting, this time in Sydney Town Hall, he also came under fire. 'The manner in which you scorned the meeting', wrote a man from Bankstown (New South Wales), 'was anything but dignified and most unbecoming of a Prime Minister', and he continued 'All this talk about the pressure of parliamentary duties is so much hooey [...] You lacked courage, Prime Minister, were you afraid or ashamed to meet those unfortunate people'.[5] In declining to face his critics, Menzies made them even angrier, as he appeared cowardly, evasive and uninterested in ordinary voters' everyday problems. 'You, as a man', decided another pensioner, 'have not very much heart, a rather ruthless spirit [...] with very little interest in human beings'.[6]

Menzies was highly skilled at silencing hecklers with a sardonic retort or a witty comment. This was a well-developed technique of any successful parliamentarian involved in the cut-and-thrust of debate and the challenge of addressing public meetings. Listening as he dismissed sincere grievances, however, was not to everybody's taste. His responses suggested an unjustified sense of his own superiority. 'You enjoy belittling people who ask questions at your meetings', wrote Mrs Malseed from Melbourne. 'They have not all had the education you were fortunate to have <u>while many were away fighting for their country and for you</u>.'[7] Menzies' failure to enlist in the First World War regularly came back to haunt him. Mrs Malseed, on the other hand, had a brother killed in the war of 1914–18.

ANGRY LETTERS AND POLITICAL PROTEST

Menzies was denounced as a snob and an egoist. He had a well-known 'propensity for pontificating before church gatherings on moral virtues', according to one letter, although admittedly this was from Evatt's private secretary who was under suspicion at the time for communist leanings.[8] An anti-Catholic correspondent was incensed when Menzies recommended giving Cardinal Gilroy, Catholic Archbishop of Sydney, precedence over Protestant clergymen in the coronation ceremonies. 'Doubtless', he wrote, 'your ego prompted the belief that your plausible tongue could be used with the oratory for which you are famed to soothe the Protestant voters [...]?'[9] He made it clear that smooth talking would not deceive such keen observers as himself who were alert to Menzies' treacherous betrayal of the Empire.

Menzies seemed aloof. He lacked a personal rapport with ordinary voters and showed little sympathy for their concerns. 'I know you have great ability', began Owen Johnston of Melbourne,

> and worked like a nigger for what you got, but I doubt if you have any sympathy with or understanding of ordinary people who battle and scratch for an existence [...] Decent hard-working men often ask me and I ask them why wealthy and successful men like you and Dr Evatt go into politics. <u>I reply because they want power and want to push little people about</u>.[10]

Angry letter-writers deployed every technique available for metaphorically stamping their foot in rage, including the red ink of fury, the capital letters of indignation and, as in this case, emphatic underlining. In this case, too, Menzies was again the target for hostility towards the entire political elite. Talking to people on the radio was no substitute for going out and meeting the electorate face to face, Michael Sawtell of Sydney told Menzies. Instead of hiding behind a microphone, he should 'go out into the street & walk up to some stranger & talk to him. In other words, be a real dinkum Aussie bloke'.¹¹ This level of fraternisation, however, was not Menzies' forte.

Florence Jowett rounded on Menzies for his poor treatment of the unemployed, and her anger was sharpened by the fact that she was forced to sell her home to pay off debts. Capital letters crystallised her resentment, as she wrote: 'It is positively CRUEL the GLIB WAY in which you speak of the "comparatively" small "fringe" of UNEMPLOYMENT. It is CREUL [sic] the way they are TREATED. Do you not CALL yourself a <u>CHRISTIAN</u>?' She reminded Menzies of the parable of the labourers who were all hired to work in the vineyard for equal pay. Yet Florence Jowett had to live for seven months on unemployment benefit of £3-5-0 per week. She challenged Menzies to do the same: 'COULD <u>YOU</u> MANAGE ON THAT OR £3-15-0 PER WEEK <u>OVER</u> A SIX to FIFTEEN MONTH <u>PERIOD</u>? This is ONE story – <u>MY</u> story. <u>What</u> are the <u>OTHERS</u>?'¹² Timothy Western's criticism of the White Australia Policy was muted by comparison, as he levelled the familiar charge that Menzies was out of touch with the people. 'The government's attitude to Asian migration to Australia', he wrote, 'is so far out of tune to be raucous'. He went on to condemn 'the present stumbling, bungling, incompetent, unimaginative, but yet complacent band of politicians'.¹³

In 1959, the government raised postal and telephone charges, an apparently minor measure which aroused the ire of many constituents and businesses. It added to company running costs while individuals grew anxious about the cost of sending Christmas cards. This, too, demonstrated Menzies' callousness. 'The general public have been treated [...] with cold and calculated indifference', wrote Edgar Conkey about the rise in postal charges, 'and thousands of your best supporters have been given a further kick in the pants'.¹⁴ The fact that postal charges could provoke so much anger is a reminder of the high value placed on letter-writing generally. The issue also angered a Western Australian correspondent who wrote to convey his 'dismay and disgust'. 'We have reached our limit of patience', he assured Menzies, 'with being sucked dry to maintain a government in Canberra who are so out of touch with the people'.[15] Menzies assured him rather weakly that all taxes were becoming more affordable than in the past.

'Weeping tears of blood'

The resentment of 'battling' workers against the privileged political elite in distant Canberra reached fever pitch over the issue of politicians' salaries. Before the establishment of the independent Remuneration Tribunal in 1973, parliamentary salaries were determined by a series of *ad hoc* reviews, such as those which reported in 1955 and 1959 (the Richardson Report). Correspondents were especially infuriated by the increases in salaries and allowances for Commonwealth members of Parliament recommended by the Richardson Report in 1959, which was subsequently adopted by Parliament. The report recommended an increase in basic pay of £400 per annum for members of the House of Representatives and senators, as well as an increase in their tax-deductible electorate expenses. This represented a raise of 17 per cent, and brought a parliamentary member's annual salary to £2750. Voters were treated to the unusual sight of a parliamentary session in which there were no hostile interjections, as members formally and without demur voted themselves a pay rise. The outcry against self-serving politicians was immediate.

Mr Ball of Cooma (New South Wales) denounced Menzies' speech on the question as nonsense and identified with the general state of public cynicism about politicians.[16] From Sydney's North Shore, Mrs Curgenven expressed her outrage on the adoption of the Richardson Report:

You must think we are all dull and stupid to believe the weak and juvenile explanation you gave us.

You have let us down, we can't forget that. You do know how wrong it is to take such big rewards, and burden the taxpayer to make the cost of living go up higher and higher.

If you loved your country, and had its welfare at heart you could not do anything so wicked and cruel.[17]

'You aren't the leader of the people', added Alice Dodd, but rather 'the leader of Parliamentary grabbers'.[18]

The public response was further irritated by the fact that there had been no warning of this measure in the 1958 federal election campaign. It was not helpful either that the announcement appeared to have been deliberately timed to coincide with the Easter holiday so as to minimise the scope for public reaction. Mr Hobson of Sydney protested in a letter loaded with sarcasm:

> I am sure many people will weep tears of blood when they have heard from you the sacrifices politicians and their wives make for the love of their country [...]
>
> What has stirred the possum in 90% of the people is the fact that you and Fadden [the Treasurer] have been impressing on the people the state economically the country was in. Everyone must tighten his belt yet what have the politicians done? They have accepted fantastic increases in salary whilst most workers have their wages pegged [...]
>
> The sneaking way you suppressed the Richardson report before the State election for fear of damaging to the Liberals, got the people's goat.[19]

ANGRY LETTERS AND POLITICAL PROTEST

The legislation was 'callous' and 'contemptuous', Menzies had underestimated the general 'revulsion' against the measure, and Mr Suttor concluded in disgust, 'I had thought of you as a Statesman now I realize you are only a politician, out for all you can get'.[20] Correspondents did not fail to point out that the politicians' pay rise would give new ammunition to the communists.

The sheer volume of protests from loyal followers on this issue was impressive. Their arguments mainly rested on a comparison between the ease with which politicians were granted more money and the difficulty which pensioners had experienced in obtaining the slightest rise for themselves. There were also economic arguments against it; it would encourage wage demands and add to inflation and, in general, the government was overspending and causing a budget deficit. Fundamentally, however, the protest emerged from general resentment against a privileged elite blatantly awarding themselves further comfort and luxury.

Menzies added fuel to the flames by accusing the press of exaggerating and encouraging public hostility. This was interpreted as an insult – Australian electors could make up their own minds and did not need the media to identify an injustice for them. 'You cannot sincerely believe that the Press is responsible for whipping public feeling', wrote Edith Jones, 'there are, strange as it may seem to you, a large number of people capable of thinking for themselves'.[21] This angry and alarmed letter was remarkable because it came not from a Labor stalwart but from a fellow-Presbyterian whose family had once been acquaintances of Menzies' parents. 'It was your wish in those days', Edith Jones added, 'to serve the people and not dominate them'. Another loyal Liberal Party member felt badly let down. 'Your diatribe against the press,' he wrote, 'is looked upon, and I think rightly, as only a smoke screen, as the press was only echoing the feelings of the electorate'.[22] The author resigned his party membership and thenceforth washed his hands of the Liberal Party altogether. The tide of vociferous rage which surged through the correspondence in April 1959 was perhaps a turning-point in Menzies' fortunes. In 1961, he would achieve the narrowest of all his electoral victories, securing a majority of only two in the lower house. Unpopularity on this issue inflicted serious damage on Menzies' mystique as a dignified imperial statesman above the political fray. Even the Liberal Party faithful were shaken by it.

Political letters

A consistent number of letters came from loyal supporters and officials within the coalition parties. Liberal Party letters, however, made up only a small proportion of Menzies' total mailbag. In 1949–50, there were 39 of them, or 4.5 per cent of all incoming mail; in 1955, a year sampled for this purpose, they numbered just 48, only 2.4 per cent of incoming correspondence. They often embodied a protest or a warning. Usually political letters originated with local party branches or from members of the various state legislatures. Candidates in state elections asked for a personal endorsement, or invited Menzies to visit their constituency. If the invitation was successful, they wrote to thank Menzies for his support; if their candidacy was unsuccessful, they occasionally wrote to explain why they were not elected. Sometimes they wrote to ask Menzies to send good wishes to a local Liberal stalwart celebrating an 80th, 90th or 100th birthday. Writers discussed the make-up of the Liberal Senate team in their state, although Menzies did not interfere in the relevant nominations.

Branches rang alarm bells if they sensed that government policy was harming Liberal credibility. Evatt's pre-election promise to abolish the pensions means test (in 1954), for example, worried them into writing to Menzies, because they knew this was a vote-winner for the Labor Party, and that Menzies was not prepared to match Labor's promise. Similarly, the Queensland Liberals sent a message of warning that Labor was campaigning on the basis of federal neglect of Queensland, implicitly asking Menzies what he was going to do about it.[23] On rare occasions, state Liberals disassociated themselves completely from federal government decisions, as when New South Wales Liberals telegrammed their opposition to the controversial decision to jail Browne and Fitzpatrick for abuse of parliamentary privilege in 1955 (see page 129).[24] This internal party correspondence reveals the vulnerabilities of the Liberal Party at state election time.

Menzies may have been complacent, but Liberal supporters were not. They remembered the failed referendum on the dissolution of the Communist Party, and they had experienced many close shaves since then, for example in the 1954 federal election. They recommended budget items and policy moves, but Menzies always replied that it was too late, that the budget had already been prepared, or the policy already worked out. Several got frustrated by a 'do nothing' approach, but Menzies always campaigned on his record, and accused the Labor Party of making unaffordable promises. This last message certainly struck home because it was echoed in the letters.

Labor voters, the Great Unwashed

Menzies' attacks on the Labor Party and its parliamentary leadership found ready endorsement from his correspondents. Some, however, thought he went too far, as this section will show. Anti-communism, as we have seen, was manipulated in order to discredit the Labor Party by association. Correspondents were particularly strident in their denunciations of Evatt's personal allegiances. 'For the love of God', pleaded R Brown of Glebe (New South Wales) in the midst of the Petrov Affair, 'for the sake of Australia and all decent people put the renegade Evatt in his place as a pro commo'.[25] Menzies replied a few days later to say that he had been very interested to hear Brown's views on Dr Evatt, and 'Mr Menzies realises that you have a great insight into political matters'.[26]

The communist issue brought out the worst in conservative, social and anti-Labor prejudice. One angry businesswoman in Broken Hill (New South Wales) denounced communist activities there, identifying local personalities and the miners in general. 'They would vote for Billy the Blackfellow if he was labour', she wrote, adding gratuitous racism to her contempt for local workers.[27] Bert Oswald referred in his letter to the 'dunder-headed illiterate barbarians who occupy the labour benches today'.[28] Labor supporters were despised as the great unwashed. Frances Warner had their representatives in mind when she offered this generalisation: 'ignorant and vulgar politicians say disgusting things'.[29] The supposed illiteracy of labour leaders was a constant refrain. According to AJH Smart, who had just heard a speech given by Evatt: 'If ever a man sounded tired, ungrammatical, lackadaisical it was Dr E. who appeared not to have any belief in what he was saying'.[30] Menzies, in comparison, was an intellectual. Gertrude Hart told him, 'You are big and brainy and you would have to look for <u>his</u> brains with an extra-powerful magnifying glass'.[31] In this letter she was referring to Evatt's successor, Arthur Calwell.

Menzies' own parliamentary duels with Evatt inspired a more profound *ad hominem* antagonism. Hubert 'Oppy' Opperman, racing cyclist and later Minister for Immigration, but when he wrote this letter simply the member for Corio in Victoria, contributed in these terms:

> after listening to Evatt puffing up Labour's [*sic*] Senate policy like a flat-chested girl trying to inflate her first pair of pneumatic bras, I have just got to get my pulse rate down ... [*Menzies replied that he was particularly amused by this paragraph*] He must have sounded synthetic even to his own claquers [...] his script was designed for the moronic, the un-thinking and the easily influenced.[32]

Nevertheless, attempted character assassinations of Evatt could backfire on Menzies. Menzies treated his opponent with undue venom which some correspondents deplored as excessive. This was not the way Menzies had customarily treated his parliamentary opponents. He and Evatt's predecessor, Chifley, for example, had regarded each other with considerable respect. According to Menzies' secretary, Hazel Craig, 'Ming' and 'Chif' would occasionally swap detective novels with each other in Canberra when Chifley was prime minister and Menzies leader of the opposition.[33] It is hard to imagine any such intimacy between Menzies and Evatt.

The letters make it clear that the Liberal Party believed that certain standards of respect and courtesy should be upheld in political life. In his attacks on Evatt, however, Menzies seemed merciless and ungracious. This was not how correspondents wanted to imagine Menzies. They frequently characterised him as calm, detached and statesmanlike, above the fray of petty political squabbles, not as a relentless fighter who did not hesitate to draw blood and humiliate the enemy. Yet this was the new Menzies revealed by his attacks on Evatt. Lilian Jones protested that she was an admirer, but

> there has been a regrettable weakness from which I have hoped you would outgrow [sic] in your years of greatness: a yielding to the temptation to cleverly score little personal triumphs by making your opponents look foolish, triumphs so base and beneath the dignity of a man of your eminence. Dr Evatt has come so low that you can afford to be a gracious victor.

This reproach came at the time of Menzies' response to the Molotov letter affair (see page 178), which had severely discredited Evatt during the Petrov Affair. 'I just fear', Mrs Jones went on, 'to see a taint on one who I think could be the saviour of our age'.[34]

Menzies was in danger of compromising his reputation for dignity and composure. His attacks on Evatt demonstrated to 86-year-old Lachlan Croft 'what a warped, vindictive mind you posess [sic]. You must hate Dr Evatt. Is it because he has far higher qualifications than yourself?'³⁵ Menzies replied tersely: 'your comments have been noted'. In 1955, Menzies' stocks were high after the royal visit and his successful management of the Petrov Affair. Furthermore, the Labor Party was in the process of splitting in two. Menzies seemed to be in such a position of strength in relation to the Labor Party that he could afford to proceed less aggressively. Accordingly, he was being asked to wind down the sarcasm, and to show a little magnanimity and humility – not among his most obvious qualities. Clare Keogh, like Lilian Jones before her, thought Menzies had gone too far, writing:

> I do not agree with your political opinions. Oh, but I did admire, and respect you as a clean and hard-hitting fight [sic]. A man capable of bringing out the best in his party, and his opponents. All this was very wonderful and good for Australia. Then, I saw you change your tactics. You did not care anymore how you won, as long as you won. Instead of being a big man you made yourself small, by making the political arena, a battle of personalitys [sic] not of broad political matters.
>
> I knew then you no longer had faith in the good government of your party, because if you had, you would fight and criticize your opponents but never, never would you demoralize them.³⁶

Evatt's determined defence of judicial rights had defeated the 1951 referendum, but his accusations against government manipulation and judicial bias in the aftermath of the Petrov Affair bordered on an obsession. All the same, he had some positive attributes in the eyes of correspondents. For one thing, he had resisted Catholic influences within his own party, and this was a redeeming feature in the eyes of the Protestant clergy. A priest (presumably Anglican) from Tasmania wrote on this theme:

> We are distressed that a P.M. should stoop so low as to kick a man when he is down [*referring to Evatt*] and we just wonder if the Federal Govt. is governing the Country, or displaying personal hatred.
>
> Dr. Evatt has at least stood up against 'Catholic Action' ('The Movement') in the Labor Party, while you, on the other hand have cow-towed [*sic*] at least on three occasions to the RCs with the vain hope of getting their votes.[37]

Menzies' overtures towards Catholic Laborites risked a Protestant backlash in his own political heartland. His correspondents had certain standards of dignity and decorum which they expected political life to observe, and they rebuked Menzies when he failed to meet them.

Lonely voices and 'tribune letters'

'Why should ratepayers have to pay for Royal visits? Who wants royal visits – costly or otherwise?' asked Mrs Malseed, for whom they simply represented more banquets for politicians.[38] But hers was a voice in the wilderness. It was difficult to persuade the prime minister to heed letters of protest when the consensus in his favour seemed so solid. One strategy was that of the 'tribune letter'. In ancient Rome, the people's Tribunes were elected officials with the power to veto legislation on behalf of the plebeians. In the Menzies correspondence, some writers similarly posed as the spokespersons (or 'tribunes') of popular opinion, representatives of wider discontent that deserved attention. For example, when Cosette Cummins wrote about government funding for Catholic schools, she represented herself as:

one of the 'average' Australians or the little people who go to make up the masses of the country whose policy you are elected to direct. However, it sometimes happens that after a time even those directing the people's policy tend to lose touch with those very people whom they represent [...] The view from the top of the democracy is often slightly different to the ground level view.[39]

She presented her views in tribune-letter style when she added that 'The opinion of the people should not be overlooked by the Prime Minister, and I maintain that my letter is voicing the opinion of the parents of the country'.

The most persistent example of writers in this mode was Joyce Atkinson, an inveterate correspondent who maintained a constant stream of letters over several years, and whom we have briefly encountered previously. She would send over 20 letters annually in her heyday between 1958 and 1961. Joyce Atkinson lived on a dairy farm near Nambour (Queensland) and addressed Menzies often about problems of the land, as well as about the education of the young who no longer wished to work on it. Most often, however, her letters were rambling and incoherent and it is sometimes difficult to grasp what point she was trying to make. She clearly craved recognition as a useful adviser and constantly offered to help Menzies in some capacity or other. She styled herself 'a servant for the PEOPLE', or Menzies' 'Research and Goodwill Officer'.[40] She gives the impression of a Queensland housewife looking in vain for a niche with some public responsibilities. She was waiting for a call to serve, as an appointed official or as a journalist, but the call never came. Nevertheless, she continued to write in the tribune's role. 'In my round-the-clock service to the nation' was one of her prefaces to an instruction to Menzies, and she addressed him 'as an unfettered and thoroughly independent spokesman for THE PEOPLE'.[41] She made it clear that a woman's contribution was badly needed in political leadership. International affairs were well within her scope, since she assured Menzies that with her assistance there would be an end to 'western bungling'.[42] After one long, rambling letter in both red and black ink, she concluded in this vein:

> Sir, I think I've said enough to convince you that I have a pretty fair understanding in regards to what this country needs, who it is that must provide that need [*i.e. herself*] and who it is that must and or will or ought to accept it [*i.e. Menzies*] [...] Otherwise we certainly ARE the pawns of Mr K's [*i.e. Khrushchev's*] horror 'colonialism' in its rottenest form. I recommend that I become your 'WELFARE MINISTER'.
>
> Yours respectfully, the peoples' confidant and protector, Joyce Atkinson.[43]

Her claims to be the people's protector carried such little weight that Menzies did not always condescend to reply to her. Like Cassandra, the prophetess of Greek mythology, Joyce Atkinson's insights, however acute they may have been, counted for nothing because she was never believed. Like Cassandra, Joyce Atkinson was ignored as a mad and helpless woman.

Only very rarely did correspondents criticise Menzies from a clear ideological standpoint. They protested, like Joy Sundfors, against atomic weapons testing in Australia and they usually did so from a platform of Christian pacifism.[44] In addition, she argued, the tests stirred up 'the wrath of all the Asian people against us', and Menzies was hiding the ugly truth about the dangers of radiation. Another rare exception was Melbourne journalist Rachel Hindle, who objected to conscription, military intervention in Malaya and the alleged use of napalm in Korea as a Christian opposed to all forms of militarisation. In 1950, she went further to indict the capitalist system itself for 'making a hell of this earthly paradise'. Menzies pencilled a note: 'Do not answer'.[45] Hindle's articulate critique of the system reached a climax in 1955, when she sent a series of letters and telegrams protesting about a range of injustices, including the evils of capital punishment, the 'semi-starvation of aged pensioners', and capitalist exploitation of the dockers. She was an isolated protagonist of full citizenship rights for Indigenous people and condemned 'the enslavement of our Fuzzie Wuzzies who helped us to defeat the Japanese during World War II'.[46] The impact of Hindle's repeated appeals to the principles of Christianity and British justice was no doubt diluted by the sheer variety and multiplicity of her grievances. In advancing a long shopping list of issues, she failed to hit the target with any single one of them. Nevertheless, her idealism stands out among the protest letters for its principled attack on the government for perpetuating social injustice and the subjection of the weak and vulnerable.

There was a strong political consensus in support of royalism and the Empire and against communism, so that dissident voices on these issues were few and far between. Angry letter-writers frequently threatened to withhold their vote or to tear up their Liberal Party membership. This tells us that angry letters often came from hitherto loyal supporters, who, for one reason or another, had become what Mr Williams of Coogee (New South Wales) called 'disillusionised'.[47] Yet there were certainly enough angry writers in the corpus to let Menzies know that he was falling short of their standards of fairness. His manner was too remote, his tongue too glib, his barbs too cutting to endear him to these writers with a genuine grievance to present. And so, for about a month in March and April 1959, when federal politicians awarded themselves an increase in salaries and allowances, their fury erupted.

11

'The Kingdom of God is nigh'

PARANOID LETTERS

In the belly of the whale

'Australia will never get out of the whale's belly', wrote Lily Kirkham to Menzies, 'Woe to the Bloody City It is all full of Lies and Robbery'.[1] She quoted from the Book of Nahum in which God foretold the ruin of Nineveh, and concluded in her uncertain spelling: 'Dose not those words of the Almighty fit the afares of the world today'. Prophecies of doom were commonplace in the correspondence along with fears of an imminent Judgment Day in the wake of a Third World War. It would be simple to dismiss them as the fantasies of a neurotic mentality, the obsessions of the lunatic fringe of Christian fundamentalism. Perhaps indeed that is what they were. Historians, however, have a tendency to view collective outbursts of millenarian prophecy as a symptom of deeper disorders, an indication that 'the time is out of joint'.

We do not need to search very far to find possible reasons for such a deeper anxiety. In August 1945, less than five years before Lily Kirkham's letter to Menzies, the USA detonated two nuclear bombs which destroyed the Japanese cities of Hiroshima and Nagasaki. Menzies' correspondents lived in the shadow of the atom bomb.

In the fraught political environment of the Cold War, the forces of good and evil appeared to confront each other in a Manichean conflict which carried the risk of mutual obliteration. In Berlin, in Korea and later in the Cuban missile crisis of 1962, the possibility of nuclear conflict came uncomfortably close. Some felt even less secure when Australian territory itself became the site of atomic weapon tests. Neville Shute's novel *On the Beach* was published in England in 1957 and released as a film in 1959. Set in Melbourne after a nuclear conflict had devastated the northern hemisphere, its characters lived their last days awaiting the inevitable arrival of a deadly cloud of nuclear fall-out. Suicide was their only option. Even Menzies himself reminded his radio listeners that a Third World War was possible. Only in hindsight can we say that these fears were groundless: at the time, they seemed real enough. This was the context of letters forecasting the Battle of Armageddon, the end of time.

This chapter dips into the letters of feverish prophets and prophetesses who confidently warned Menzies that the end was nigh, before it turns to different and lesser forms of paranoia which surfaced in the correspondence. Conspiracy theories about Jews and Freemasons emerged, as well as Australia's recurring nightmare, the fear of an Asian invasion. Attacks on communism, already discussed in chapter 9, sometimes overstepped the bounds of rationality. Most frequent of all, however, were attacks on the supposed Catholic subversion of Protestant Australia. The Menzies correspondence had its lunatic fringe, which will be briefly explored here.

Armageddon letters

The Third World War was just over the horizon, heralding the end of the world according to biblical prophecy. Eena Ledebur explained the divine plan to Menzies:

PARANOID LETTERS

> Two outstanding events to occur in the near future are the change in the Economic System and the third great war with Russia, ending in the battle of Armageddon. According to prophecy, this is to happen with a generation (40 years) of the release of Jerusalem in 1917.²

'Please do not think I am just a religious crank', she added, 'I am a genuine Presbyterian, who wants to see the world put right'. In Sydney, Mrs White was equally convinced of the approach of Armageddon and hence of the need for repentance and a return to obeying the will of God. 'There is no other way', she assured Menzies, 'or else more judgements will come', because the Bible foretold

> that the 3rd world war is the Might of Armageddon and Christ's soon return, and all Christians are looking forward to that Great and Glorious day when all wrongs will be righted and poor animals properly treated and fiends put back in Hell where the[y] belong.³

This correspondent offered Menzies a practical lesson. Since Armageddon was inevitably approaching, it was futile to spend more and more money on defence. Since all would soon be destroyed, he should tailor the budget accordingly. The Bible had accurately shown, GW Heslop reminded Menzies, 'how near we are to the great battle of ARMAGEDDON, (3rd World War) and the Seven Last PLAGUES'.⁴

In 1956, British nuclear testing began at Maralinga in South Australia, boosting pro-peace movements. The Australian Peace Council had been established in 1949, and 12 000 people attended its first congress in Melbourne in 1950. 'Why cannot the ordinary people of this world live happily without the threat of destruction and fear?' asked Jean Lonie.⁵ The Peace Convention held in Sydney in 1953, boycotted by the media and condemned by the government, was less successful, but the movement revived somewhat with another Melbourne congress held in 1959 in the wake of contentious nuclear weapons testing. A few correspondents poured scorn on official assurances that testing was completely safe, and quoted a United Nations report to the contrary on the dangers of radiation.[6] Both Menzies and his wife were petitioned in vain to ban nuclear testing.[7] Menzies unhesitatingly rebuffed these correspondents. Menzies distrusted the movement for peace and disarmament. ASIO suspected that it was being manipulated by communists, and Menzies concurred. Although the movement's leaders were well-meaning Protestant clerics, he considered them naive and gullible instruments of something much more sinister.[8] Fears of war did not go away. Several correspondents worried about the possibility of a Chinese attack from nuclear submarines, and urged plans to move industrial plant inland so that it would be out of range.[9]

Disaster could be averted, if Menzies would only heed his Christian correspondents, and if Australia and its leaders returned to godly ways. This thought opened the way to the homiletic letters with which Menzies was bombarded. A Queensland woman told Menzies of the need to be Born Again (her capitals), and with staggering self-assurance she offered to help Menzies 'in this Most Important Matter The Destiny of Your own Soul'.[10] F Umfreville of Tasmania gave Menzies a sermon on the need to seek divine guidance and to pray to God morning and night, in preparation for the Second Coming of Christ.[11] Miss Cameron recommended a National Day of Prayer, and cited God's admonition in 2 Chronicles 7 to turn away from wickedness.[12] Mrs Cunningham urged Menzies to invoke Our Lady of Lourdes in the Far Eastern crisis of 1958 over China's seizure of offshore islands – this was Lourdes' centenary year.[13] For one Melbourne correspondent, Menzies could show his repentance by taking the pledge (to abstain from alcohol), instead of raising taxes from the vices of his constituents.[14] Persuading Menzies to forgo the bottle was surely a forlorn cause.

PARANOID LETTERS

The Bible was often invoked as a guide to future conduct and preparation for the coming of the Messiah. The Bible was supremely relevant, according to former political cartoonist Stuart Peterson, because 'the scriptures are more positively political than the writings of Karl Marx. They give plain and intensely practical instructions for the functioning of perfect government [...] right here on this fear-ridden planet'.[15] Menzies was frequently exhorted to keep the Ten Commandments and study the Scriptures. He received letters to this effect from several messiahs themselves. One was William Cole in Pambula (New South Wales), who brought news from God that Menzies had great tasks ahead of him. Another slightly more purposeful self-styled messiah was T Mohsin from Hong Kong, who above all wanted access to mainland China to let the Chinese know that 'The Kingdom of God is nigh'.[16]

It would be tedious to recite further examples of sermons to Menzies to heed God, be conscious of his word and follow the example of Jesus Christ. It is curious, all the same, to note that correspondents attributed a special role to Britain in their sermons on the end of the world. Clare Farmer, for example, informed Menzies that God was temporarily using the communists and the Labor Party for his own purposes, intending later to destroy them, as he would also destroy all man-made parliaments. 'Very soon now', she wrote, 'Christ is coming to reign as King of Israel and Britain will appoint His own helpers'. 'We', she explained, meaning Britain, 'are the people of the book – the Bible – God's servant Nation'.[17] Another South Australian correspondent felt that Britain's support for the creation of the state of Israel had demonstrated her loyalty to the Bible and her special role in the fulfilment of God's plan.[18] The British connection was thus authorised by the Bible, and this gave the British, and by association all Australians, full justification for peppering Menzies with calls to prayer and repentance.

Paranoia

Some letters Menzies received were inspired by prejudice against certain minority groups and on occasion by outright xenophobia. The paranoid elements of the Menzies letters, however, should be put into proper perspective: they represented a small albeit very agitated minority. For example, the correspondence as a whole very rarely expressed antisemitic sentiments. Antisemitism lurked, however, behind discussions of the Middle East situation, as when one correspondent predicted that 'The Jewish Race will of course be on the side of the winner'.[19] Very occasionally, echoes of the world Jewish conspiracy surfaced. One Tasmanian writer asserted that 'all governments today [are] run and controlled by their Econimists [*sic*]'. Those 'Econimists', he alleged, were trained in schools like the London School of Economics which were financed by international Jewry. Capitalism, socialism and communism were three 'isms' being exploited by Jews to enslave the entire world.[20]

This echo of earlier antisemitic conspiracy theories based on the notorious forgery *The Protocols of the Elders of Zion* was quite exceptional.[21] In fact Menzies and his secretary Everil Wilkinson had a brief scribbled conversation about how remarkable it was and concluded the author was definitely eccentric. More frequently, correspondents were moved to praise Menzies for his support for the Jewish community, for example in the speech he delivered at Sydney's Central Synagogue in 1960. Menzies had given hope on this occasion to recent Jewish immigrants from Central and Eastern Europe, 'a suffering people', wrote one correspondent, 'whose relatives died like dogs in the gas chambers of Himmler'.[22] Menzies' own views, however, were entirely conventional and he always sought to dampen any suggestion of social tension. When the Jewish Council to Combat Fascism and Anti-Semitism reported an outbreak of swastika daubings in Melbourne, he played the incidents down and advised that giving hooligans publicity might exacerbate the problem. In any case, he typically added, it was a state not a federal problem.[23]

Freemasons and atheists only occasionally stirred the anxieties of biblical enthusiasts. The Protestant Council of New South Wales was upset when the Speaker of Parliament chose to make an affirmation of loyalty rather than taking an oath on the Christian Bible. This, of course, was perfectly permissible, but in the eyes of the writer it offended the sanctity of the Bible.[24] Freemasonry, others alleged, was in control of key social and political institutions like the church and the judiciary. It was condemned for encouraging immorality and drunkenness.[25] One Bondi (New South Wales) correspondent was genuinely paranoid about the Freemasons' 'telepathic radio sets', which in his fantasy were exerting their invisible control over the thoughts of influential people like the Queen.[26] Theories of invisible conspiracies combined with fantasies about extra-sensory perception permeated this literature of paranoia.

Exaggerated fears of an Asian invasion were less entertaining for Menzies' secretariat, but they reflected anxieties embedded deep within the Australian psyche, which David Walker has expertly analysed.[27] 'Teeming millions of Asiatics knocking at our very doors' worried Bert de Plater in 1949.[28] The fact that these millions were undernourished could only make their designs on Australian territory more insistent and more intense. Campaigns for developing Australia's north more fully and also defending it more securely were inspired by such fears of 'the hungry hordes' and 'the under-fed state of the people of Asia as a whole', not to mention the threat of the Chinese armed forces.[29] During the Korean War one former soldier volunteered for a virtual suicide mission of his own design, offering to dive-bomb North Korea with a plane stacked with explosives, and assured Menzies unconvincingly that he was fully in control of his faculties.[30] There was a persistent fear that Australia would be 'swamped with Asians, and Chinese Reds too!'[31] In fact the 1961 Commonwealth census showed that Asian people constituted a mere

0.31 per cent of Australia's total population, but this did not deter Menzies' paranoid correspondents.[32] 'You are the man', Menzies was told, 'to keep this Land from an invasion of Reds, pinks and Blacks', a veritable snooker-table full of undesirables.[33]

When I first read EW Vernon's letter, written at the height of the Cold War, asserting that Australian Labor Party votes had been in effect captured by an interfering foreign power, I automatically assumed that he was accusing Moscow and the influence of international communism. But as it turned out this was not another anti-Soviet diatribe. In fact, the foreign influence to which he referred was the world power of the papacy and its beating heart lay not in Moscow but in Rome.[34] Vitriolic anti-Catholicism was by far the dominant theme of the paranoid letters in the corpus. George Gavan's letter from his bed at the Prince of Wales Hospital in Randwick (New South Wales) gives a taste of its sectarian hatred: 'If', he wrote to Menzies,

> you are as wise a man as most folks believe you are, you will conscript every available Roman Catholic traitor, and send them to the front immeaditly [sic]. As they are the most dangerous people in this colony. They are flat out to get control of Australia. And they will wade up to their hocks in blood to get control. If you believe in God as I do, you will conscript at once. They are the most loathsome and murderous bunch of skunks, the world ever knew. Please remember that I am sworn to fight to the death against them.[35]

In this view, Catholics were inherently disloyal to Australia since they had sworn obedience to a foreign power (an accusation reminiscent of ancient antisemitic assumptions about Jewish uprootedness and lack of patriotism).

The Roman Catholic population of Australia was certainly expanding during the 1950s as a result of post-war immigration from

Europe, but it was also becoming less homogeneous. The arrival of Catholics from Croatia, Poland, Italy and elsewhere stretched the existing parish framework and challenged the traditional Irish culture of Australian Catholicism. Menzies' correspondents were certainly responding to a rise in the absolute numbers of Australian Catholics, although their relative share of the population never exceeded 27 per cent; in fact the decline in the Anglican share of the population (because of the rise in Greek Orthodoxy and of Protestant evangelicalism) might have worried them more.[36]

In the view of anti-Catholic extremists, the Pope was the Anti-Christ and the Lutheran Reformation was apparently in danger of being reversed. Furthermore, insidious Catholic doctrines threatened to alienate their followers and turn people to atheism and communism in disgust. Some writers urged Menzies to protect their vision of a Protestant Australia, ideally uncontaminated either by paganism or the 'Marian cult'. 'If any preference is shown to the Roman Catholic pagan movement or to Communism', wrote one correspondent, 'then there will be weeping and wailing and gnashing of teeth'.[37] Menzies' secretary was astounded. 'MR MENZIES', she wrote, 'This is a corker!' Menzies agreed and advised her to send a short acknowledgment with thanks.

Fundamentalists were responding to Menzies' speeches about restoring spirituality to Australian politics, but they saw this through a strictly Protestant lens. For example, the suggestion to appoint Dame Enid Lyons as Minister for Immigration provoked a howl of protest from Protestant activists, who peppered Menzies with telegrams of protest. Any reservations they may have had about having a woman in government were trivial compared to their insistence that there should not be a Catholic in the cabinet. Menzies in fact appointed Harold Holt (Enid Lyons was born a Methodist but converted to Catholicism; Holt was baptised an Anglican but his subsequent religious loyalties, if any, were vague).

In the eyes of such extremists, Menzies' campaigns against

communism were focusing on the wrong target. One writer urged him to 'forget about the "Red Herring" of Communism on the world horizon and face up to the evil of the Black Hand Gang in this country'.[38] The context of this remark shows that the writer was referring to the global machinations of the Vatican. 'I see no difference between it [*i.e. Roman Catholicism*] and Communism', wrote Lurline Allee, 'They will capture Australia if we do not look out'. Then, shifting her register in a manner typical of the correspondence as a whole, she requested a licence to import a Cadillac.[39] Writers argued that both Catholicism and communism were equally obnoxious: they were both foreign powers, both were authoritarian organisations and both were enemies of religious freedom. They were a twin menace and there was little to separate them as fundamental threats to the country. Mrs Cardwell identified the double menace succinctly when she wrote, 'The Irish demons are the so called communists in the Empire'.[40]

Menzies always remained personally on good terms with Vatican diplomats, and in his intermittent correspondence with the Apostolic Delegate, relations with the Holy See were friendly and courteous.[41] He kept in touch with members of the Catholic hierarchy in Australia, like Sydney's Cardinal Gilroy. He sent Daniel Mannix, Catholic Archbishop of Melbourne, a telegram on his 95th birthday.[42] Sometimes he received messages of support from Catholic convents, including the Carmelites and the Little Sisters of the Poor, to whom he made donations.[43] Miss Massingham of Coogee (New South Wales) sent him a scapular in 1955, but he apparently never wore it because it remains in the correspondence file.[44] Long before the Commonwealth government began funding independent schools in 1964, Menzies maintained a good rapport with his Catholic constituents. He certainly did not share the sectarian attitudes of a few of his supporters and correspondents. But when he spoke out deploring sectarian conflict, he attracted fire-and-brimstone rebukes from Protestant extremists.

PARANOID LETTERS

After the Labor Party split in 1955, Menzies relied on the electoral preferences of the Catholic-leaning Democratic Labor Party, but his overtures to Catholics created a backlash in his own Protestant heartland. Protestants repeatedly accused him of 'kow-towing' to the Catholic Church. When, in 1954, the ceremony of dedicating the colours at Duntroon military college was carried out not by a Protestant clergyman but by a layman, in deference to the presence of Catholic cadets, they interpreted the gesture as caving in to Catholic pressure. Favouring the immigration of Greeks and Italians was another sign of weakness at the knees and a betrayal of Australia's Protestant heritage.[45] Protestant fanatics were also outraged in 1953, when the initials 'F.D.' temporarily disappeared from newly minted coins. 'F.D.', standing for Defender of the Faith (*fidei defensor* or *defensatrix*), identified the Queen as the upholder of the (Anglican) Church in Britain. The omission was most probably the result of incompetence and confusion at the Mint, as it was in the process of reminting the coinage at the accession of a new monarch. It seemed to some like another fatal concession to non-Protestant elements. The title disappeared permanently when the coinage was decimalised in 1966, and on this occasion there was thankfully no outcry.

'You have read the Bible prophecies', wrote one correspondent from Queensland in response to the coinage scandal, 'and know, or should know, that in a short time the Pope will be the most powerful man in the world, and we will have the Dark Ages over again'.[46] 'Your flirting with Rome is now apparent to thousands of Protestant voters', another disgusted Sydney correspondent complained, and added abusively, 'Of all the snivelling, unctuous humbugs you take the bun [...] If you are as simple as you profess you should be in an asylum and not in a position of responsibility [...] you have the effrontery to get up and say you hate sectarianism'.[47] Clearly a number of supporters felt that Catholic influence was growing and that this threatened Australia's democratic heritage and Protestant traditions. The fear was intensified by their perceptions that Menzies himself was backsliding. Will Blandford sent an unorthodox letter which abandoned linearity and in which his ideas appeared in circles like thought bubbles. He addressed Menzies amicably as the 'Hon Big Bob' and urged him to beware of all 'Sanatic Led forces [sic]'.[48] In the same vein, others warned that a Catholic totalitarian conspiracy was at work, using 'Machiavellian subtlety and as deadly and ruthless as any devised by the Borgia'.[49] Moreover, Prince Charles would need a special bodyguard on his next visit because Catholics might try to kidnap him.[50]

The selection examined in this chapter revealed an unexpected function of the letters to Menzies. They took on a homiletic character, as writers delivered earnest sermons about the need to follow the Christian commandments and to seek the kingdom of Christ. Unlike others who wrote upwards with deference and humility, they confidently lectured him as though he was their Sunday school pupil. These epistolary preachers drew their texts from the Book of Revelation, if their theme was the imminent battle of Armageddon, or from the Old Testament prophets, if they were emphasising the need for personal repentance and the moral regeneration of society. The Bible, in other words, was a constant resource. It was plundered by Christian fundamentalists whose letters sought to put pressure on Menzies to maintain the fight against the twin dangers of atheistic communism and predatory Catholicism. Vitriolic language surfaced, reminiscent of the religious wars of the 16th century. The two-headed beast of Moscow and Rome had to be slain.

Telepathy and weird inventors

Masters of telepathy and strange inventors conclude this brief parade of the bizarre and deluded. One man in Gosford (New South Wales), for example, wrote to Menzies about his work on a flying saucer which would prove enormously useful in aerial bombardments and naval engagements.[51] Another inventor claimed, like many before him, to have discovered the secret of perpetual motion and requested an interview with the prime minister.[52] As for the telepaths, a woman in Birmingham (UK) offered to use her telepathic expertise to bring rain to drought-stricken Australian farmers. All she needed was a detailed map, but she apologised because, in view of the great distance involved, her extraordinary rainmaking powers might need a few weeks to take effect.[53] In a strange and garbled telegram from Sydney, Agnes Foskett told Menzies that he and her 'astral friend' President Dwight D Eisenhower appeared in visions in her sleep and both should work to end war. 'Thank you darling', she affectionately concluded.[54]

In a final example, Mr Haines asked Menzies to introduce legislation to prohibit women from wearing pants. The Old Testament, a continual reference point for writers considered in this chapter, had condemned cross-dressing as an abomination.[55] It is not clear exactly what provoked this attack, for the Menzies years are not commonly associated with any serious challenge to traditional gender roles. Nevertheless, the *Matrimonial Causes Act* of 1959 did extend the causes of divorce, including the controversial provision that a two-year desertion by one of the spouses could justify a divorce petition. This too generated further correspondence from members of all religious denominations and genders objecting to the change.

Menzies clearly attracted letters from correspondents who were irrational and bigoted. A few even appear mentally unhinged, although completely illegible and incomprehensible letters received from inmates of lunatic asylums fall into another category altogether, and I have not included them here. Nevertheless, the letters considered in this chapter were not always unreasonable; the new destructive power of nuclear weapons generated a genuine fear of annihilation and, during the Cold War, events continued to remind Australians of the risks of international conflict.

12

STRUCTURES OF BELIEF

Menzies' mailbag

Menzies belonged to a small but select company of modern and contemporary Western leaders who valued and respected the written word. His situation, however, was a little different from those like Barack Obama who received mountains of correspondence. For one thing, it was more secure; unlike Obama, Menzies did not need to have his incoming correspondence screened for toxic substances.[1] For another thing, it was less highly organised; unlike François Mitterrand, he did not require his secretariat to develop over a hundred formula responses to letters from the general public.[2] In comparison to these other two leaders, Menzies' mailbag was much thinner: he received about 22 000 letters over 16 years, whereas every day over 12 years between 1983 and 1995 Mitterrand received about 1000 letters and Obama received about 10 000 daily for the eight years between 2009 and 2017. Menzies' secretariat was far more rudimentary, and its operations were less bureaucratised and more spontaneous, homely and personal than procedures necessarily adopted by leaders in France and the USA, who, after all, had to deal with incoming correspondence on a massive scale. Even so, the volume of Menzies' correspondence is quite large enough to intimidate researchers. It has required persistence to encompass the whole corpus, and some strategic sampling to find statistical answers to a few specific questions.

In spite of the contrasts between Australia, France and the USA, the Menzies correspondence shared important characteristics with

STRUCTURES OF BELIEF

letters received by other 20th- and 21st-century leaders. Every case, for instance, served to underline the importance which ordinary people everywhere attached to writing and receiving letters. In spite of the asymmetrical power relationship between the citizen and the political leader, people put their faith in writing to bridge the gap. Writing was invested with the power to communicate grievances and influence future policy. It could shock or persuade, insult or congratulate. Although writers were far too optimistic about their ability to make personal contact with their leader, writing nevertheless gave them a sense, however illusory, of empowerment. Letters to Barack Obama, according to one White House adviser, were 'voices in the president's head', suggesting that they had an enduring resonance beyond the merely trivial or ephemeral.[3] The efforts exerted by all the leaders mentioned to send replies to their correspondents shows that they themselves well understood the importance of the act of writing. In France, the USA or Australia, writing to one's political leader or head of state, and receiving some form of epistolary response from them, reflected the significance attached everywhere to writing upwards.

The contents of each corpus were naturally very different. They reflected the preoccupations of a particular time and the context of a particular country. The main preoccupations of the Menzies correspondence have clearly emerged in previous chapters: firstly, pensions, their inadequacy and the problematic means test which disqualified many from their benefits; secondly, the British connection in all its ramifications, from emotional attachment to the monarchy to the implementation of the restricted immigration policy; and thirdly, communism and its allegedly sinister attempts to undermine Australian democracy and the British Empire. I list those primary concerns in very approximate order of their importance to correspondents.

The legacy of the Second World War also casts a long shadow over the correspondence. It can be seen, for example, in the many letters about war pensions and repatriation problems. It can be seen, too, in the continuing correspondence from the RSL and organisations of disabled veterans, the so-called TPIs (Totally and Permanently Incapacitated personnel). Menzies, as we have seen, was popular in Britain, not only with upper-class Tory politicians, but also with many ordinary people who had seen him on TV and others seeking an assisted passage to emigrate. This popularity derived from his role as a close ally, present at the government's side in London, during the Second World War itself. Wartime memories lived on in correspondents' expressions of reverence for Winston Churchill and in the many comparisons they made between him and Menzies, as well as in the occasional reference to a Menzies speech as 'Churchillian'. To some extent, Menzies tried to put the war to rest, for instance in developing friendly commercial relationships with Japan. But perhaps he never fully succeeded until January 1965, when he cut short a Pacific holiday and sped to London for the funeral of Churchill, giving him a final tribute in his speech in the crypt of St Paul's Cathedral. Or perhaps the Second World War did not fully end in Australia until Menzies retired in 1966.

Correspondence defines an individual's social and professional world. In fact, it does not merely define a network, but it also acts to perpetuate and perform that network. In this sense, the letters tell us something about Menzies himself, because they situate him within a significant web of interconnected interests. They present all the connected threads of his important networks – the Scots, the Presbyterians, his Kooyong constituency, the cricketers and the gentlemen's clubs, as well as the circle of 'imperocrats' (the politicians and administrators of the British Commonwealth) – with whom he was closely linked. These social ties defined his identity, and the letters activated these significant networks.

Structures of belief

No correspondence, however private, is ever perfectly transparent. Letters always conceal as much as they express, and sometimes their omissions are as eloquent as what they actually include. There were significant lacunae in the letters to Menzies. World events which in hindsight seem of major significance were passed over in almost complete silence by correspondents at the time. When a new prime minister took office in Britain, writers were well aware of it, but similar events elsewhere did not surface in their letters. The death of Josef Stalin in 1953 went virtually unmentioned, which is a surprise considering the general interest in communism at this stage of the Cold War. Eisenhower's accession to the US presidency in place of Truman in the same year went similarly unnoticed in the letters. We cannot attribute this to the insular outlook of Australians and their general indifference to foreign affairs, because there were clearly occasions when correspondents took a great interest in events abroad. If Australian troops were committed overseas, for instance in Malaya, public interest certainly followed them. The Suez crisis of 1956, together with the debate over apartheid after 1960, generated plenty of discussion in the correspondence, completely defying Menzies' own pronouncements that apartheid was a South African domestic issue which did not concern Australia. African affairs have probably never figured so prominently in the Australian consciousness as they did in this period. Writers' interest in foreign issues, however, remained selective.

Discussion of Aboriginal problems was significantly lacking in the correspondence. Only a few lone voices raised the question of Indigenous rights and welfare. David Munro was one of them, a former Presbyterian minister who asked, 'Cannot something be done immediately to relieve the hunger and thirst of the native of N.W. Australia?' Menzies replied in his usual evasive way, indicating that the condition of Aboriginal people in the Warburton

Ranges of Western Australia was purely a state matter.[4] This was constitutionally correct, but it could be remedied, as one Tasmanian correspondent who had been prompted to resign from the Liberal Party pointed out, writing: 'The stock answer that this is not a Federal matter is technically correct, but unsatisfying. I have gained the impression from your published statements and broadcasts that you personally do not like coloured people'.[5] Menzies left Indigenous affairs to Paul Hasluck, who, as long-serving Minister for Territories from 1951 to 1963, promoted a policy of assimilation involving the closure of Aboriginal reserves, the continuing removal of children on the basis of alleged neglect, and the extension after 1959 of social security benefits to the Indigenous population.[6]

Michael Sawtell, who was a member of the Aborigines Welfare Board of New South Wales, asked Menzies for an interview about Indigenous affairs, as well as writing to Dame Pattie Menzies on the subject of Indigenous pensions. 'I know', he wrote, 'that "the milk of human kindness is not yet dried up" in the Prime Minister'.[7] This was wishful thinking, and no interview eventuated. Sawtell was a champion of Aboriginal citizenship rights, and an opponent of detribalisation, which he knew could leave individual Aboriginal men and women bereft and disorientated. 'I could tell you', he wrote, 'why it is so cruel, even with the best of intentions to get those unsophisticated and innocent bush girls down to the big cities'.

Sawtell was a former soapbox orator in the Sydney Domain and a friend of Indigenous artist Albert Namatjira. In 1958, Namatjira's conviction and prison sentence for making alcohol available to his kin network (he shared a bottle of rum with a ward) were well publicised.[8] His fate did provoke a ripple of correspondence, but, overall, Indigenous topics remain distinguished by their absence. Activism on the behalf of Indigenous people was discouraged. When a writer from Hobart recommended a Royal Commission to formulate 'measures aimed at atoning for the historical injustice through which they have been decimated and degraded', Menzies' secretary Heseltine passed his letter on to the security services (a decision which now seems inexplicable).[9]

Lying beneath what the letters either said or did not say was a geological stratum in which were embedded, like fossils from a prehistoric era, a series of assumptions about Australia and the world. These assumptions, whether implicit or explicit, which have emerged in previous chapters, formed the structure of beliefs and values shared by Menzies and most of his correspondents. The letters therefore introduce us to the heart of Australia's Liberal-voting middle class, and the priorities which shaped their world view.

Their structure of belief was first and foremost a Christian structure, based around the Protestant faith, with special reference to Menzies' own Presbyterianism. Historian David Hilliard has already emphasised the importance of religion in post-war Australia, and the letters reflect this. In the 1954 census, only one in 300 Australians declared they had 'no religion', and he suggests that 30 per cent of the population probably attended church regularly on Sundays.[10] Correspondents tended to see the hands of both God and the Devil everywhere, and they frequently cited biblical texts to support their points and admonish Menzies. Common prejudices against Roman Catholics as puppets of a foreign power, and the homiletic letters which urged Menzies to follow the path of Christian righteousness, were aspects of these fundamental ideas. Christian philanthropy also inspired more positive letters urging global peace and greater fairness towards the aged, the vulnerable and, very occasionally, Aboriginal people. The opposition to apartheid, too, sprang essentially from Christian notions of human dignity and equality, while Christian values were always a reference point for the struggle against communism.

The correspondence has also revealed a second important tendency. Writers shared a natural propensity to think in terms of conspiracies at every corner. The profusion of conspiracy theorists did not originate in the age of 5G and COVID-19; it has a much longer history. Phobic tendencies were most obvious in the case of alleged communist conspiracies, regularly portrayed as the global machinations of a secret alliance manipulating the naive and the gullible. In the events surrounding the Petrov Affair, Cold War suspicions reached a climax when several personal denunciations found their way to Menzies, reminiscent of the secret operations of some totalitarian societies. Fears of conspiratorial subversion, however, were not directed exclusively at world communism. They occasionally targeted Jews and Freemasons, and at times they embraced the Australian Labor Party leadership as potential agents of subversion.

Correspondents felt comfortable in a white-dominated world, in which the settler nations of the English-speaking world united in the British Empire. They wrote without compunction about preserving the White Australia Policy and they were not afraid to defend the ideal of white supremacy. This is what they had grown up with and they took it for granted. A proportion of international correspondents, especially from southern Africa, reinforced the white-supremacist element in the corpus. This world view could not endure. Correspondents were forced onto the defensive by the Suez crisis, which, even if they did not immediately realise it, reflected Britain's diminished world-imperial capabilities. They faced changes in the immigration intake which diluted the 'whiteness' of Australia and they resisted growing pressure from Asian nations to go even further towards opening Australia's borders. The fear that white control was slipping away no doubt reinforced the conspiracy phobia already mentioned.

Fourthly, Menzies' correspondents were simultaneously both British and Australian patriots and saw nothing ambiguous or contradictory about their dual loyalty. Menzies himself, imbued with a genuine anglophilism, personified this duality. When historian Richard White analysed the appearance after the Second World War of the notion of an 'Australian way of life', he was impressed most of all by the vagueness of the concept.[11] Menzies' correspondents gave it a little more solidity by identifying it as the 'British way of life', implying an affection for the crown, a solidarity with Britain and a respect for British democratic and judicial institutions. To be proudly British was for them an integral part of their Australian identity. This was not just royalist sentimentality; patterns of trade and investment as well as membership of the sterling currency area all gave British-Australian patriotism very real substance and significance. As White also argued, the British-Australian way of life was a defensive, conservative idea. It was a concept under threat, from communism, from immigrants who failed to assimilate and eventually from creeping Americanisation. Defending their hazy notion of Britishness informed letter-writers' core values.

Correspondents were motivated by a well-entrenched work ethic. This clearly emerged in their respect for the hard labour of Australia's pioneer settlers. It was also accompanied by the belief that others were abusing their faith in the value of work. Politicians who awarded themselves salary increases fell into this category, but so too, on occasion, did age pensioners. One correspondent rounded on pensioners as parasites feeding on the taxpayer, branding them as 'loafers and schemers [who] were never an asset to Australia in any shape or form'.[12] Pensioners, however, were rarely a target; workers were much more commonly accused of 'bludging'. On a small card, Margaret Heath suggested that when the opposition asked Menzies when he was going to deliver on his promise to 'put the value back into the pound', he should reply: 'When the worker puts value back into the "hour"'.[13] The work ethic was always supported by a belief in thrift and the importance of saving for the future, which have been core values of the Liberal Party since its foundation. This fundamental perspective framed much of the criticism of the age pension means test. In a talk on the BBC in 1953, Menzies insisted that the capital for future development had to be earned and saved, and this was music to the ears of his own constituency. But others disagreed, reminding him that banks were necessary for loans as well as deposits, and that credit, not savings, fuelled the economy.[14]

The world view of Menzies' correspondents was structured according to traditional gender expectations. The Liberal Party's family ideology rewarded the married male breadwinner while granting him tax concessions on behalf of his dependent spouse. Letter-writers expressed no dissent from this model of the wage-earning man and his female partner principally devoted to home duties and childcare. In 1953, for example, the idea of building a new apartment complex which provided residents with a crèche and a baby-sitting facility so that women could go out to work had shocked one conservative (female) correspondent.[15] The norms of heterosexual relationships and the nuclear family were not challenged in the letters.

Only a handful of letters broke the conservative mould, including one from the United Associations of Women, who complained that Australian men were responsible for retarding the progress of women in politics by denying them selection as party candidates. Hazel Craig replied in justification that there were four Liberal women in the Senate and several in the New South Wales General Assembly. In the light of today's aspirations to gender parity, this weak response serves only to justify the original complaint.[16]

This was an isolated protest. If we did not turn to other sources, we would be quite unaware that the pattern of gender relations was changing. In reality, the proportion of married women who were in paid employment more than doubled from 8.6 per cent in 1947 to 18.7 per cent in 1961. The traditional pattern persisted most strongly for the Australian-born population, but its hold over immigrant families was weaker. For them, survival depended on securing a second income, and women from immigrant families were more likely than others to enter the workforce.[17] Perhaps the prevailing tendency towards male domination is best illustrated by the fact that men wrote the majority of the letters to Menzies. Women wrote less than 30 per cent of letters he received from individuals throughout his term of office.

STRUCTURES OF BELIEF

Correspondence and the New History from Below

The importance of the letters to Menzies has hitherto been ignored. We should situate them within a specific genre of letter-writing – namely, writing upwards. I have simplified Menzies correspondents' many motives for writing upwards by identifying five chief genres in the typology of their letters. They wrote to congratulate Menzies and to share in his electoral successes. They praised his oratorical performances and sent gifts in appreciation. Secondly, they sent supplicatory letters, asking for a favour or a special intervention by Menzies on their behalf to resolve a problem, perhaps to connect them to the telephone network or secure an invitation to a royal garden party. Many supplicatory letters outlined a more serious situation, as when age pensioners sought urgent relief from hardship and poverty. A third variety was the 'political letter', which typically came from a Liberal Party branch, warning of the electoral dangers of following a certain policy line. Angry letters were similar to the political letters but their harder edge of protest was more hostile and incisive. Lastly, I have identified eccentric and paranoid letters, which included a great deal of sermonising and prophecies of catastrophe. Although this typology is not necessarily exhaustive, it effectively supports an analysis of the various purposes of writing to Menzies.

As we have seen, writers of all types of letters deployed a range of rhetorical devices to bring their messages to Menzies' attention. They used the rhetoric of apology and self-abasement, a typical strategy of the weak when addressing those in power. They tried to persuade Menzies that there was some past affinity binding him to the writer. They advertised aspects of themselves which they imagined would carry weight with him: their Britishness, their dedicated loyalty to the Liberal Party in the past, or the history of past sacrifices for the nation made by their family. All these rhetorical appeals for attention and sympathy formed essential building blocks which structured the correspondence.

Historians have customarily used correspondence as a window on some other reality, and they have mined it for data on whatever subject they were seeking to illuminate. I have followed exactly the same path here, excavating the Menzies correspondence for information on the prejudices and preoccupations of grassroots Liberal supporters in this period. This kind of data mining, however, is only one approach to the historical study of correspondence. Letters do not merely constitute evidence about something beyond their own existence, they also speak about themselves and about the importance of writing. Scholars have accordingly turned their attention to the function and purpose of letter-writing *per se*, and to its inherent rules and conventions. Writing is a social practice, which means that letters define a social relationship between writer and reader – in this case, the relationship between prime minister and ordinary citizen was a very unequal one. Forms of address and farewell are crucial in shaping that relationship and indicate how the writer interprets the relationship and wishes it to be conducted. Leaving a large blank space at the head of the letter, to take another example, is part of the social grammar of letter-writing by which the sender expresses deference to the addressee. The larger the expanse of empty white space, the more deferential the writer. Letters also define and perpetuate social networks.[18] The corpus gives us an outline of Menzies' own networks, whether familial, religious, tied to his political party or his Scottish ancestry. Supplicants attempted to insert themselves convincingly into one of these networks. Correspondence, therefore, is not a transparent window onto some other reality, but a highly coded and ritualised medium which demands elucidation in its own right. Attention must accordingly be paid to its unspoken rules and structures as well as to its contents. The material and textual form of correspondence reveals much about its social function.

STRUCTURES OF BELIEF

The analysis of writings upwards provides an alternative to conventional political history. It changes the perspective, focusing on the assumptions and concerns of the so-called silent masses and finding them to have been not so silent after all. Writings like the corpus of letters to Menzies form part of the New History from Below. The traditional histories from below of the 1960s and 1970s treated the subordinate classes as anonymous masses, or else they focused on the collective movements which advanced workers' struggles. They were primarily interested in public action rather than private lives. In contrast, the New History from Below puts a higher value on individual subjective experience. And when historians do claim value for the lives of ordinary people, they ultimately discover that nobody is truly 'ordinary'.

Today, the New History from Below is making great efforts in various parts of the world to unearth more direct evidence of their existence and their culture in the writings of the poor and the marginal themselves – the writings, in fact, of those who often in the past have not been credited with the ability to write competently at all.[19] This kind of history re-evaluates their individual experience and searches for the personal voices of common people. Those voices may be mediated, as in this case, through written correspondence; and they may struggle to express themselves because of their unfamiliarity with writing technology or with epistolary literacy in general. But ordinary readers and writers can only be fully understood if we listen to their voices, however inarticulate they may seem, and regard them as active agents in their own history rather than passive receptacles for official ideologies. The writings of humble people are there if we care to look for them. The letters to Menzies are one small part of a submerged continent of ordinary writings now becoming increasingly accessible.

NOTES

1 Menzies' Forgotten People

1. National Library of Australia (NLA), Menzies papers ms 4936, Box 42, folder 51, Reg Longden, 26 December 1949. All future citations from the Menzies letters refer to this collection and this call number. I normally use correspondents' real names, in the interests of transparency and to enable researchers to locate my sources. If a letter is extremely offensive or racially prejudiced, I withhold the author's name in order not to embarrass their descendants.
2. Cameron Hazlehurst, *Menzies Observed*, George Allen & Unwin, Sydney, 1979, p. 182.
3. John Howard, *The Menzies Era: The Years that Shaped Modern Australia*, HarperCollins, Sydney, 2014, pp. 3, 385, 631–35.
4. Paul Keating, speech to House of Representatives at question time, 27 February 1992, <australianpolitics.com/1992/02/27/keating-blasts-liberal-party-fogies.html>, read 18 July 2019.
5. Allan W Martin, *Robert Menzies: A Life: Volume 2, 1944–1978*, Melbourne University Press, Melbourne, 1999.
6. Troy Bramston, *Robert Menzies: The Art of Politics*, Scribe, Melbourne, 2019.
7. John Murphy, *Imagining the Fifties: Private Sentiment and Political Culture in Menzies' Australia*, UNSW Press, Sydney, 2000, pp. 2–6.
8. David Lowe, *Menzies and the 'Great World Struggle': Australia's Cold War, 1948–1954*, UNSW Press, Sydney, 1999.
9. Martyn Lyons, 'A New History from Below? The Writing Culture of Ordinary People in Europe', *History Australia*, vol. 7, no. 3, 2010, 60.1–60.9.
10. Armando Petrucci, *Scrivere lettere: Una storia plurimillenaria*, Laterza, Bari, 2008, pp. x–xi.
11. Maarten van Ginderachter, '"If Your Majesty Would Only Send Me a Little Money to Help Buy an Elephant": Letters to the Belgian Royal Family (1880–1940)', in Martyn Lyons (ed.), *Ordinary Writings, Personal Narratives, Writing Practices in 19th and Early 20th-century Europe*, Peter Lang, Bern, 2007, pp. 69–83.
12. Henrik Eberle (ed.), *Letters to Hitler*, English version edited by Victoria Harris, trans. Steven Randall, Polity, Cambridge UK, 2012, pp. 94 and 174.
13. Anne Wingenter, '*Voices of Sacrifice*: Letters to Mussolini and Ordinary Writing under Fascism', in Lyons, *Ordinary Writings, Personal Narratives*, 2007, pp. 155–72.
14. Sudhir Hazareesingh, *In the Shadow of the General: Modern France and the Myth of De Gaulle*, Oxford University Press, Oxford, 2012.
15. Béatrice Fraenkel, '"Répondre à tous"? Une enquête sur le service du courrier présidentiel', in Daniel Fabre (ed.), *Par écrit. Ethnologie des écritures quotidiennes*, Maison des Sciences de l'Homme, Paris, 1997, pp. 243–71.
16. Jeanne Marie Laskas, *To Obama: With Love, Joy, Hate and Despair*, Bloomsbury Circus, London, 2018.
17. Ibid., pp. 65–66 and chapter 14.
18. Ibid., p. 71.

19 Martyn Lyons, 'Writing Upwards: How the Weak Wrote to the Powerful', *Journal of Social History*, vol. 49, no. 2, winter 2015, pp. 317–30.
20 Camillo Zadra and Gianluigi Fait, *Deferenza, Revendicazione, Supplica: le lettere ai potenti*, Pagus, Treviso, 1992.
21 James C Scott, *Weapons of the Weak: Everyday Forms of Peasant Resistance*, Yale University Press, New Haven CT, 1985.
22 Hazlehurst, *Menzies Observed*, pp. 109–110, 168, 312–15.
23 Robert Menzies, *The Forgotten People and Other Studies in Democracy*, with introduction by David Kemp, Liberal Party of Australia, Melbourne, 2011, first published by Angus & Robertson in 1943, p. 33.
24 Murphy, *Imagining the Fifties*, 2000, chapter 10, 'The Meanings of Home'.
25 Menzies, *Forgotten People*, 2011, p. 33; Judith Brett, *Robert Menzies' Forgotten People*, Melbourne University Press, Melbourne, 2007 [1992], p. 65.
26 Box 76, folder 338, Sydney Moss, Beverly Hills (NSW), 26 November 1956.
27 Box 43, folder 62, HA Roope, 21 December 1949.
28 Box 56, folder 173, Zora Cross, 17 November 1954.
29 Box 59, folder 193, Patricia Heggarty, 6 May 1954.
30 Box 88, folder 439, Alice Morgan, North Carlton (Vic), 21 April 1959.
31 Box 62, folder 221, reply to Mrs R Powell, 5 July 1954.
32 Box 78, folder 348.
33 Box 46, folder 82, EJ Hallstrom, Chairman of the Taronga Park Trust, November 1951, and Box 42, folder 52, Kathleen McCary, Freeport (Texas), May 1950.
34 Box 55, folder 161, Robert Bone, Gosford (NSW), January 1954 and Box 123, folder 713, Shri Vijayadev, Bombay, 6 February 1964.
35 Box 135, folder 732, Glyn Matthews, Birmingham (UK), 28 January 1965.
36 Box 121, folder 701, Mrs B Moran, Wingello (NSW), 17 September 1964.
37 Box 164, folder 1049, Lillias Griffiths, Balranald (NSW), 18 May 1971.
38 Box 52, folder 133, Stanhope Hotel, New York, 26 June 1953.
39 Steven King, *Writing the Lives of the English Poor, 1750s–1830s*, McGill-Queen's University Press, Montréal, 2019, chapter 7.
40 Box 58, folder 187, Bruce Graham, 1 December 1953.
41 Moral Re-Armament was a religious, non-denominational movement for peace, reconciliation and harmonious relations between capital and labour. It saw Christianity as the best alternative to the perceived evils of communism.
42 Until independence was achieved in 1975, 'Papua and New Guinea' was an Australian-administered territory.
43 James C Scott, *Domination and the Arts of Resistance: Hidden Transcripts*, Yale University Press, New Haven CT, 1990, pp. 3–16.
44 Box 48, folder 103, reply of 20 November 1953.

2 **The profile of the ordinary writer**
1 Box 47, folder 98, Lawrence Johnston, 11 September 1953.
2 Box 61, folder 214, Harbord (NSW), 15 February 1954.
3 The year-by-year classification of the archive is not foolproof – some dossiers include letters from previous years where there is a long exchange of correspondence over a protracted matter, or in cases where an individual author is unusually persistent. So each annual box contains a few letters written in previous or subsequent years – but I have counted the letters in the year in which they were actually written, and annual totals have been adjusted accordingly.

4   Percentages include letters sent by married couples and jointly by families so they add up to more than 100.
5   Box 122, folder 702.
6   Box 95, folder 496, 30 November 1960.
7   Box 69, folder 281, 24 September 1955.
8   Given the difficulty of distinguishing writing by superior ball-point pens from that of fine-nibbed fountain pens, there is some margin of error in this figure.
9   Box 41, folder 46, King's Cross, Sydney, June 1950.
10 Martyn Lyons, *The Writing Culture of Ordinary People in Europe, c.1860–1920*, Cambridge University Press, Cambridge UK, 2013, gives many examples from soldiers' letters in the First World War and from the correspondence of Spanish emigrants to the Americas.
11 Box 43, folder 59, Merrylands (NSW), 1 March 1950.
12 Box 164, folder 1049, Balranald (NSW), 18 May 1971.
13 Box 50, folder 124, 14 April 1953.
14 Box 122, folder 704, MS Parvati, 5 August 1964.
15 Box 118, folder 673, Colombo, August 1964; Box 120, folder 686, 3 February 1964; Box 121, folder 693, 17 April 1964, among others.
16 Box 120, folder 690, 19 May 1964 ('aloha'); Box 84, folder 401, Sister Wooly, Townsville (Qld), 22 August 1958 ('Bro Menzie').
17 'Yours very sincerely', 'Sincerely yours', 'Sincerely', 'Always yours sincerely' and so on.
18 Box 123, folder 713, Shri Vijayadev, Bombay, 6 February 1964; Box 122, folder 708, Thelma Saunders, Sunbury (Vic), 8 December 1964.
19 Box 123, folder 710, Major AW Smith, Essex (UK), 1 July 1964.
20 Box 117, folder 668, 26 September 1963.
21 Box 93, folder 480, AM Hamilton, Canberra, 22 April 1960.
22 Box 108, folder 596, John Harris, Torquay (Devon, UK), 21 May 1962.
23 Box 120, folder 689, 12 May 1964.
24 Box 98, folder 514, Nambour (Qld), 9 June 1961.
25 Box 63, folder 231, Nambour (Qld), 10 December 1955.

3   Fan mail and congratulations
1   Box 62, folder 219, Lance Pearse of Melbourne Baby Carriages, Bendigo (Vic), 8 May 1954.
2   Box 123, folder 711, St Ives (NSW), 31 October 1964.
3   Box 99, folder 524, Agnes Cleary, Kew (Vic), 22 June 1961.
4   Box 42, folder 51, 18 January 1950.
5   Box 43, folder 59, 12 December 1949.
6   Box 43, folder 53, JL Skerman, Maleny (Qld), 20 February 1950.
7   Box 49, folder 114, 12 May 1953.
8   Box 51, folder 129, A Shayler, 5 May 1953.
9   Box 55, folder 164, JC Burn, Balmain (NSW), 12 May 1954.
10 Box 76, folder 337, 28 November 1957.
11 Box 85, folder 411, Mrs Brett, Glenroy (Vic), 24 November 1958.
12 Box 86, folder 419, Joseph Derwin, Brisbane, 16 September 1959; Box 42, folder 54, AG Moyes of *Sporting Life*, 23 May 1950.
13 Series 5, Boxes 246–250.
14 Box 246, folder 3, 13 March 1963.

15 Box 122, folder 704, 3 July 1964.
16 Box 42, folder 51, reply to Alasdair Loch, London, 9 March 1950.
17 Box 41, folder 41, Miss Pamela Davenport, 9 June and 9 July 1950, with reply of 30 June 1950.
18 Box 48, folder 103, SA Lombard, Pretoria, 11 December 1953.
19 Box 51, folder 129, George Simmons, Rockhampton (Qld), 23 December 1953.
20 Box 49, folder 110, Mary Morgan, Unley Park (SA), 1953.
21 Box 61, folder 210, Sister Mary, St Cecily (Qld), 9 August 1954.
22 Box 61, folder 213, Myra Mullaney, St Kilda (Vic), 8 August 1954.
23 Box 106, folder 578, Toorak (Vic), July 1962.
24 Box 76, folder 334, Frances Lambert, Hurstpierpoint (Sussex), 19 March 1957.
25 Box 113, folder 634, V Balfour, Mosman (NSW), 6 December 1963.
26 Box 104, folder 564, Curlewis (NSW), 19 November 1961.
27 Box 42, folder 47, Gertrude Hart, Sassafras (Vic), 23 October 1950.
28 Box 71, folder 196, Peter Szabo, Newcastle (NSW), October 1955.
29 Box 85, folder 405, M Ashby, Tourist Class, SS *Orcades*, 13 May 1959.
30 Box 87, folder 422, Federated Clothing Industries Council, Canberra, 20 March 1959.
31 Box 110, folder 607, Brisbane Caledonian Society, 3 November 1962.
32 Box 112, folder 626, Charles Vete, Stanmore (NSW), no date 1962.
33 Box 105, folder 571, Sydney, 29 June 1961.
34 Box 74, folder 317, 3 September 1957.
35 Box 45, folder 75, 2 March 1951.
36 Box 74, folder 324, Melbourne, 17 August 1958, and reply of 21 August 1957.
37 Box 47, folder 102, Armadale (Vic).
38 Box 90, folder 455, Subiaco (WA), 13 March 1959.
39 Box 86, folder 421, JD Eales, Morpeth (NSW), 1 May 1959.
40 Box 115, folder 650, Rosemary Kepecz, Welland (Ontario), 8 October 1963.
41 Box 66, folder 251, 11 November 1955.
42 Box 41, folder 46, Petty Officer Leslie Groves, Crib Point (Vic), 10 September 1950.
43 Martin Francis, 'Tears, Tantrums and Bared Teeth: The Emotional Economy of Three Conservative Prime Ministers, 1951–1963', *Journal of British Studies*, vol. 41, no. 3, July 2002, p. 358.
44 Box 55, folder 158, Brisbane, 9 September 1953.
45 Box 57, folder 177, Leichhardt (NSW), 30 May 1954.
46 Box 42, folder 48, Robertson (NSW), 28 October 1950.
47 Box 54, folder 150, Nalin Abeyesekere, January 1954.
48 Box 81, folder 376, Merriwa (NSW), 29 January 1958.
49 Box 59, folder 191, Gertrude Hart, Sassafras Gully (Vic), 3 April 1954.
50 Troy Bramston, *Robert Menzies: The Art of Politics*, Scribe, Melbourne, 2019, pp. 118 and 123.
51 Frank Jennings, Interview with Barry York for the Museum of Australian Democracy Oral History Collection, Part 5, 29 October 2007.
52 Box 71, folder 197, J Nevin Tait for JC Williamson Theatres, 1955. On this occasion, he saw *Macbeth*.
53 Box 42, folder 50, Norman Kater, London, 26 May 1950, and reply of 4 July 1950.
54 Box 70, folder 287, Portland Cement, 25 April 1955.
55 Box 71, folder 293, Kenneth Slessor, 6 October 1955. 'Robert Menzies rewrites the Trial Scene from *The Merchant of Venice*' was published in *Southerly*, no. 2, 1956.

56 Box 63, folder 227, Mrs EA Adams, Highcliffe (Hants), 31 January 1955.
57 Box 66, folder 253, MA Fagnani, Bristol (UK), 28 January 1955.
58 Box 121, folder 698, Elizabeth Bay (NSW), 22 July 1964.
59 Box 99, folder 520, Mrs Pat Brooks, Heidelberg (Vic), 9 June 1961.
60 Box 46A, folder 93, 3 August 1953.
61 Box 48, folder 103, Mollie Livingston, Chatswood (NSW), 1953.
62 Box 48, folder 105, Sister E McGrath, Goulburn (NSW), 11 February 1953.
63 Box 55, folder 164, 12 November 1954.
64 Box 43, folder 63, undated March 1950.
65 Box 67, folder 258, 4 September 1955.
66 Box 47, folder 97, Auburn (NSW), 21 April 1953.
67 Box 50, folder 121, A Rathbone-Proctor, 11 April 1953.
68 Box 43, folder 57, 29 December 1949, and reply of 4 February 1950.
69 Box 88, folder 436, Sir Daniel McVey, Sydney, 25 August 1959. McVey was a fellow Scot and former chief of the Postmaster-General's Department.
70 Box 78, folder 353, Florence Brown, Kyneton (Vic), 13 March 1958.
71 Box 75, folder 331, Alma Isaacs, Windsor (Vic), 28 November 1946, and Box 42, folder 51, FW Larner, Fairlight (NSW), 19 February 1950.
72 Box 42, folder 49, Miss F Jude, Melbourne, 20 April 1950.
73 Box 59, folder 191, G Hart, Sassafras (Vic), 29 November 1954.
74 Box 108, folder 597, Waratah (NSW), 5 March 1962.
75 Box 127, folder 750, Canberra, 21 January 1966.
76 Box 83, folder 391, July 1958.
77 Box 91, folder 467, WS Bengtsson of the British Tobacco Co, Kensington (NSW), 15 July 1959.
78 Box 92, folder 473, Alice Springs, April 1960.
79 Box 92, folder 473, reply to Sidney Conger, Honolulu, 25 April 1960.
80 Box 82, folder 389, 25 August 1958. 'Blue books' contained official government surveys of various social problems in industrialising Britain, much exploited by British social historians.
81 Box 121, folder 696, Pymble (NSW), 21 May 1964, and reply.

4 The personal hotline
1 Box 126, folder 737, Bolton (UK), 20 June 1965.
2 Béatrice Fraenkel, '"Répondre à tous": une enquête sur le service du courier présidentiel', in Daniel Fabre (ed.), *Par Écrit. Ethnologie des écritures quotidiennes*, Maison des Sciences de l'Homme, Paris, 1997, para 30.
3 Box 51, folder 130, 12 June 1953.
4 Box 66, folder 257, 22 August 1955.
5 Box 46A, folder 92, London, 6 June 1953.
6 Box 48, folder 107, Pagewood (NSW), 22 October 1953.
7 Box 79, folder 355, Warren Carey, University of Tasmania, 13 February 1958.
8 Box 69, folder 278, Beverly Hills (NSW), 28 May 1955.
9 Box 88, folder 436, Longueville (NSW), 22 April 1959.
10 Box 89, folder 448, H Roberts, Kew (Vic), 30 March 1959.
11 Box 76, folder 334, Joan Lewis, Cardiff (Wales), 17 July 1957.
12 Box 87, folder 427, John Harris, Paignton (Devon), 10 October 1959.
13 Box 52, folder 135, 2 June 1953.

14 Box 98, folder 514, Nambour (Qld), 7 October 1961.
15 Box 90, folder 457, Potts Point (NSW), 13 September 1958.
16 Box 47, folder 102, Dagmar Levy, Armadale (Vic), 1 January 1953.
17 Box 81, folder 372, Glen Iris (Vic), 19 July 1958.
18 Stephen Holt, 'From Typists to Trusted Advisers', *Public Sector Informant* (supplement to *The Canberra Times*), 2 July 2013, pp. 14–15.
19 NLA ORAL TRC 3562, John Farquharson, Interviews with Hazel Craig, Tape 1, 20 February 1997.
20 Ibid., Tape 3, 25 February 1997.
21 Ibid., Tape 5, 4 March 1997.
22 Ibid., Tape 6, 1 April 1997.
23 Short, James Robert (Senator), Tribute to Geoff Yeend, 10 October 1994, <parlinfo.aph.gov.au/parlInfo/search/display/display.w3p;query=Id%3A%22chamber%2Fhansards%2F1994-10-10%2F0098%22>, read 9 September 2020.
24 Frank Jennings, Interviews with Barry York for the Museum of Australian Democracy Oral History Collection, parts 1–7, October 2007, at <oralhistories.moadoph.gov.au/frank-jennings-1930-2014>.
25 Box 55, folder 160, December 1954.
26 Box 119, folder 678, Mrs M Clout, London, 29 March and 4 May 1964.
27 Box 65, folder 246, Bunbury (WA), 1 September 1955.
28 Box 63, folder 231, Note from Craig, 27 July 1955, on Joyce Atkinson of Nambour (Qld).
29 Box 64, folder 239, Ascot Vale (Vic), 10 August 1955.
30 Box 62, folder 221, 30 June 1954 and reply of 5 July.
31 Box 92, folder 473, Tasmania, 9 March 1960.
32 Box 105, folder 570, 20 September and reply of 28 September 1961.
33 Box 44, folder 67, EG Linehan to Mrs DM Rae of the Australian Women's Movement Against Socialisation, 7 January 1950.
34 Box 42, folder 48, Walter Henderson, Robertson (NSW), 28 October 1950.
35 Box 42, folder 48, Edward Hirst, Sydney, reply of 20 July 1950.
36 Box 89, folder 441, reply to Spencer Nall, 25 August 1959.
37 Box 43, folder 62, Adelaide, 29 November 1949.
38 Box 90, folder 459, Glenbrook (NSW), 14 September 1959.
39 Jeanne Marie Laskas, *To Obama, with Love, Joy, Hate and Despair*, Bloomsbury Circus, London, 2018, pp. 15–16.
40 Box 123, folder 711, Georgetown (Tas), 9 May 1964.
41 Box 123, folder 717, several letters, 10 February to 3 September 1964.
42 Boxes 164–165.
43 Box 133, folder 638, Helen Coates, Brisbane, December 1963.
44 Box 42, folder 52, Kathleen McCary, Freeport (Texas), May 1950. In the early 1950s, myxomatosis ('myxo') effectively reduced the rabbit population.
45 Fraenkel, '"Répondre à tous"', 1997, para 1.

5 The rhetoric of apology
1 Box 41, folder 46, Petty Officer Leslie Groves, Crib Point (Vic), 10 September 1950.
2 Martyn Lyons, 'Writing Upwards: How the Weak Wrote to the Powerful', *Journal of Social History*, vol. 49, no. 2, winter 2015, pp. 317–18.
3 James C Scott, *Weapons of the Weak: Everyday Forms of Peasant Resistance*, Yale University Press, New Haven CT, 1985, pp. 285–6.

4   Box 43, folder 57, Rhoda Payne, 29 December 1949.
5   Box 49, folder 116, Elwood (Vic), undated March 1953.
6   Box 42, folder 52, Millendon (WA), 7 May 1950.
7   Box 55, folder 162, Mary Brown, Burwood (Vic), 29 September 1954.
8   Box 42, folder 50, Charles Kennedy, Gympie (Qld), 3 April 1950.
9   Box 97, folder 510, 15 December 1960.
10 Box 84, folder 401, Sister Wooly, Townsville (Qld), 22 August 1958.
11 Box 71, folder 294, Wingham (Kent), 24 May 1955.
12 Box 70, folder 285, CK Punjabi, Kandla Port, 11 June 1955.
13 Box 119, folder 682, Arthur D'Ombrain, Sydney, 4 February 1964.
14 Box 75, folder 333, Robert Jaya Kumar, Eluru (Andhra Pradesh), 15 April 1957.
15 Box 106, folder 577, Balamban, Cebu (Philippines), 4 November 1961.
16 Box 71, folder 295, Blackheath (Greater London), 1 February 1955.
17 Box 42, folder 52, Mrs WJ McAuley, North Sydney, 2 May 1950.
18 Box 45, folder 76, Chullora Railway Camp (NSW), 14 June 1951.
19 Box 42, folder 54, Melbourne, 9 April 1950.
20 Box 80, folder 366, Mundaring (WA), 17 March 1958.
21 Box 42, folder 48, Toorak (Vic), 16 June 1950.
22 Box 68, folder 266, IC Kempe, Ramco (SA), 20 July 1955.
23 Box 80, folder 369, Redcliffe (Qld), 7 November 1958.
24 Box 42, folder 48, LA Houghton, undated September 1950; Box 56, folder 166, E Campbell, 27 April 1954.
25 Box 86, folder 413, South Yarra (Vic), February 1959.
26 Box 51, folder 130, East Melbourne, 25 April 1953.
27 Box 81, folder 367, Oyster Bay (NSW), 27 October 1958.
28 Box 57, folder 175, Mitcham (Vic), 25 January 1954.
29 Box 85, folder 405, George Arnoldt, Hobart, 11 January 1959; Box 86, folder 421, Miss JFD Eales, Morpeth (NSW), 1 May 1959.
30 Box 88, folder 432, Manning (WA), November 1959.
31 Box 81, folder 367, Little River (Vic), 2 April 1958.
32 Box 119, folder 678, Agnes Cleary, Kew (Vic), 7 April 1964.
33 Box 86, folder 413, South Yarra (Vic), undated February 1959.
34 Box 76, folder 334, Mrs Joan Lewis, Cardiff (Wales), 17 July 1957.
35 Box 50, folder 119, Miss E Porter, London, 5 June 1953.
36 Box 48, folder 105, 19 March 1953.
37 Box 70, folder 283, undated July 1955.
38 Box 44, folder 71, Sir Ernest Fisk, Hayes (Middlesex), 12 February 1951.
39 Box 48, folder 105, Mrs RJ McGarvie, Pomborneit (Vic), 30 September 1953.
40 Box 54, folder 143, 3 August 1953.
41 Box 51, folder 134, Hylda Summerbell, London, 18 June 1953.
42 Box 71, folder 293, Scottish Secretariat, Glasgow, 21 January 1955, for example.
43 Box 42, folder 51, Florence Love, Middle Park (Vic), 11 April 1950; Box 42, folder 52, Mrs McGlashan, 16 January 1950.
44 Box 52, folder 136, Mrs MC Thomson, Northbridge (NSW), 7 October 1953.
45 Box 42, folder 50, John Fraser Kelly, 14 December 1949.
46 Box 89, folder 448, GA Robertson, Brisbane, 24 April 1959.
47 Box 50, folder 118, London, 28 June 1953.
48 Box 48, folder 105, Rev Ian McLellan, 25 June 1953.

49 Box 80, folder 365, E Gray, Paddington (Qld), 18 January 1958.
50 Box 48, folder 105, Melbourne, 30 January 1953.
51 Box 42, folder 48, Orford (Vic), 11 December 1950. The original reads:
But bring a Scotchman frae his hill,
Clap in his cheek a Highland gill,
Say, such is royal George's will,
An' there's the foe!
He has nae thought but how to kill
Twa at a blow.
52 Box 41, folder 42, East Malvern (Vic), 5 July 1950.
53 Box 41, folder 43, IF Heathershaw, Secretary of the Council of Elders of the Presbyterian Church of Victoria, 31 March 1950.
54 Box 56, folder 166, 1 February 1954.
55 Box 68, folder 272, 6 October 1955.
56 Box 47, folder 100, Kew Traders' Committee (Vic), 10 December 1953.
57 Sybil Nolan, 'The Snub: Robert Menzies and the Melbourne Club', *Australian Historical Studies*, vol. 48, no. 1, 2017, pp. 3–18.
58 Box 64, folder 239, Ascot Vale (Vic), 10 August 1955.
59 Box 51, folder 134, Ashburton (Vic), undated August 1953.
60 Box 87, folder 426, Jean Robinson Guy, Surrey Hills (Vic), 15 August 1959.
61 Box 60, folder 205, Roseville (NSW), 17 May 1954.
62 Box 63, folder 233, 20 December 1955.
63 Box 66, folder 249, undated January 1955.
64 Box 67, folder 261, Australian Textile Mills, 18 November 1955; Box 65, folder 242, Beryl Carlyon, 18 April 1955.
65 Box 63, folder 230, 19 April 1955.
66 Box 64, folder 238, 24 October 1955.
67 Box 66, folder 257, 13 May 1955.
68 Box 69, folder 275, 11 letters in 1955.
69 Box 43, folder 57, February 1957 (exact date unknown).
70 Box 46, folder 85, Menzies to Governor-General Sir William McKell, 15 January 1952.
71 Maarten van Ginderachter, '"If your Majesty Would Only Send Me a Little Money to Help Buy an Elephant": Letters to the Belgian Royal Family (1880–1940)', in Martyn Lyons (ed.), *Ordinary Writings, Personal Narratives: Writing Practices in 19th and early 20th century Europe*, Peter Lang, Bern 2007, p. 69.
72 Box 100, folder 528, Bob Demaine, Melbourne, 11 August 1961.
73 Box 47, folder 100, 3 June 1953.
74 Box 50, folder 124, Dorothy Rookwood, Finsbury Park, London, 14 June 1953.
75 Box 51, folder 130, Mrs Sydney Smith, London, 9 June 1953. England won by eight wickets.
76 Box 48, folder 103, Mrs E Lowe, East Brunswick (Vic), 3 August 1953.
77 Box 63, folder 229, Betty Amer, Romford (Essex), 23 July 1953.
78 Box 49, folder 113, Mrs F Norris, Totnes (Devon), date unknown 1953.
79 Box 48, folder 107, Panania (NSW), 30 November 1953.
80 Box 51, folder 131, Wendy Solling, Maitland (NSW), 18 February 1953.
81 Box 42, folder 51, 10 April 1950.
82 Box 75, folder 328, Mrs H Herbert, North Carlton (Vic), 5 November 1957.
83 Box 51, folder 131, Waldemar Sommer, 26 August 1953.

NOTES TO PAGES 102–112

84 Box 44, folder 66, WTK Thomson, Bexley (NSW), 17 February 1950.
85 Box 52, folder 137, PG Tolley, London, undated June 1953.
86 Box 47, folder 98, Owen Johnston, 29 October 1953.
87 Box 62, folder 221, Anka Popovich, Fairfield (NSW), undated June 1954.
88 Box 58, folder 185, 8 March 1954.

6 The cry of the distressed pensioner
1   Box 76, folder 338, 26 November 1956 and undated October 1957.
2   Box 52, folder 135, Tamworth (NSW), 10 February 1953.
3   Thomas Henry Kewley, *Social Security in Australia: The Development of Social Security and Health Benefits from 1900 to the Present*, Sydney University Press, Sydney, 1965, p. 382, Table 8.
4   Ibid., p. 285.
5   Ibid., pp. 220–29.
6   John Murphy, 'Shaping the Cold War Family: Politics, Domesticity and Policy Interventions in the 1950s', *Australian Historical Studies*, vol. 26, no. 105, 1995, p. 562.
7   Kewley, *Social Security*, 1965, p. 210.
8   Box 115, folder 652, Helensburgh (NSW), undated July 1963.
9   Box 42, folder 51, 31 March 1950.
10 Box 55, folder 160, LM Beggs, Swan Hill (Vic), 19 June 1954.
11 Box 64, folder 239, Victoria Brown, Ascot Vale (Vic), 10 August 1955.
12 Box 50, folder 125, RSL, Melbourne, telegram 10 September 1953.
13 Box 51, folder 134, E Hardy, Ashburton (Vic), undated August 1953.
14 Box 80, folder 366, Bairnsdale (Vic), 12 June 1958.
15 Box 66, folder 250, Canterbury (Vic), 25 April 1955.
16 John Murphy, *Imagining the Fifties: Private Sentiment and Political Culture in Menzies' Australia*, UNSW Press, Sydney, 2000, pp. 110–13.
17 Arthur Fadden, *They Called me Artie: The Memoirs of Sir Arthur Fadden*, Jacaranda, Milton Qld, 1969, p. 66.
18 Murphy, *Imagining the Fifties*, 2000, p. 107.
19 Box 59, folder 196, JF Horner, Fitzroy (Vic), undated January 1954.
20 Greg Whitwell, 'Economic Policy', in Scott Prasser, JR Nethercote and John Warhurst (eds), *The Menzies Era: A Reappraisal of Government, Politics and Society*, Hale & Iremonger, Sydney, 1995, pp. 166–84.
21 Gwen Gray, 'Social Policy', in Prasser et al., *The Menzies Era*, 1995, pp. 211–27.
22 Box 81, folder 372, AE Kerley, Semaphore (SA), 6 November 1958.
23 Box 42, folder 54, 23 March 1950.
24 Box 71, folder 293, Kew (Vic), 20 July 1955.
25 Box 78, folder 354, Cumberland (NSW), 22 October 1958.
26 Box 80, folder 366, Mundaring (WA), 17 March 1958.
27 Box 80, folder 366, Bairnsdale (Vic), 3 February 1958.
28 Box 53, folder 149, 6 October 1953.
29 Box 68, folder 268, Evelyn Lampard, West Ryde (NSW), 19 May 1955. She referred Menzies to Matthew 25: 44–45 and James 5: 1–3.
30 Box 47, folder 97, 3 September 1953.
31 Stephen Garton, *Out of Luck: Poor Australians and Social Welfare*, Allen & Unwin, Sydney, 1990, p. 146.
32 Ibid., p. 149, citing John Stubbs, *The Hidden People: Poverty in Australia*, Lansdowne Press, Sydney, 1966.

33 Ibid., p. 150.
34 Box 70, folder 283, Sydney, 26 April 1955.
35 Box 75, folder 330, H Howard, Bronte (NSW), 24 September 1957.
36 Box 44, folder 72, I Hume, Kew (Vic), 27 June 1951.
37 Box 97, folder 510, FB Williams, 15 December 1960.
38 Box 80, folder 370, Miss Marie Irwin, 5 August 1958.
39 Box 83, folder 395, Penrith (NSW), 7 August 1958.
40 Box 54, folder 153, AT Armstrong, 24 May 1954.
41 Box 46A, folder 94, Belmore (NSW), 4 August 1953.
42 Box 56, folder 169, Mrs D Clarke, 15 May 1954.
43 Box 83, folder 395, Mrs DW Taylor, Iluka (NSW), 16 October 1958.
44 Box 88, folder 439, North Carlton (Vic), 21 April 1959.
45 Box 97, folder 510, Warrnambool (Vic), 15 December 1960.
46 Box 58, folder 184, Mary Flamank, Rowland Flat (SA), undated May 1954.
47 Box 64, folder 239, Ascot Vale (Vic), 10 August 1955.
48 Box 88, folder 438, Mrs EB Missing, Maryborough (Qld), 30 October 1958.
49 Kewley, *Social Security*, 1965, p. 237.
50 Box 50, folder 121, HR Raymond, Greenwich (NSW), undated October 1953.
51 Box 64, folder 238, Lilian Bradford, Blackwood (SA), 8 June 1955.
52 Box 48, folder 105, Murdoch McDonald, Hawthorn (Vic), 24 August 1953.
53 Box 81, folder 372, AE Kerley, Semaphore (SA), 6 November 1958.
54 Box 55, folder 160, LM Beggs, Swan Hill (Vic), 19 June 1954.
55 Box 115, folder 652, WM McGee, Helensburgh (NSW) undated July 1963.
56 Box 56, folder 168, B Chapple, Quirindi (NSW), 16 March 1954.
57 Box 58, folder 190, R Hamilton, Heidelberg West (SA), 27 April 1954.
58 Box 79, folder 362, Ettalong Beach (NSW), 19 October 1958.
59 Dean E McHenry, 'The Australian General Election of 1954', *Australian Quarterly*, vol. 27, no. 1, 1955, pp. 14–23.
60 Box 49, folder 110, Gertrude Morrissey, Kew (Vic), 27 August 1953.
61 Kewley, *Social Security*, 1965, p. 188. Writing while Menzies was still in office, Kewley offered little adverse criticism of the government's record on social welfare. Later perspectives have been less generous (see Garton, *Out of Luck*, 1990, and Gray, 'Social Policy', in Prasser et al., *The Menzies Era*, 1995).
62 Ibid., p. 299.
63 Box 125, folder 733, 22 January 1965.
64 Box 81, folder 375, Gympie (Qld), 21 March 1958.
65 Box 44, folder 77, I Hume, Kew (Vic), 27 June 1951.
66 Box 55, folder 160, LM Beggs, Swan Hill (Vic), 19 June 1954.
67 Box 48, folder 106, Alice McLean, Barnawartha South (Vic), 2 May 1953.
68 Box 53, folder 142, Victoria Park (WA), undated June 1953.
69 Box 42, folder 51, Sydney, 31 March 1950.
70 Box 53, folder 149, Bankstown (NSW), 6 October 1953.
71 Box 88, folder 438, Maryborough (Qld), 30 October 1958.
72 Box 47, folder 98, Lawrence Johnston, 11 September 1953.
73 Box 47, folder 98, postmarked 11 September 1953.
74 Box 57, folder 177, Boronia (Vic), 26 March 1954.
75 Box 165, folder 1062, Ultimo (NSW), 6 August 1965.
76 Kewley, *Social Security*, 1965, p. 251.
77 Box 67, folder 262, Prahran (Vic), 25 October 1955.

7 Britain and the Empire

1. Box 78, folder 353, 13 March 1958.
2. Neville Meaney, 'Britishness and Australian Identity: The Problem of Nationalism in Australian History and Historiography', *Australian Historical Studies*, vol. 32, no. 116, 2001, p. 79.
3. Jon Stratton, 'Not Just Another Multicultural Story', *Journal of Australian Studies*, vol. 24, no. 66, 2000, p. 32.
4. Richard White, 'The Australian Way of Life', *Australian Historical Studies*, vol. 18, no. 73, 1979, pp. 528–45, defined the notion as inherently defensive and conservative.
5. Box 43, folder 61, Capt F Rhodes, Rockhampton Newspaper Co. (Qld), 3 January 1950.
6. Box 81, folder 372, Einar Kampmann-Arnild, Coon Rapids (Minnesota), from his poem 'The "Jervis Bay" Attacks'.
7. Box 41, folder 39, Derek H Palmer, 10 December 1949.
8. Box 83, folder 394, AA Sweeney, 30 May 1958.
9. Geoffrey Bolton, *The Oxford History of Australia, vol. 5: The Middle Way, 1942–1988*, Oxford University Press, Melbourne, 1990, p. 91; Jenny Stewart, 'Trade and Industry Policies', in Scott Prasser et al. (eds), *The Menzies Era: A Reappraisal of Government, Politics and Society*, Hale & Iremonger, Sydney, 1995, pp. 185–201.
10. Box 71, folder 294, Wingham (Kent), 24 May 1955.
11. David Lowe, '1954: The Queen and Australia in the World', *Journal of Australian Studies*, vol. 19, no. 46, 1995, p. 4.
12. Judith Brett, *Robert Menzies' Forgotten People*, Melbourne University Press, Melbourne, 2007, pp. 116–27. Menzies had described Churchill as a menace and a publicity-seeker – see Cameron Hazlehurst, *Menzies Observed*, George Allen & Unwin, Sydney, 1979, p. 182.
13. Box 41, folder 46, Thelma Garbett, Killara (NSW), 18 December 1949.
14. Box 42, folder 49, Coburg (Vic), 9 March 1950.
15. Box 42, folder 51, Mrs EM Lawrence, Turramurra (NSW), 18 January 1950.
16. Box 48, folder 103, Peter Liddell-Chinn, undated 1953.
17. Box 53, folder 141, 12 November 1953.
18. Box 60, folder 204, 12 May 1954.
19. Box 47, folder 97, Brisbane, 18 October and 29 November 1953.
20. Box 67, folder 260, Balwyn (Vic), 9 April and 14 June 1955 for example.
21. Box 85, folder 407, Council of Australian Jewry, Melbourne, 20 August 1959.
22. Box 85, folder 406, 20 January 1959.
23. Box 66, folder 252, reply to Gladys Ebbs, East Brisbane, 31 May 1955.
24. Brett, *Robert Menzies' Forgotten People*, 2007, p. 191.
25. Box 121, folder 699, New Milton (Hants), 5 July 1964.
26. Box 122, folder 705, Frank Price, Auckland NZ, 19 June 1964.
27. Box 44, folder 68, WH Bunning to Miss EG Linehan, 11 April 1954, for one example.
28. Box 46A, folder 93, Sassafras (Vic), 28 April 1953.
29. Box 51, folder 130, 25 April 1953.
30. Box 56, folder 166, Alice Campbell, Hurstville (NSW), 22 March 1954.
31. Box 58, folder 189, WK Gregory, Hartwell (Vic), 3 March 1954, for one example.
32. Box 55, folder 164, Mrs F Brown, Abbotsford (Vic), February 1954.
33. Box 57, folder 175, Wangaratta (Vic), 8 March 1954.
34. Jane Connors, 'The 1954 Royal Tour of Australia', *Australian Historical* Studies, vol. 25, no. 100, 1993, pp. 371–82.

35 Mark McKenna, 'Monarchy: From Reverence to Indifference', in Deryck Schreuder and Stuart Ward (eds), *Australia's Empire*, Oxford University Press, Oxford, 2008, p. 273; Peter Spearritt, 'Royal Progress: The Queen and Her Australian Subjects', in SL Goldberg and FB Smith (eds), *Australian Cultural History*, Cambridge University Press, Cambridge, UK, 1988, p. 140.
36 Box 55, folder 159, Sydney, 26 February 1954.
37 Box 60, folder 207, East Malvern (Vic), 21 February 1954.
38 Box 57, folder 176, Leichhardt (NSW), 6 February 1954.
39 Box 91, folder 461, 9 October 1959.
40 McKenna, 'Monarchy: From Reverence to Indifference' 2008, pp. 279–84; Spearritt, 'Royal Progress' 1988, pp. 152–54.
41 Box 42, folder 54, Kent, 7 January 1950.
42 Box 82, folder 389, 7 May 1958.
43 Lowe, '1954', 1995, p. 8.
44 Box 41, folder 39, 3 July 1950 and Box 80, folder 366, Anthony Hamilton, South Africa House, 6 May 1958.
45 Allan W Martin, *Robert Menzies: A Life, Volume 2, 1944–1978*, Melbourne University Press, Melbourne, 1999, *passim*.
46 Box 74, folder 317, Sydney, 2 January 1957.
47 Box 46A, folder 92, 9 December 1952.
48 Box 90, folder 458, PF Walsh, Steeple Aston (Oxon), January 1959.
49 Box 41, folder 40, Wallsend (NSW), 1 May 1950.
50 Box 57, folder 178, Mrs MD Duff, Drummoyne (NSW), 22 September 1954.
51 Box 79, folder 362, North Ryde (NSW), 10 April 1958.
52 Box 53, folder 147, Menzies' reply to Paul Williams, 16 November 1953.
53 Box 92, folder 474, 1960.
54 Box 66, folder 252, London, 7 July 1955 and Box 80, folder 371, Norman Eggar, 19 June 1958.
55 Box 114, folder 646, letter to Sir Jack Hobbs, 12 December 1963.
56 Box 65, folder 248, Molly Cowdrey, Sutton (Surrey), 25 February 1955.
57 Box 75, folder 332, name withheld, Bristol (UK), 24 June 1957.
58 Box 75, folder 332, name withheld, Bristol (UK), 14 November 1957.
59 Box 47, folder 100, Martin-Kramer, 9 March 1953.
60 Box 50, folder 119, LT Pitman, 25 September 1953.
61 ANL ORAL TRC 3562, Hazel Craig interviewed by John Farquharson, Canberra, Tape 4, 25 February 1997.
62 Box 124, folder 722, London, 14 June 1965.
63 Sara Wills, 'Passengers of Memory: Constructions of British Immigrants in Post-Imperial Australia', *Australian Journal of Politics and History*, vol. 51, no.1, 2005, pp. 94–107.
64 A James Hammerton and Alistair Thomson, *Ten Pound Poms: Australia's Invisible Migrants*, Manchester University Press, Manchester, 2005, pp. 1–34.
65 Box 124, folder 720, Report of Australian High Commission, 5 February 1965.
66 Hammerton and Thomson, *Ten Pound Poms,* 2005, chapter 4; Wills, 'Passengers of Memory' 2005, p. 103; Stratton, 'Not Just Another Multicultural Story' 2000, pp. 23–47; Andrew Hassam, 'From Heroes to Whingers: Changing Attitudes to British Migrants, 1946–1977', *Australian Journal of Politics and History*, vol. 51, no. 1, 2005, pp. 79–93.
67 Box 87, folder 422, GP Files, Rossendale (Lancs), April 1959.

68 Box 79, folder 362, James Fitton, Ettalong Beach (NSW), 19 October 1958.
69 Box 78, folder 353, 14 August 1958.
70 Box 84, folder 399, Joseph Ward, West Ryde (NSW), 3 March 1958.
71 Andrew Markus, 'Everybody Became a Job: Twentieth-Century Immigrants', in Verity Burgmann and Jenny Lee (eds), *A People's History of Australia since 1788: Making a Life*, Penguin, Ringwood Vic, 1988, p. 97.
72 Box 58, folder 189, name withheld, 11 December 1953.
73 Box 50, folder 123, CB Riley, Surrey Hills (Vic), 19 January 1953.
74 Box 80, folder 368, R Hedge, St Kilda (Vic), 12 July 1958.
75 Box 90, folder 454, name withheld, 12 September 1959.
76 Box 59, folder 192, Sydney, 4 March 1954.
77 Box 81, folder 378, Mrs WE Mate, Ivanhoe Liberal Party, 6 March 1958.
78 Linda Colley, *Britons: Forging the Nation, 1701–1837*, Yale University Press, New Haven CT, 1992.
79 Box 53, folder 146, Mrs Marjorie Williams, Bellevue Hill (NSW), 5 May 1953; Box 71, folder 292, Maberley Scott, Malanda (Qld), 27 July 1955.
80 John Murphy, *Imagining the Fifties: Private Sentiment and Political Culture in Menzies' Australia*, UNSW Press, Sydney, 2000, p. 157.
81 Box 91, folder 464, Crystal Palace, 7 May 1960.
82 Box 98, folder 514, Nambour (Qld), 29 September 1961.
83 Box 88, folder 436, AM McLay, Bellevue Hill (NSW), 7 August 1959.
84 AW Martin, 'R.G. Menzies and the Suez Crisis', *Australian Historical Studies*, vol. 23, no. 92, 1989, p. 169.
85 Box 76, folder 338, Enid M Morgan, Kensington (London), 3 July 1957.
86 Box 76, folder 339, Ealing (Greater London), 3 December 1956.
87 Box 74, folder 325, Dumfriesshire, 11 February 1957.
88 Box 75, folder 330, JJ Hughes, 7 December 1956.
89 Box 86, folder 416, Sydney Cotton, London, 24 June 1959.
90 Box 133, folder 637, P Cambridge, Penshurst (NSW), undated February 1963.
91 EFTA originally comprised Britain, Norway, Denmark, Sweden, Switzerland, Austria and Portugal.
92 Box 74, folder 324, Miss Mary H Gray, Wigtownshire (Scotland), 26 June 1957.
93 Box 120, folder 685, Tonbridge (Kent), 6 July 1964.
94 Box 68, folder 266, Rev Neil Glover, St Matthias Church, Richmond (Vic), 13 February 1955.
95 Box 71, folder 195, Joy Sundfors, Burwood (Vic), 2 April 1955.
96 Ewan Morris, 'Forty Years On: Australian and the Queen, 1954', *Journal of Australian Studies*, vol. 18, no. 40, 1994, pp. 1–13.
97 Box 88, folder 436, Mrs CF Malseed, Canterbury (Vic), 20 April 1959.
98 Box 92, folder 476, name withheld, Johannesburg, 28 April 1960.
99 Box 42, folder 49, GE Jones, South Yarra, undated (?January 1950).

8 Immigration and the White Australia Policy

1 AC Palfreeman, *The Administration of the White Australia Policy*, Melbourne University Press, Melbourne, 1967; Gwenda Tavan, *The Long, Slow Death of White Australia*, Scribe, Melbourne, 2005; Neville Meaney, 'The End of "White Australia" and Australia's Changing Perceptions of Asia, 1945–1990', *Australian Journal of International Affairs*, vol. 49, no. 2, 1995, pp. 171–89.

2   Sean Brawley, 'Finding Home in White Australia: The O'Keefe Deportation Case of 1949', *History Australia*, vol. 11, no. 1, 2014, pp. 128–48; Gwenda Tavan, '"Poor Little Nancy": The Nancy Prasad Case and the Commonwealth Immigration Department', *Australian Historical Studies*, vol. 44, no. 2, 2013, pp. 227–44.
3   Palfreeman, *Administration of the White Australia Policy*, 1967, p. 84.
4   Ibid., p. 140; David Lowe, 'Canberra's Colombo Plan: Public Images of Australia's Relations with Postcolonial South and Southeast Asia in the 1950s', *South Asia: Journal of South Asian Studies*, vol. 25, no. 2, 2002, p. 203.
5   David Walker, *Anxious Nation: Australia and the Rise of Asia, 1850–1939*, University of Queensland Press, St Lucia Qld, 1999; and the same author's *Stranded Nation: White Australia in an Asian Region*, University of Western Australia Publishing, Crawley WA, 2019.
6   Box 91, folder 465, 27 April 1960.
7   Box 92, folder 474, Gertrude A Dahle, Kew (Vic), 23 April 1960.
8   Box 92, folder 476, Hilary Ellis, North Balwyn (Vic), April 1960.
9   Box 96, folder 498, Ronald Reid, Dar-es-Salaam (Tanganyika), 14 April 1960.
10 Box 95, folder 493, Chelsea (UK), 30 March 1960.
11 Box 123, folder 714, 28 February 1964. Riots targeting West Indian immigrants broke out in Nottingham and Notting Hill in 1958.
12 Box 95, folder 493, EN Neville, Chelsea (UK), 30 March 1960.
13 Box 91, folder 463, Mrs Isla Atherley, Epsom (Surrey), 6 May 1960.
14 Box 96, folder 503, Hallyburton Stretton, Eastbourne (Kent), 26 April 1960.
15 Box 104, folder 562, Newport (Monmouthshire), 19 March 1961.
16 Box 100, folder 533, name withheld, 22 March 1961.
17 Box 92, folder 471, Vaucluse (NSW), 13 September 1960.
18 Box 100, folder 528, Lancaster (UK), 21 March 1961.
19 Box 105, folders 572 and 573.
20 Box 105, folder 573, Lady Manifold, 13 April 1961.
21 Box 92, folder 473, 11 April 1960.
22 Box 95, folder 493, Naboth Nyadioe-Makgatle, 28 April 1960.
23 Box 95, folder 495, 30 March 1960.
24 Box 89, folder 450, Thomas Sawyer, Hendon (Middlesex), 4 June 1959.
25 Box 91, folder 464, name withheld, 7 May 1960.
26 Box 92, folder 473, Miss F Creen, 24 April 1960.
27 Box 94, folder 486, 3 December 1959.
28 Box 122, folder 709, 2 June 1964.
29 Box 122, folder 709, 6 July 1964.
30 Box 121, folder 695, London, 7 July 1964.
31 Box 121, folder 693, name withheld, Bristol (UK), 1 July 1964.
32 Brawley, 'Finding Home in White Australia', 2014.
33 Tavan, '"Poor Little Nancy"', 2013.
34 Tavan, *The Long, Slow Death of White Australia,* 2005, pp. 95–96. Although Hubert Oppermann, Minister for Immigration, proposed reform in 1965, the Menzies correspondence, in which he frequently appears, gives no inkling of this.
35 On ALP policy, see Neville Kirk, 'Traditionalists and Progressives: Labor, Race and Immigration in Post-World War II Australia and Britain', *Australian Historical Studies*, vol. 39, no. 1, 2008, pp. 53–71.

36 Gwenda Tavan, 'Immigration: Control or Colour Bar? The Immigration Reform Movement, 1959–1966', *Australian Historical Studies*, vol. 32, no. 117, 2001, pp. 181–200; Kate Darian-Smith and James Waghorne, 'Australian-Asian Sociability, Student Activism and the University Challenge to White Australia in the 1950s', *Australian Journal of Politics and History*, vol. 62, no. 2, 2016, pp. 203–18.
37 Tavan, 'Immigration: Control or Colour Bar?', 2001, p. 189.
38 Box 91, folder 467, name withheld, 16 September 1960.
39 Walker, *Stranded Nation*, 2019, pp. 52–53.
40 Ibid., pp. 317–18.
41 Lowe, 'Canberra's Colombo Plan' 2002, p. 203.
42 Box 55, folder 160, Beaumaris (Vic), 22 May 1954.
43 Box 61, folder 215, Melbourne, undated May 1954.
44 Ai Kobayashi, 'Australia and Japan's Admission into the Colombo Plan', *Australian Journal of Politics and History*, vol. 60, no. 4, 2014, pp. 518–33.
45 In 1962, Australia had sent a training team to South Vietnam. In 1965, Menzies announced the departure of a battalion of Australian combat troops.
46 Box 124, folder 721, MCR Butler, Liverpool (UK), 14 June 1965.
47 Box 126, folder 737, V Reilly, Blackburn (Vic), 4 April 1965.
48 Darian-Smith and Waghorne, 'Australian-Asian Sociability' 2016, pp. 203–18.
49 Palfreeman, *Administration of the White Australia Policy*, 1967, p. 126.
50 Box 82, folder 383, Ivanhoe (Vic), 12 May 1958.
51 Box 105, folder 570, Camberwell (Vic), 20 September 1961.
52 Box 100, folder 529, 7 March 1961.
53 Box 105, folder 572, Unley Park (SA), 6 April 1961.
54 Box 95, folder 495, G Phillips (Suffolk), 30 March 1960.
55 Box 120, folder 687, Southern Rhodesia, 1 July 1964.

9 The changing face of anti-communism
1 Box 47, folder 99, 22 October 1953.
2 Box 58, folder 187, Sydney, 1 December 1953.
3 Box 68, folder 267, Wilfred King, Ballarat (Vic), 3 December 1955.
4 Box 56, folder 175, Miss Marjorie Dalgarno, Canberra, 4 March, and reply of 12 March 1954.
5 Allan W Martin, *Robert Menzies: A Life, Volume 2, 1944–1978*, Melbourne University Press, Melbourne, 1999, p. 81.
6 John Murphy, *Imagining the Fifties: Private Sentiment and Political Culture in Menzies' Australia*, UNSW Press, Sydney, 2000, p. 98.
7 Meredith Burgmann, 'Dress Rehearsal for the Cold War', in Ann Curthoys and John Merritt (eds), *Australia's First Cold War, 1945–1953: Vol. 1: Society, Communism and Culture*, George Allen & Unwin, Sydney, 1984, p. 79.
8 Box 41, folder 40, 27 April 1950.
9 Box 56, folder 169, Mrs D Clarke, 15 May 1954.
10 Box 42, folder 53, Rev Wilson Macaulay, Camberwell (Vic), 7 January 1950.
11 Box 79, folder 360, 15 December 1958.
12 On the People's Union, see Keith Richmond, 'Response to the Threat of Communism: The Sane Democracy League and the People's Union of New South Wales', *Journal of Australian Studies*, vol. 1, no. 1, 1977, pp. 70–83.
13 Box 49, folder 117, People's Union, Sydney, 10 August 1953.

14 Box 49, folder 117, People's Union, Sydney, 28 April 1953.
15 Box 67, folder 259, People's Union, Sydney, 29 June and 15 December 1955.
16 Box 41, folder 40, G Foster, 6 May 1950.
17 Box 41, folder 40, MM McEneroe, 28 April 1950.
18 Box 43, folder 57, Mrs HA Parrott, Lower Mitcham (SA), undated (May 1950).
19 Murray Goot and Sean Scalmer, 'Party Leaders, the Media, and Political Persuasion: The Campaigns of Evatt and Menzies on the Referendum to Protect Australia from Communism', *Australian Historical Studies*, vol. 44, no. 1, 2013, pp. 71–88; Frank Bongiorno, 'Herbert Vere Evatt and British Justice: The Communist Party Referendum of 1951', *Australian Historical Studies*, vol. 44, no. 1, 2013, pp. 54–70.
20 Murphy, *Imagining the Fifties* 2000, pp. 98–99.
21 Frank Cain and Frank Farrell, 'Menzies' War on the Communist Party, 1949–1951', in Curthoys and Merritt, *Australia's First Cold War: Volume 1,* 1984, pp. 132–33.
22 Victoria and South Australia also returned a 'No' majority. Overall, the referendum was lost by 2.37 million votes to 2.318 million.
23 Box 52, folder 140, 9 October 1953.
24 Box 59, folder 195, EJ Hogan, East St Kilda (Vic), 8 February 1954. The 'Comintern' was short for The Communist International, an international organisation, dominated by the USSR, which promoted world communism. Stalin had actually abolished it in 1943 so as not to antagonise his wartime allies.
25 Box 46A, folder 88, 2 September 1953.
26 Box 50, folder 121, 9 March 1953.
27 Box 84, folder 402, Rathmines (NSW), undated August 1958.
28 Box 116, folder 662, Melbourne, undated 1963.
29 John Warhurst, 'Catholics, Communism and the Australian Party System: A Study of the Menzies Years', *Politics*, vol. 14, no. 2, 1979, pp. 232–33.
30 Robert Manne, *The Petrov Affair*, Text Publishing, Melbourne, new ed. 2004.
31 Ibid., chapters 3–4.
32 Box 55, folder 160 (Beazley) and Box 58, folder 187 (Gorton).
33 Box 59, folder 191, 21 April 1954.
34 Murphy, *Imagining the Fifties*, 2000, p. 69.
35 Box 76, folder 337, 30 September 1957.
36 Barbara Carter, 'The Peace Movements of the 1950s', in Ann Curthoys and John Merritt (eds), *Better Dead than Red: Australia's First Cold War, 1945–195: Vol. 2*, Allen & Unwin, Sydney, 1986, pp. 58–73; Phillip Deery, 'Menzies, the Cold War and the 1953 Convention on Peace and War', *Australian Historical Studies*, vol. 34, no. 122, 2003, pp. 248–69.
37 Ralph Summy and Malcolm Saunders, 'The 1959 Melbourne Peace Congress: Culmination of Anti-communism in Australia in the 1950s', in Curthoys and Merritt, *Better Dead than Red*, 1986, pp. 79–83.
38 Fiona Capp, *Writers Defiled*, McPhee-Gribble, Melbourne, 1993, pp. 117–33. Waten had received £600 and used it to produce *The Unbending*, published in 1954.
39 Allan Ashbolt, 'The Great Literary Witch-hunt of 1952', in Curthoys and Merritt, *Australia's First Cold War: Vol. 1*, 1984, pp. 153–82.
40 Box 65, folder 248, name withheld, 28 October 1955.
41 Box 48, folder 105, WG MacDiarmid, Guildford (NSW), 21 September 1953.
42 Box 52, folder 136, G Thorley, Olinda (Vic), 9 November 1953.
43 Box 59, folder 193, 5 May 1954.

NOTES TO PAGES 177–189

44 Box 68, folder 267, name withheld, Caulfield (Vic), 5 April 1954.
45 Box 70, folder 283, 30 February 1955.
46 Box 72, folder 306, 23 September 1954.
47 Box 63, folder 239, PP Buckland, Chelsea (Vic), 20 October 1955.
48 Box 65, folder 245, probably Lakemba (NSW), 12 November 1955.
49 Box 56, folder 172, 22 December 1954.
50 Box 56, folder 174, J Crowley, undated November 1954.
51 Box 41, folder 41, Coburg (Vic), 21 October 1950.
52 Box 41, folder 40, Coburg (Vic), undated 1950.
53 Box 58, folder 183, Burwood (NSW or Vic?), 2 April 1954.
54 Warhurst, 'Catholics, Communism and the Australian Party System' 1979, cited p. 222.
55 Box 56, folder 166, Kootingal (NSW), 27 April 1954.
56 Box 57, folder 178, MD Duff, 22 September 1954.
57 Box 58, folder 190, Edith Hannan, Waratah (NSW), 1 June 1954.
58 Box 83, folder 397, South Melbourne, 13 November 1958. Today historians prefer the figure of 4.5 million. See Anne Applebaum, *Red Famine: Stalin's War on Ukraine*, Allen Lane, London, 2017, and Sheila Fitzpatrick's review in *The Guardian*, 2 August 2017. Australia is one of 15 countries which recognise the famine (*holomodor* in Ukrainian) as a genocide.
59 Box 62, folder 217, East Kew (Vic), 16 October 1954.
60 Box 85, folder 409, Newborough (Vic), 21 September 1959.
61 Murphy, *Imagining the Fifties*, 2000, p. 93.
62 Box 49, folder 111, 4 September 1953.
63 Box 49, folder 110, County Londonderry, 4 June 1953.
64 Box 61, folder 215, May 1954.
65 Box 80, folder 367, Sydney, 16 and 24 January 1958.
66 Box 87, folder 427, Launceston (Tas), February 1959.
67 Box 73, folder 313, People's Union, Sydney, 24 January 1956.
68 Box 75, folder 327, People's Union, Sydney, 1957.
69 Box 80, folder 367, People's Union, Sydney, 27 August 1958.
70 Box 101, folder 538, People's Union, Sydney, 14 December 1961.
71 Box 101, folder 538, People's Union, Sydney, 17 April and 28 August 1961.
72 Box 164, folder 1047, 8 March 1965.
73 Box 41, folder 42, 25 October 1950.
74 Box 44, folder 64, Moonee Ponds (Vic), 30 April 1950.
75 Box 44, folder 64, 28 August 1950.
76 Box 67, folder 258, Bickley (Kent), 23 April 1954.
77 Geoffrey Bolton, *The Oxford History of Australia, vol. 5: The Middle Way, 1942–1988*, Oxford University Press, Melbourne, 1990, p. 21.
78 Box 87, folder 428, People's Union, Sydney, 16 March 1959.
79 Box 90, folder 457, Melbourne, 20 August 1959.
80 Box 59, folder 191, Milsons Point (NSW), 21 April 1954.
81 Box 56, folder 166, Kootingal (NSW), 27 April 1954.

10 Angry letters and political protest
1 Renato Monteleone, *Lettere al Re*, Editori Riuniti, Rome, 1973.
2 Box 50, folder 124, Elizabeth Roskell, Romford (Essex), 7 February 1953.

3   Box 105, folder 561, no address, no date (1961).
4   Box 70, folder 287, Brisbane, 7 December 1955.
5   Box 53, folder 149, George Young, 6 October 1953.
6   Box 57, folder 177, Miss JF Donald, Boronia (Vic), 26 March 1954.
7   Box 88, folder 436, Canterbury (Vic), 20 April 1959.
8   Box 57, folder 175, AJ Dalziel, telegram, 13 August 1954.
9   Box 53, folder 146, CF Williams, Coogee (NSW), 17 May 1953.
10 Box 59, folder 198, Camberwell (Vic), 26 April 1954.
11 Box 83, folder 390, Sydney, 30 March 1958.
12 Box 102, folder 543, Upper Fern Tree Gully (Vic), 28 November 1961. The parable is found in Matthew 20: 1–16.
13 Box 105, folder 570, Camberwell (Vic), 20 September 1961.
14 Box 86, folder 416, Cootamundra (NSW), 16 September 1959.
15 Box 85, folder 408, WS Beall, Narrogin (WA), 1 October 1959.
16 Box 85, folder 408, JPA Ball, Cooma North (NSW), 17 April 1959.
17 Box 86, folder 417, Mrs M Curgenven, Mosman (NSW), 16 April 1959.
18 Box 86, folder 420, Kew (Vic), 31 March 1959. The Richardson Report raised the prime minister's salary to £10 000 per annum.
19 Box 87, folder 429, GL Hobson, Narrabeen (NSW), 14 April 1959.
20 Box 86, folder 421, RF Every, Bendigo (Vic), 16 April 1959; Box 86, folder 420, Mrs Margaret Dyson, Thorngate (SA), 20 April 1959; Box 90, folder 453, MGF Suttor, Willoughby (NSW), 26 March 1959.
21 Box 88, folder 432, Mornington (Vic), 14 April 1959.
22 Box 90, folder 455, Clr Thompson, Blackheath (NSW), 22 April 1959.
23 Box 69, folder 277, 13 September 1954.
24 Box 66, folder 249, Bernard Deane, MLA for Hawkesbury (NSW), 9 January 1955.
25 Box 55, folder 164, 13 May 1954.
26 Box 55, folder 164, reply to R Brown, 18 May 1954.
27 Box 55, folder 161, name withheld, 25 April 1954.
28 Box 49, folder 115, Hawthorn (Vic), 1 April 1953.
29 Box 54, folder 143, St Kilda (Vic), April 1952.
30 Box 83, folder 394, Armidale (NSW), 17 October 1958.
31 Box 101, folder 538, Ferny Creek (Vic), 10 October 1961.
32 Box 49, folder 115, 7 April 1953.
33 NLA ORAL TRC 3562, John Farquharson, Interview with Hazel Craig, Tape 2, 20 February 1997.
34 Box 67, folder 265, East Malvern (Vic), 21 October 1955.
35 Box 65, folder 248, West Wyalong (NSW), 9 December 1955.
36 Box 75, folder 332, Clearview (SA), 14 September 1957.
37 Box 64, folder 236, Rev JW Bethune, Kingston Beach (Tas), 2 April 1955.
38 Box 88, folder 436, Canterbury (Vic), 20 April 1959.
39 Box 92, folder 473, Casterton (Vic), 2 May 1960.
40 Box 98, folder 514, 30 January and 5 February 1961.
41 Box 98, folder 514, 12 May and 9 June 1961.
42 Box 98, folder 514, 19 September 1961.
43 Box 91, folder 463, Nambour (Qld), 7 November 1960.
44 Box 71, folder 195, Burwood (Vic), 2 April 1955.
45 Box 44, folder 72, Balwyn (Vic), 23 August 1950.

46 Box 67, folder 260, 9 April and 17 August 1955 among others. Hindle referred to supporters of the Australian war effort in Papua New Guinea, known as the 'Fuzzie Wuzzie Angels'.
47 Box 53, folder 146, 17 May 1953.

11 Paranoid letters
1 Box 32, folder 50, Sydney, 21 February 1950. 'Woe to the bloody city! It is all full of lies and robbery; the prey departeth not; the noise of a whip, and the noise of the rattling of the wheels, and of the pransing horses, and of the jumping chariots.' (Nahum 3:1–2)
2 Box 42, folder 51, Brisbane, 17 January 1950.
3 Box 53, folder 145, North Sydney, 21 February 1953.
4 Box 120, folder 690, Blacktown (NSW), 14 January 1964.
5 Box 81, folder 375, Canterbury (Vic), 19 March 1958.
6 Box 84, folder 402, Richard Zakharov, Camberwell (Vic), 18 August 1958.
7 Box 83, folder 395, Mrs Terpstra to Mrs Menzies, O'Connor (ACT), 9 October 1958; Box 83, folder 397, Union of Australian Women, Melbourne, undated 1958; Box 81, folder 372, Kew-Hawthorn West Peace Group (Vic), 3 November 1958.
8 Phillip Deery, 'Menzies, the Cold War and the 1953 Convention on Peace and War', *Australian Historical Studies*, vol. 34, no. 122, 2003, pp. 248–69; Barbara Carter, 'The Peace Movement of the 1950s', in Ann Curthoys and John Merritt (eds), *Better Dead Than Red: Australia's First Cold War, 1945–1959, vol. 2*, George Allen & Unwin, Sydney, 1986, pp. 58–73; Ralph Summy and Malcolm Saunders, 'The 1959 Melbourne Peace Congress: Culmination of Anti-communism in Australia in the 1950s', in *Better Dead Than Red*, 1986, pp. 74–95.
9 Box 79, folder 360, DH Drummond, 1 October 1958; Box 96, folder 498, G Richmond, Vancouver Island, 29 April 1960.
10 Box 99, folder 523, Amy Chilvers, Camp Hill (Qld), 10 July 1961.
11 Box 45, folder 75, Kaoota (Tas), 19 October 1950.
12 Box 49, folder 113, Dorothy Cameron, Lindfield (NSW), 18 November 1951. 'If my people, which are called by my name, shall humble themselves, and pray, and seek my face, and turn from their wicked ways; then will I hear from heaven, and will forgive their sin, and will heal their land.' (2 Chronicles 7:14)
13 Box 79, folder 357, RM Cunningham, Mt Lawley (WA), 19 September 1958.
14 Box 83, folder 392, Edith Tennyson Smith, South Yarra (Vic), 25 August 1958.
15 Box 95, folder 495, Coogee (NSW), 25 August 1960.
16 Box 99 folder 524, undated September 1961 (Cole); and Box 165, folder 1060, 10 January 1965 (Mohsin).
17 Box 41, folder 44, North Adelaide, 25 June 1950.
18 Box 48, folder 106, Mary Nairn McLiesle, Blackwood (SA), 2 March 1953.
19 Box 80, folder 367, name withheld, 3 November 1958.
20 Box 41, folder 45, name withheld, 30 October 1950.
21 First published in 1905, it outlined an alleged Jewish plan for world domination.
22 Box 91, folder 465, Eric Baume, 8 February 1960.
23 Box 93, folder 483, 20 July 1960.
24 Box 62, folder 223, JS Hayes, Sydney, 17 September 1954.
25 Box 62, folder 220, Ruth Pfeiffer, Nuriootpa (SA), 9 April 1954.
26 Box 54, folder 152, James Andrew, 12 January 1954.

27 David Walker, *Anxious Nation: Australia and the Rise of Asia, 1850–1939*, University of Queensland Press, St Lucia Qld, 1999, and the sequel, *Stranded Nation: White Australia in an Asian Region*, University of Western Australia Publishing, Crawley WA, 2019.
28 Box 43, folder 59, Allawah (NSW), 12 December 1949.
29 Box 47, folder 101, John Lamberth, Quamby (Qld), 29 July 1953.
30 Box 41, folder 46, JG Gart, Melbourne, 18 July 1950.
31 Box 76, folder 337, Constance K Moir, no place, undated 1957.
32 AC Palfreeman, *The Administration of the White Australia Policy*, Melbourne University Press, Melbourne, 1967, p.151.
33 Box 76, folder 337, Constance K Moir, no place, undated 1957.
34 Box 53, folder 141, Harbord (NSW), 12 November 1953.
35 Box 41, folder 46, 2 July 1950.
36 According to the 1961 Commonwealth Census, 34.9 per cent of the population identified themselves as Anglicans, as opposed to 39 per cent in 1947. Roman Catholics accounted for 26.2 per cent.
37 Box 45, folder 75, Thomas Agst, United Protestant Association, Sydney, 18 May 1951.
38 Box 47, folder 99, Gordon K Kelly, Bentleigh (Vic), 23 March 1953.
39 Box 63, folder 228, Camberwell (Vic), 8 July 1954.
40 Box 65, folder 242, no place, undated (probably 1955).
41 Box 54, folder 153.
42 Box 88, folder 436, 1959.
43 Box 88, folder 439, Mrs and George Willier-Moran, Port Pirie (SA), 19 December 1958.
44 Box 69, folder 273, Elizabeth Massingham, Coogee (NSW), 1 November 1955.
45 Box 67, folder 164, William James, Frankston (Vic), 25 July 1955; Box 67, folder 260, George Hillyard, Camden (NSW), 16 December 1955.
46 Box 51, folder 129, W Sinclair, Baldercombe (Qld), 4 November 1953.
47 Box 71, folder 298, name withheld, 23 May 1955.
48 Box 64, folder 237, Cottesloe (WA), 27 November 1955.
49 Box 54, folder 152, Mrs GM Anderson, East Malvern (Vic), 8 March 1954.
50 Box 125, folder 731, Freda May Leeds, Nedlands (WA), 10 December 1965.
51 Box 55, folder 161, Robert Bone, undated January 1954.
52 Box 56, folder 173, FH Crawford, Kamarah (NSW), 3 August 1954.
53 Box 49, folder 111, Alice Muir, 14 June 1953.
54 Box 66, folder 254, Brickfield Hill (NSW), 20 April 1955.
55 Box 58, folder 190, HC Haines, Auburn (NSW), 22 February 1954. He cited Deuteronomy 22:5 in support.

12 Structures of belief
1 Jeanne Marie Laskas, *To Obama, with Love, Joy, Hate and Despair*, Bloomsbury Circus, London, 2018, p. 68.
2 Béatrice Fraenkel, '"Répondre à tous": une enquête sur le service du courier présidentiel', in Daniel Fabre (ed.), *Par Écrit. Ethnologie des écritures quotidiennes*, Maison des Sciences de l'Homme, Paris, 1997, paras. 63–65.
3 Laskas, *To Obama*, 2018, p. 18.
4 Box 76, folder 339, Balwyn (Vic), 12 February 1957.
5 Box 115, folder 652, N McCelland, New Town (Tas), 16 August 1963.
6 John Murphy, *Imagining the Fifties: Private Sentiment and Political Culture in Menzies' Australia*, UNSW Press, Sydney, 2000, chapter 12; Will Sanders, 'Aboriginal Policy', in

Scott Prasser, JR Nethercote and John Warhurst (eds), *The Menzies Era: A Reappraisal of Government, Politics and Policy*, Hale & Iremonger, Sydney, 1995, pp. 258–72.
7   Box 83, folder 390, Sydney, April and May 1958.
8   Julie T Wells and Michael F Christie, 'Namatjira and the Burden of Citizenship', *Australian Historical Studies*, vol. 31, no. 114, 2000, pp. 110–30.
9   Box 80, folder 369, Martin Holman, 17 September 1958.
10 David Hilliard, 'God in the Suburbs: The Religious Culture of Australian Cities in the 1950s', *Australian Historical Studies*, vol. 24, no. 97, 1991, p. 400.
11 Richard White, 'The Australian Way of Life', *Australian Historical Studies*, vol. 18, no. 73, 1979, pp. 528–45.
12 Box 41, folder 46, JG Greenwood, Elwood (Vic), 8 June 1950.
13 Box 42, folder 47, Geelong (Vic), 26 October 1950.
14 Box 53, folder 147, KF Williamson, place unknown, 5 June 1953.
15 Box 46A, folder 88, Florence Cardell-Oliver, Perth, 2 September 1953.
16 Box 123, folder 723, Sydney, 27 April 1964.
17 John Murphy, 'Shaping the Cold War Family: Politics, Domesticity and Policy Interventions in the 1950s', *Australian Historical Studies*, vol. 26, no. 105, 1995, pp. 565–66.
18 Cécile Dauphin et al., *Ces Bonnes Lettres: Une correspondance familiale au XIXe siècle*, Albin Michel, Paris, 1995; Cécile Dauphin, 'Les correspondances comme objet historique: un travail sur les limites', *Sociétés et Représentations*, vol. 13, no. 1, 2001, pp. 43–50.
19 Tim Hitchcock, 'A New History from Below', *History Workshop Journal*, no. 57, 2004, pp. 294–99; Thomas Sokoll, *Essex Pauper Letters, 1731–1837*, Oxford University Press, Oxford, 2011; Antonio Gibelli, 'C'era una volta la storia del basso …', in Quinto Antonelli and Anna Iuso (eds), *Vite de Carta*, L'Ancora, Naples, 2000, pp. 160–61; Martyn Lyons, *The Writing Culture of Ordinary People in Europe, c. 1860–1920*, Cambridge University Press, Cambridge UK, 2013; Martyn Lyons, 'A New History from Below? The Writing Culture of Ordinary People in Europe', *History Australia*, vol. 7, no. 3, 2010, pp. 60.1–60.9; Steven King, *Writing the Lives of the English Poor, 1750s–1830s*, McGill-Queens University Press, Montréal, 2019.

BIBLIOGRAPHY

Primary sources

National Library of Australia (NLA), Canberra

NLA 4936 Papers of Sir Robert Menzies:
Series 2:
Boxes 41–128 Correspondence arranged by year, 1949–1966
Boxes 164–165 'No-reply correspondence' 1965–1978
Series 5:
Boxes 246–259 Messages of congratulation on Knighthood of the Order of the Thistle, 1963
Series 12:
Box 382 Get Well Messages and replies, 1962–1963 and 1968
Box 389 Congratulations on record term of office, 1957 (folder 3)
　　　　Requests for photographs, 1955–1965 (folder 9A)
Box 391 Birthday greetings, 1964 and 1965
NLA ORAL TRC 3562
Farquharson, John, interview with Hazel Craig, Canberra, 20 February to 1 April 1997 (six tapes)

Interviews for the Museum of Australian Democracy Oral History collection

Begg, Ken, Interview with Hazel Craig, recorded Monday 25 March 1996, <oralhistories.moadoph.gov.au/hazel-craig-1914-2013>
York, Barry, Interviews with Frank Jennings, recorded October 2007, 12 parts, <oralhistories.moadoph.gov.au/frank-jennings-1930-2014>

Secondary sources

Agutter, Karen, 'Her Majesty's Newest Subjects: Official Attempts to Assimilate Non-English Speaking Migrants In Post-war Australia', *History Australia*, vol. 16, no. 3, 2019, pp. 480–95.
Antonelli, Quinto and Anna Iuso (eds), *Vite de Carta*, L'Ancora, Naples, 2000.
Balint, Ruth and Zora Simic, 'Histories of Migrants and Refugees in Australia', *Australian Historical Studies*, vol. 49, no. 3, 2018, pp. 378–409.

Bolton, Geoffrey, *The Oxford History of Australia, vol. 5: The Middle Way, 1942–1988*, Oxford University Press, Melbourne, 1990.
Bongiorno, Frank, 'Herbert Vere Evatt and British Justice: The Communist Party Referendum of 1951', *Australian Historical Studies*, vol. 44, no. 1, 2013, pp. 54–70.
Bramston, Troy, *Robert Menzies: The Art of Politics*, Scribe, Melbourne, 2019.
Brawley, Sean, 'Finding Home in White Australia: The O'Keefe Deportation Case of 1949', *History Australia*, vol. 11, no. 1, 2014, pp. 128–48.
Brett, Judith, *Robert Menzies' Forgotten People*, Melbourne University Press, Melbourne, new edition, 2007, first published 1992.
—— 'The Menzies Era 1950–66', in Alison Bashford and Stuart Macintyre (eds), *The Cambridge History of Australia, vol. 2, The Commonwealth of Australia*, Cambridge University Press, Cambridge UK, 2013, pp. 112–34.
Burgmann, Verity and Jenny Lee (eds), *A People's History of Australia since 1788: Making a Life*, Penguin, Ringwood Vic, 1988.
—— *A People's History of Australia since 1788: Constructing a Culture*, Penguin, Ringwood Vic, 1988.
—— *A People's History of Australia since 1788: A Most Valuable Acquisition*, Penguin, Ringwood Vic, 1988.
Capp, Fiona, *Writers Defiled*, McPhee-Gribble, Melbourne, 1993.
Connors, Jane, 'The 1954 Royal Tour of Australia', *Australian Historical Studies*, vol. 25, no. 100, 1993, pp. 371–82.
Curthoys, Ann and John Merritt (eds), *Australia's First Cold War, 1945–1953: Vol. 1, Society, Communism and Culture*, George Allen & Unwin, Sydney, 1984.
—— *Better Dead Than Red: Australia's First Cold War, 1945–1959: Vol. 2*, George Allen & Unwin, Sydney, 1986.
Darian-Smith, Kate and James Waghorne, 'Australian-Asian Sociability, Student Activism and the University Challenge to White Australia in the 1950s', *Australian Journal of Politics and History*, vol. 62, no. 2, 2016, pp. 203–18.
Dauphin, Cécile, 'Les correspondances comme objet historique: un travail sur les limites', *Sociétés et Représentations*, vol. 13, no. 1, 2001, pp. 43–50.
Dauphin, Cécile et al, *Ces Bonnes Lettres: Une correspondance familiale au XIXe siècle*, Albin Michel, Paris, 1995.
Deery, Phillip, 'Menzies, the Cold War and the 1953 Convention on Peace and War', *Australian Historical Studies*, vol. 34, no. 122, 2003, pp. 248–69.
Eberle, Henrik (ed.), *Letters to Hitler*, English version edited by Victoria Harris, trans. Steven Randall, Polity, Cambridge UK, 2012.
Fadden, Arthur, *They Called Me Artie: The Memoirs of Sir Arthur Fadden*, Jacaranda, Milton Qld, 1969.
Farquharson, John, Obituary of Hazel Craig, *Sydney Morning Herald*, 23 May 2013.
Fraenkel, Béatrice, '"Répondre à tous": une enquête sur le service du courier présidentiel', in Daniel Fabre (ed.), *Par Écrit. Ethnologie des écritures quotidiennes*, Maison des Sciences de l'Homme, Paris, 1997, pp. 243–71.
Francis, Martin, 'Tears, Tantrums and Bared Teeth: The Emotional Economy of Three Conservative Prime Ministers, 1951–1963', *Journal of British Studies*, vol. 41, no. 3, July 2002, pp. 354–87.
Garton, Stephen, *Out of Luck: Poor Australians and Social Welfare*, Allen & Unwin, Sydney, 1990.
Goot, Murray and Sean Scalmer, 'Party Leaders, the Media, and Political Persuasion:

BIBLIOGRAPHY

The Campaigns of Evatt and Menzies on the Referendum to Protect Australia from Communism', *Australian Historical Studies*, vol. 44, no. 1, 2013, pp. 71–88.

Hammerton, A James and Alistair Thomson, *Ten Pound Poms: Australia's Invisible Migrants*, Manchester University Press, Manchester, 2005.

Hassam, Andrew, 'From Heroes to Whingers: Changing Attitudes to British Migrants, 1947–1977', *Australian Journal of Politics and History*, vol. 51, no. 1, 2005, pp. 79–93.

Hazareesingh, Sudhir, *In the Shadow of the General: Modern France and the Myth of De Gaulle*, Oxford University Press, Oxford, 2012.

Hazlehurst, Cameron, *Menzies Observed*, George Allen & Unwin, Sydney, 1979.

Herscovitch, Andrew and David Stanton, 'History of Social Security in Australia', *Family Matters*, vol. 80, 2008, pp. 51–60.

Hilliard, David, 'God in the Suburbs: The Religious Culture of Australian Cities in the 1950s', *Australian Historical Studies*, vol. 24, no. 97, 1991, pp. 399–419.

Hitchcock, Tim, 'A New History from Below', *History Workshop Journal*, no. 57, 2004, pp. 294–99.

Holt, Stephen, 'From Typists to Trusted Advisers', *Public Sector Informant* (supplement to *The Canberra Times*), 2 July 2013, p. 4.

Howard, John, *The Menzies Era: The Years that Shaped Modern Australia*, HarperCollins, Sydney, 2014.

Jones, Jennifer, 'Voluntary Organisations and the Assimilation of non-British Migrant Women in Rural Australia: The Efforts of the Country Women's Association of New South Wales, 1952–1966', *Australian Historical Studies*, vol. 48, no. 3, 2017, pp. 381–98.

Keating, Paul, speech to House of Representatives at Question Time, 27 February 1992, at <australianpolitics.com/1992/02/27/keating-blasts-liberal-party-fogies.html>.

Kewley, Thomas Henry, *Social Security in Australia: The Development of Social Security and Health Benefits from 1900 to the Present*, Sydney University Press, Sydney, 1965.

King, Steven, *Writing the Lives of the English Poor, 1750s–1830s*, McGill-Queens University Press, Montréal, 2019.

Kirk, Neville, 'Traditionalists and Progressives: Labor, Race and Immigration in Post-World War II Australia and Britain', *Australian Historical Studies*, vol. 39, no. 1, 2008, pp. 53–71.

Kobayashi, Ai, 'Australia and Japan's Admission into the Colombo Plan', *Australian Journal of Politics and History*, vol. 60, no. 4, 2014, pp. 518–33.

Laskas, Jeanne Marie, *To Obama, with Love, Joy, Hate and Despair*, Bloomsbury Circus, London, 2018.

Lee, David, 'The 1949 Federal Election: A Reinterpretation', *Australian Journal of Political Science*, vol. 29, no. 3, 1994, pp. 501–19.

Lowe, David, '1954: The Queen and Australia in the World', *Journal of Australian Studies*, vol. 19, no. 46, 1995, pp. 1–10.

—— *Menzies and the 'Great World Struggle': Australia's Cold War, 1948–1954*, UNSW Press, Sydney, 1999.

—— 'Canberra's Colombo Plan: Public Images of Australia's Relations with Postcolonial South and Southeast Asia in the 1950s', *South Asia: Journal of South Asian Studies*, vol. 25, no. 2, 2002, pp. 183–204.

Lyons, Martyn (ed.), *Ordinary Writings, Personal Narratives, Writing Practices in 19th and early 20th-century Europe*, Peter Lang, Bern, 2007.

—— 'A New History from Below? The Writing Culture of Ordinary People in Europe', *History Australia*, vol. 7, no. 3, 2010, pp. 60.1–60.9.

—— *The Writing Culture of Ordinary People in Europe, c. 1860–1920*, Cambridge University Press, Cambridge UK, 2013.
—— 'Writing Upwards: How the Weak Wrote to the Powerful', *Journal of Social History*, vol. 49, no. 2, winter 2015, pp. 317–30.
Manne, Robert, 'Is there an End to the Petrov Affair?' *Quadrant*, July-August 1991, pp. 15–21.
—— *The Petrov Affair*, Text Publishing, Melbourne, new ed. 2004.
Markus, Andrew and Margaret Taft, 'Postwar Immigration and Assimilation: A Reconceptualisation', *Australian Historical Studies*, vol. 46, no. 2, 2015, pp. 234–51.
Martin, Allan W, 'R.G. Menzies and the Suez Crisis', *Australian Historical Studies*, vol. 23, no. 92, 1989, pp. 163–85.
—— *Robert Menzies: A Life, Volume 2, 1944–1978*, Melbourne University Press, Melbourne, 1999.
Martin, Jean Isobel, *The Migrant Presence: Australian Responses, 1947–1977*, George Allen & Unwin, Sydney, 1978.
McHenry, Dean E, 'The Australian General Election of 1954', *Australian Quarterly*, vol. 27, no. 1, 1955, pp. 14–23.
McKenna, Mark, 'Monarchy: From Reverence to Indifference', in Deryck M Schreuder and Stuart Ward (eds), *Australia's Empire*, Oxford University Press, Oxford, 2008, pp. 261–87.
McQueen, Humphrey, '*Time* and Bob Menzies' Essence: Lifting the Cover on Australia 1960', *Honest History*, 30 August 2016 [2000], <honesthistory.net.au/wp/time-and-bob-menzies-essence-lifting-the-cover-on-australia-1960/>.
Meaney, Neville, 'The End of "White Australia" and Australia's Changing Perceptions of Asia, 1945–1990', *Australian Journal of International Affairs*, vol. 49, no. 2, 1995, pp. 171–89.
—— 'Britishness and Australian Identity: The Problem of Nationalism in Australian History and Historiography', *Australian Historical Studies*, vol. 32, no. 116, 2001, pp. 76–90.
Menzies, Robert, *The Forgotten People and Other Studies in Democracy*, with introduction by David Kemp, Liberal Party of Australia, Melbourne, 2011, first published by Angus & Robertson in 1943.
Milne, RS, 'The Australian 1958 General Election', *Parliamentary Affairs*, vol. 12, no. 2, 1959, pp. 230–39 (part one).
—— 'The Australian 1958 General Election', *Parliamentary Affairs*, vol. 12, no. 3, 1959, pp. 417–27 (part two).
Monteleone, Renato, *Lettere al re*, Editori Riuniti, Rome, 1973.
Morris, Ewan, 'Forty Years On: Australia and the Queen, 1954', *Journal of Australian Studies*, vol. 18, no. 40, 1994, pp. 1–13.
Murphy, John, 'Shaping the Cold War Family: Politics, Domesticity and Policy Interventions in the 1950s', *Australian Historical Studies*, vol. 26, no. 105, 1995, pp. 544–67.
—— *Imagining the Fifties: Private Sentiment and Political Culture in Menzies' Australia*, UNSW Press, Sydney, 2000.
Nolan, Sybil, 'The Snub: Robert Menzies and the Melbourne Club', *Australian Historical Studies*, vol. 48, no. 1, 2017, pp. 3–18.
Palfreeman, AC, *The Administration of the White Australia Policy*, Melbourne University Press, Melbourne, 1967.

BIBLIOGRAPHY

Petrucci, Armando, *Scrivere lettere: Una storia plurimillenaria*, Laterza, Bari, 2008.
Prasser, Scott, JR Nethercote and John Warhurst (eds), *The Menzies Era: A Reappraisal of Government, Politics and Policy*, Hale & Iremonger, Sydney, 1995.
Rawson, David William, *Australia Votes: The 1958 Federal Election*, Melbourne University Press, Melbourne, 1961.
Reynolds, Wayne, 'Loyal to the End: The Fourth British Empire, Australia and the Bomb, 1943–1957', *Australian Historical Studies*, vol. 33, no. 119, 2002, pp. 38–54.
Richmond, Keith, 'Response to the Threat of Communism: The Sane Democracy League and the People's Union of New South Wales', *Journal of Australian Studies*, vol. 1, no. 1, 1977, pp. 70–83.
Sainsbury, KAF, 'The Australian Elections of 1954', *Parliamentary Affairs*, vol. 7, no. 4, 1954, pp. 401–08.
Scott, James C, *Weapons of the Weak: Everyday Forms of Peasant Resistance*, Yale University Press, New Haven CT, 1985.
—— *Domination and the Arts of Resistance: Hidden Transcripts*, Yale University Press, New Haven CT, 1990.
Short, James Robert (Senator), Tribute to Geoff Yeend, 10 October 1994, <parlinfo.aph.gov.au/parlInfo/search/display/display.w3p;query=Id%3A%22chamber%2Fhansards%2F1994-10-10%2F0098%22>.
Spearritt, Peter, 'Royal Progress: The Queen and her Australian Subjects', in SL Goldberg and FB Smith (eds), *Australian Cultural History*, Cambridge University Press, Cambridge UK, 1988, pp. 138–57.
Strachan, Lachlan, *Australia's China: Changing Perceptions from the 1930s to the 1990s*, Cambridge University Press, Cambridge UK, 1996.
Stratton, Jon, 'Not Just Another Multicultural Story', *Journal of Australian Studies*, vol. 24, no. 66, 2000, pp. 23–47.
Tavan, Gwenda, '"Good Neighbours": Community Organisations, Migrant Assimilation and Australian Society and Culture, 1950–61', *Australian Historical Studies*, vol. 28, no. 109, 1997, pp. 77–89.
—— 'Immigration: Control or Colour Bar? The Immigration Reform Movement, 1959–1966', *Australian Historical Studies*, vol. 32, no. 117, 2001, pp. 181–200.
—— *The Long, Slow Death of White Australia*, Scribe, Melbourne, 2005.
—— '"Poor Little Nancy": The Nancy Prasad Case and the Commonwealth Immigration Department', *Australian Historical Studies*, vol. 44, no. 2, 2013, pp. 227–44.
Van Ginderachter, Maarten, '"If Your Majesty Would Only Send Me a Little Money to Help Buy an Elephant": Letters to the Belgian Royal Family (1880–1940)', in Martyn Lyons (ed.), *Ordinary Writings, Personal Narratives, Writing Practices in 19th and early 20th-century Europe*, Peter Lang, Bern, 2007, pp. 69–83.
Walker, David, *Anxious Nation: Australia and the Rise of Asia, 1850–1939*, University of Queensland Press, St Lucia Qld, 1999.
—— *Stranded Nation: White Australia in an Asian Region*, University of Western Australia Publishing, Crawley WA, 2019.
Walter, James, 'Designing Families and Solid Citizens: The Dialectic of Modernity and the Matrimonial Causes Bill, 1959', *Australian Historical Studies*, vol. 32, no. 116, 2001, pp. 40–56.
Warhurst, John, 'Catholics, Communism and the Australian Party System: A Study of the Menzies Years', *Politics*, vol. 14, no. 2, 1979, pp. 222–42.
Wells, Julie T and Michael F Christie, 'Namatjira and the Burden of Citizenship',

Australian Historical Studies, vol. 31, no. 114, 2000, pp. 110–30.
White, Richard, 'The Australian Way of Life', *Australian Historical Studies*, vol. 18, no. 73, 1979, pp. 528–45.
Wills, Sara, 'Passengers of Memory: Constructions of British Immigrants in Post-Imperial Australia', *Australian Journal of Politics and History*, vol. 51, no. 1, 2005, pp. 94–107.
Wingenter, Anne, *'Voices of Sacrifice*: Letters to Mussolini and Ordinary Writing under Fascism', in Martyn Lyons (ed.), *Ordinary Writings, Personal Narratives, Writing Practices in 19th and early 20th-century Europe*, Peter Lang, Bern, 2007, pp. 155–72.
Zadra, Camillo and Gianluigi Fait, *Deferenza, Revendicazione, Supplica: le lettere ai potenti*, Pagus, Treviso, 1992.

INDEX

2UE, RGM talks on 11

Aboriginal affairs, relative lack of interest in 23, 221–3
address, forms of 34–40, 64, 84
affinity, rhetoric of 20, 90–6
age pensions *see* pensioners
Alderman, Harry 161
Alexandra, Princess 133
Allee, Lurline 214
Allies Works Council 98
Amery, Leo 135
anti-Catholicism *see* religious issues
anti-communism *see also* Cold War; Communist Party of Australia
  letters relating to 103, 163
  political actions 53
  praise for 51
  rhetoric of 20–1
antisemitism 210–11 *see also* racism
apartheid *see* racism
apologetic mode 19–20, 81–9
Ashby, Mrs 48
Ashkanasy, Maurice 129
'Asians'
  attitudes towards 149, 211–12 *see also names of countries*
  relations with 158–9
Assisted Passage Migration Scheme 89, 136, 138–41
Atkinson, Joyce
  as problem correspondent 72–3
  invitation to Dame Pattie 67
  on White Australia Policy 141, 202–3
  serial letters from 15, 39
Attlee, Clement 135
Australia Day Committee 130
Australia House in London 100, 131
Australian Capital Territory, letters originating from 30–1
Australian Communist Party 53, 117, 166–8, 184–5 *see also* anti-communism; Cold War
Australian Consolidated Press 98 *see also* Packer, Frank

Australian Labor Party (ALP)
  attacks on 197–8
  branches condemn RGM 154
  DLP splits from 3, 173, 215
  links to communism 21, 164–6
  loses power 3
  media support for 98
  removes White Australia Policy from platform 157
  threats to vote for 120
  under Chifley 5
  voters support monarchy 132
  welfare policies 116–18
Australian National University 177
Australian Security Intelligence Organisation (ASIO) 26, 175
Australian Wine Producers' Association 97

Bagot, GE 141
Bake, Herbert 51
Balfour, Mrs 46
Ball, Mr 193
Bandaranaike, Mrs Sirimavo 138
Barking Young Liberal Association 150
Barnes family 139
Barredo, José 85
Barwick, Sir Garfield 132
Bate, Jeff 177
Beazley, Kim Snr 173
Bedser, Alec 136
Beggs, Mrs 106–7
Belgian Royal Family, letters to 7
Bell, KH 159
Bendas, AN 180
Bengtsson, Thomas 59
Beniams, Mrs 72
Berlin Blockade 5
Bevan, Aneurin 181
Bible quotes 184, 205, 207, 209, 215–16
Bilinsky, Irene 46
biographers, would-be 59
birthday and Christmas cards 47–8
Blandford, Will 216
Bradman, Don 90

Bramston, Troy 4
Brett, Judith 11–12, 130
'Bring out a Briton' campaign 88
Brisbane
   poverty in 5
Brisbane, Archbishop of 50–1
Bristol Aviation Services 97
Britain *see* United Kingdom
British Empire/Commonwealth *see also names of countries*
   declining importance 160–1
   diminished faith in 13
   effect of apartheid on 152–3
   letters originating from 30
   letters relating to 123–47
   rhetoric of 20
British Empire Service League 133
British Immigration League 140
Broken Hill, anti-communism in 198
Brooks, Austen 156
Brooks, Mrs 54–5
Brotherhood of St Lawrence 111
Brown, Allen 70
Brown, Mrs 57, 83, 123, 131–2
Brown, R 197
Brown, Victoria 73, 95, 115
Browne, Frank 129
Buckland, PP 178
Bureau of Public Relations 167
Burgess, Lloyd 109
Burgmann, Meredith 166
Burns, Dulcie 55
Bury, Leslie 145
business correspondence 96–9

Cahill, Joseph J 132–3
Caithness, DS 45
Caldwell, Ron 48
Calwell, Arthur 198
Camberwell Business Men's Club 94
Cameron, Miss 208
Campbell, Enid 87, 135, 179, 186
Cantor, Margie 88–9
Cardell-Oliver, Florence 171
Cardwell, Mrs 214
Carey, Warren 64–5
Carmelites 214
Casanova nightclub in Mayfair 97
Casey, Richard 68
Castle Menzies 92
Catholic Church *see* religious issues
Ceylon, gifts from PM of 135
'Chacha', RGM addressed as 84–5

Chamberlayne, MF 138
Chambers of Commerce and Manufacture 97
Chapple, Mrs 117
Chifley, Ben 44, 69, 166, 199
Chifley Labor government 5
Child Endowment 105, 114, 120, 122
China, attitudes towards 181 *see also* 'Asians'
Churchill, Winston
   as historian 60
   as Warden of the Cinque Ports 130
   letter of introduction to 100
   RGM attends funeral of 135, 220
   RGM compared with 51–2, 54, 57–8, 220
   RGM in War Cabinet 126–7
   RGM's relations with 3
Clarke, Mrs 113
Clune, Frank 153
Cold War *see also* anti-communism
   Australian politics and 4–5
   letters relating to 172–81
   paranoia generated by 205–7
   perceived Soviet threat 170–1
   rhetoric of anti-communism 20–1
   thawing relations 185–6
Cole, William 209
Colley, Linda 141
Colombo Plan 136, 149, 157–9
Commonwealth *see* British Empire/Commonwealth; United Kingdom
Commonwealth Literary Fund 175
Commonwealth Prime Ministers' Conferences 135, 138, 150, 153
Communist Party of Australia 153–4, 163, 168–70 *see also* anti-communism
complaints
   about politicians' salaries 193–6
   about smugness and complacency 189–93
   from or about pensioners 103–22
   letters of anger and protest 17–18
   'monarchist' view of the world 62–8
   political complaints 188–90
Congo, the 156
congratulatory letters 17, 41–5, 61
Conkey, Edgar 192–3
Connellan, Eddie 59–60
Conney, Louis 178–9
Connors, Jane 132
'Control or Colour Bar?' pamphlet 160
Cooper, Ernest 72
correspondence *see* letters; secretarial staff
Country Party, UAP relations with 2–3
Cowdrey, Molly 137
Cowling, B 73

INDEX

crackpots, letters from 72–3
Craig, Hazel
  background of 69
  direct responses from 50, 72–3, 100
  in secretariat 8
  letters addressed to 66, 89
  notes to RGM 78–9
  on Chifley 199
  on female politicians 226
  on Prime Ministers' Conferences 138
  on right to correspondence 14–15
  on supposed acquaintances 91–2
cricket, RGM's interest in 100, 136
Croft, Lachlan 199–200
cross-writing 33, 64
Cross, Zora 12
Crowley, Miss 179
Cummins, Cosette 201
Cunningham, Mrs 208
Curgenven, Mrs 193–4
Curtin Labor government 164

Dahrencourt, Marie 179
Danahay, Beryl 88
Davies, Vernon 132
Dawson, Ada 133
de Gaulle, Charles 7, 143
de Plater, Bert 43, 211
decimal currency 130
Defence Preparations Bill 112
Democratic Labor Party 3, 173, 215
Denne, Reverend 153
Dennis, A 107
dictation test 148
Diefenbaker, John 135
divorce, partial deregulation of 217
Dobell, William 59–60
Dodd, Alice 194
Donald, Miss 121
Dougan, Mrs 167
Drayton, WW 51
Drummond, Edith and Margaret 93
Drury, Nigel 160, 162
Duff, Mrs 136, 179
Dulles Plan 142

Eales, Mrs 50
Eberle, Henrik 7
Eisenhower, Dwight 52, 221
Elizabeth II, Queen *see also* monarchy
  Heseltine becomes secretary to 70
  letters relating to 100, 131–2
  RGM's relations with 52

  Royal Visit, 1954 20
emotional restraint, RGM praised for 51
epistolatory competence 32–4, 88
'epistolatory pact' 25
European Economic Community 143
European Free Trade Organisation 144
Evatt, Herbert Vere
  accused of supporting Communism 21, 197–200
  campaigns against dissolution of Communist Party 170
  campaigns on means test 117–18
  discredited by Petrov Affair 173, 178–9
  outshone by RGM 69

Fadden, Arthur 55, 108
Fagnani, Miss 53–4
Fait, Gianluigi 10
fan mail 45–50
farewell, forms of 34–40
Farmer, Clare 209
Farrer, Jas 179
favours, requests for *see* supplicatory letters
'F.D.' initials on coins 215
Featherstone, HS 145
Federation of Ukrainian Associations 180
Findlay, Fredrick 136
Finschhafen, battle of 95
Fitton, James 117
Fitzpatrick, Ray 129
Flamank, Mary 114–15
Foenander, Peter 37
'forgotten people'
  letters from 29–30
  pensioners as 104
  RGM as advocate for 10–11
  speech out of print 79
forms of address and farewell 34–40, 64
Forson, Obiba 102
'Forty Club', RGM joins 137
Foskett, Agnes 217
Fraenkel, Béatrice 7–8
Francis, Babette 158
Francis, Martin 51
Freemasonry 211

Gadd, Mrs 161
Gamboa case 157
Garbett family 127
Gard, Doreen 166
Garton, Stephen 111
Gavan, George 212
gender disparities

in letters received 29–30, 226
in party policies 226
women disadvantaged by means test 117–18
Ghana 154
gifts for RGM 46–7, 92–3, 96
Gilmore, Dame Mary 33, 175–6
Gilroy, Cardinal 191, 214
Glancy, Neville 49
Gorton, John 173
Graham, Bruce 164
Gray, Mary 145
Gray, Mrs 92–3
Gray's Inn 94
Graziers' Corporation 97
Griffiths, Lillias 34
Groser, Oswald 143
Groves, Petty Officer 81
Guy, Jean 95

Haddon, Robert 184
Haines, Mr 217
Hall, Leonora 56
Hallam, Chris 182
Hamilton, Louis 135
Hamilton, Mr 117
Hampel, Edward 86, 109–10
Hancocks, Violet 107, 110
Hann, Alice 64
Hannan, Miss 58
Hannan, Mrs 179–80
Harding, Nellie 174, 186
Hardy, Mrs 95, 107
Harlem Globetrotters 21, 164
Harrison, Eric 133–4
Hart, Gertrude
  invites RGM to tea 47
  praise for RGM 58, 198
  welcomes RGM home 55
  wishes RGM a lovely time 131
Hasluck, Paul 222
Hassett, Lindsay 4
Hay, Sir Philip 39
Hazareesingh, Sudhir 7
Hazlett, Anita 58
Heath, Margaret 225
Hebblewhite, AG 167, 182–3, 185
Hedge, Mrs 140
Heggarty, JW 113
Heggarty, Patricia 177
Henderson, Ronald 112
Henderson, Walter 51–2, 75–6
Henry, Duke of Gloucester 133
Herbert, Mrs 101

Heseltine, William
  in secretariat 8
  on Mrs Dougan 167
  on rude letters 78
  on success 49
  replaces Yeend 70
  response to call for Royal Commission 222–3
Heslop, GW 207
The Hidden People 111–12
High Commissioner for South Africa 39
High Court, blocks dissolution of Communist Party 168
Hilliard, David 223
Hindle, Rachel 129, 203–4
Hitler, Adolf, letters to 7
Hobson, Mr 194
Hodge, George 73, 78
Holt, Harold 70, 157, 213
Honolulu Cricket Club 37
Hood, CA 93
Horne, Donald 190
Horner, Mr 108
Hosking, Julia 122
Houghton, Mr 87
Howard, John, praise for RGM 4
Howard, Mrs 112
Hudson, Syd 179
Hughes, Billy 160
Hughes, Squadron Leader 143
Hume, Mrs 112, 120
Hungarian immigrants 175
Hurrell, Mrs 87
Hyland, AE 87

Iles, Lillian 127–8
immigration *see also* racism; White Australia Policy
  from southern Europe 139–40
  from UK 124, 136, 138–41
  letters about 148–62
  opinions of 120
Immigration Reform Group 157, 160
Immigration Restriction Act 1901 see White Australia Policy
Imrie, Lieutenant-Colonel 56
India, letters from 84–5
Indonesia, attitudes to 182–3
industrial action 165–6
inflation 107–8
Institute of Public Affairs (IPA) 111
inventions, claims about 216–17
Irwin, Marie 112
Isaacs, Alma 58

INDEX

Jackson, Mrs Elizabeth 128–9
Japan, Australian relations with 97–8
Jardine, Douglas 137
JC Williamson Theatres 97
Jefferson Oration 44
Jennings, Frank 8, 52, 70
Jeparit, Victoria, RGM born in 2
Jewish community *see* religious issues
Johnston, Lawrence 27
Johnston, Owen 191
Jones, Edith 195
Jones, Gladys 136
Jones, Leonard 88
Jones, Lilian 199
Jones, Mr 146
Jowett, Florence 192

Kater, Norman 53
Keates, E 163–4
Keating, Paul 4
Kempe, Mr 87
Kennedy, Gladys 67
Kenya 156
Keogh, Clare 200
Kerley, Mrs 108–9, 116
Kew, RGM's support for 94
Kewley, Thomas 119
Khrushchev, Nikita 171–2
King, Steven 19
King, Walter 100
Kirkham, Lily 205
knighthood *see* Order of the Thistle
Kooyong electorate
    letters originating from 31, 62, 65–6, 93–4
    Menzies elected to represent 2
Korean War 181, 211

Labor Party *see* Australian Labor Party
Lake Burley Griffin, water-skiing on 15
Lambert, Frances 46
Lampard, Mrs 110–11
Laskas, Jeanne Marie 8–9
Lawrence, Mrs 42–3
Leckie, Pattie *see* Menzies, Pattie
Ledebur, Eena 206–7
legal profession, affinity based on 94–5
Leslie, J 106, 120
letters
    about anti-communism 103, 163
    about immigration 148–62
    about the Cold War 172–81
    about the Commonwealth 123–47
    about the monarchy 100, 131–2

    about the Petrov Affair 43, 184
    about the White Australia Policy 148–62
    addressed to Menzies family members 14, 67, 83–4, 222
    analysis of 5–10
    birthday and Christmas cards 47–8
    business correspondence 96–9
    citizen's rights to 14–15
    congratulatory 17, 41–5, 61, 75
    delays in replying 74–5
    epistolary competence 32–4, 88
    fan mail 45–50
    forms of address and farewell 34–40
    from and about war veterans 20, 95–6, 107, 219–20
    from British Empire/Commonwealth 30
    from crackpots 72–3
    from 'forgotten people' 29–30
    from India 84–5
    from Joyce Atkinson 15, 39
    from Kooyong electorate 31, 62, 65–6, 93–4
    from Liberal branches and supporters 16, 22–3, 41, 196–7
    from NSW 30–1
    from or about pensioners 12–13, 23, 99, 103–22
    from or about war veterans 20, 95–6
    from private individuals 29–30
    from South Africa 63, 137–8, 146
    from the ACT 30–1
    from United Kingdom 30, 39, 66, 100
    from Victoria 30–1
    gender disparities in 29–30, 226
    gifts sent to RGM 46–7, 92
    intended as education 21–2
    letters as texts 22
    letters from overseas 30
    letters from paupers 19
    material quality of letters 25–6
    'no reply' file 79
    numbers of 14, 27–8, 30–1
    of anger and protest 17–18, 62–8, 103–22, 189–201
    of introduction, requests for 99–100
    paper sizes and types 31–3, 87–8, 120
    paranoid letters 18–19, 205
    photograph requests 45–6
    poems and songs in 46–7, 86, 125, 131
    power of writing 13–17
    proportion from overseas 30
    proportion of replies to 74
    relating to monarchy 131–2
    repeat correspondence 31–2

    requests for recipes 48–9
    requests to meet 47
    RGM welcomed home from UK 153
    signs of intimacy in 64
    supplicatory 18, 99
    to secretarial staff 36, 66, 89
    treatment by secretariat 68–71
    'tribune letters' 18, 201–4
    types of 17–22
    white space in 228
Levy, Dagmar 49
Lewis, Joan 66, 89
Liberal Party of Australia
    1949: takes office 3, 42–3
    1951: gains control of Senate 3
    1953: retains control of Senate 43
    1954: retains power 3, 177–8
    1955: retains power 3
    1961: reduced majority 3, 196
    Aboriginal affairs policies 221–2
    affinity based on 94–5
    cultural ties to UK 127–8
    disillusionment with 195–6, 204–5
    establishment of 3
    gender bias in policies 226
    industrial relations policies 167
    letters from supporters and branches 16, 22–3, 41, 196–7
    welfare policies 109–10
Lilley, Thomas 61
Lincoln, Peter 155
Linehan, Eileen G 8, 68–9
Little, A 119–20
Little Sisters of the Poor 214
lobby groups 16, 96–8
Longden, Reg 1–2
Lonie, Jean 207–8
Lowe, Mrs 100
Loyal Orange Institution of Victoria 128
The Lucky Country 190
Lunacy Laws 12
Lutyens, Lady Emily 23–4
Lyons, Dame Enid 213
Lyons, Joseph 2, 68
Lyons, Madge 101

Macmillan, Harold 143, 153, 185
Macquart, AHA 100–1
Malayan Emergency 126, 181
Malet, Wing Commander 130
Malseed, Mrs 190, 201
'Man to Man' broadcasts 56–7, 111

mangoes sent as gifts 46
Mannix, Daniel 214
Mansell, Byram 33
Maralinga atomic tests 126–7, 145, 207–8
Margaret, Princess 134
Marina, Princess 133
Martin, Allan 4, 135
Mary, Sister 46
Mason, John 64
Massingham, Miss 214
McAuley, Mrs 86
McClure, Alexander 95
McConville, John 65
McCurrie, Harry 52
McDonald, DG 183
McDonald, Neville 83
McEneroe, Mrs 168–9
McFerran, WR 130
McGarvie, RJ 91
McGee, WM 106
McGregor, Sam 93
McInnes, Stewart 90
McKell, William 77–8
McKenna, Mark 134
McKillop, Gordon 88
McKinnon, GD 32
McKinnon, George 132–3
McLay, Mrs 142–3
McNamara, Father 94
McNaughton, Mrs 88
McNicoll, Frances 54
Meaney, Neville 123
Melbourne
    antisemitism in 210
    Peace Congresses 175, 208
    poverty in 5, 13, 111–13
    RGM's early life in 5
    RGM's visits to 92
Melbourne Club 95
Melbourne Scots Club 92
Melbourne University 2, 111–13, 160
Menzies, Belle 16
Menzies, Frank 16
Menzies, Heather
    congratulations on wedding 48
    included in greetings 37
    letters addressed to 14, 83–4
    requests to paint 101
Menzies, Pattie
    cook application referred to 101
    included in greetings 37, 44
    letters addressed to 67, 222

INDEX

marriage to RGM 2
Menzies, Robert Gordon, personal history and views
  appointed Warden of the Cinque Ports 69
  as anti-communist crusader 168–70, 183–4
  background and early life 2–3
  Christian faith 42–3, 110, 216
  fashion sense 48
  health issues 45, 49–50
  interest in cricket 137
  knighthood 26–7, 45
  links to UK culture 130, 143
  on Egyptians 142–3
  perceived complacency 189–92
  praise for personal qualities 50–1
  Presbyterianism 78
  relations with Catholic officials 214
  relations with Evatt 170
  Scottish connections 90, 92–3
  seen as protector of Empire 136
  view of correspondence 23–4
  writers' connections with 81–2
Menzies, Robert Gordon, political career
  anniversary year 45
  as statesman 58
  becomes Liberal Prime Minister 3
  correspondence seen by 71
  in UK War Cabinet 69, 126
  planned retirement 58
  Prime Minister for UAP 2–3
  Prime Ministers' Conferences 135
  retains power in 1954 51
  secretarial staff and 8, 68
  trips to UK 91
  visits Japan 97–8
  welcomed home from UK 153
Menzies, Robert Gordon, public life
  books and speeches 44
  eulogy for Churchill 220
  on importance of savings 225–6
  on relations with Asia 158–9
  on Royal visits 133–4
  predicts third world war 168
  public speaking skills 52–8, 190–1
  radio broadcasts 55–6
  supports Jewish community 210–11
  television appearances 54–5, 57
  'wind of change' speech 153
Merchant of Venice, modernised court scene 53
Meredith, Fortescue 98
Messel, Harry 44
Missing, Mrs 120

Mitchell, Josephine 174
Mitterrand, François 7–8, 63, 80
Mohsin, T 209
Molotov, Vyacheslav 178
'monarchist' view of the world 63
monarchy, Australian connections to 131–4 *see also* Elizabeth II, Queen
monkey skin, RGM offered 102
Moore, Les 8, 74
Moral Re-Armament World Summit 67
Morgan, Alice 113–14
Morgan, Charles 129
Morgan, Enid 143
Morgan, Mary 46
Morgan, Mrs 109
Morris, Ewan 145
Morrissey, Miss 118
Morrisson, Hugo 181
Moss, Sydney 65
Mount Pleasant Winery 97
Muir, Joy 119
Muller, Henry 104
Munro, David 221–2
Murphy, Father 86
Murphy, John 5
Murphy, Linda 134
Murphy, Veronica 181
Mussolini, Benito, letters to 7
Mustill, Beatrix 143

Namatjira, Albert 222
Nash, Walter 135
Nasser, Gamal Abdel 142
National Gallery Society 176
National Insurance scheme, proposed 116
Nehru, Jawaharlal 137
Neville, EN 151
'New Australians' *see* immigration
New History From Below 229
New South Wales, letters from 30–1
New South Wales Liberal Party 197
New South Wales Quarrymens' Union 168
Newcastle, anti-communism in 164
Newland Oration 44
Newling, Bill 27
Nicolson, Norman 159, 181
Nkrumah, Kwame 154
'no reply' file 79
Non-Aligned Movement 137
Northern Rhodesia 155
nuclear testing *see* Maralinga atomic tests
Nyasaland 154–5

Obama, Barack, letters to 8–9, 78, 218–19
O'Brien, Archbishop 32
O'Brien, Norman 43
O'Keefe case 157
old age pensioners *see* pensioners
On the Beach 206
Opeltz, Frank 180
Opperman, Hubert 'Oppy' 198
oratory *see* public speaking skills
Order of the Thistle
    awarded to RGM 26–7, 130
    congratulations on 45
    forms of address following 35
Oswald, Bert 198
Our Lady of Lourdes 208
overseas letters, proportion of 30

Packer, Frank 45, 98 *see also* Australian Consolidated Press
Pain, Mrs 83
Palmer, Vance 175
pants, women wearing 217
paper sizes and types 31–3, 87–8, 120
paranoid letters 18–19, 205
Parramatta Art Society 176
Parry, GH 33–4
patriotism, rhetoric of 20
paupers, letters from 19
Payne, Rhoda 56–7
Peace Convention 207–8
peaches, maggots in 189
pensioners
    letters from or about 12–13, 23, 99, 103–22
    means test for 116–19
    poverty among 111–12
Pensioners' Amenities Society 112
People's Union of New South Wales 167, 182–4
Pepys, Helen 92
Peterson, Stuart 209
Petrov Affair
    anti-communism and 21
    effect on attitudes 172–81
    effects on Evatt and ALP 117–18, 199–200
    letters prompted by 43, 184
Petrov, Evdokia 174
Petrucci, Armando 5
Phillips, G 154
photographs, requests for 45–6
Plast 177
Plummer, CE 90
poems and songs 46–7, 86, 125, 131
political advice and warnings 18, 196 *see also* Liberal Party of Australia

politicians, salary raise for 193–5
Poor Law overseers, letters to 19
Porritt, Barbara 138
Porter, E 89
portrait painters, requests from 59, 101
postal rates, rise in 192–3
poverty, responses to 111–22
Powell, Mrs 73
Prasad, Nancy 157
Presbyterian Home for the Elderly 42
Press Conference program 54
Prichard, Katherine Susannah 175
Protestant Council of New South Wales 141, 211
protests *see* complaints
Protocol of Sèvres 143
The Protocols of the Elders of Zion 210
Prunier's of London 97
public speaking skills 52–8
Punjabi, Mr 84–5

Queensland
    perceived neglect of 196–7
    Royal Visit to 133
Queensland Liberal Party 196–7

rabbit problem 80
racism *see also* White Australia Policy
    antisemitism 210
    apartheid in South Africa 124, 150–2
    assumed superiority of Britons 147
    in immigration policies 139–43, 157–8
Radcliffe, Mrs 63–4
Raymond, Mr 115
Reader's Digest 173
recipes, RGM asked for 48–9
Reeves, George 62
Refoy, Elizabeth 190
Reid, Alan 179
Reilly, Mrs 159
Reisman, H 171
religious issues
    anti-Catholicism 140–1, 212–16
    antisemitism 210–11
    approaching Armageddon 206–9
    behavioural exhortations 208–9
    Bible quotes 184, 205, 209
    'Catholic Action' 201
    Christianity linked with anti-communism 178–9
    cultural significance of faith 223
    Presbyterianism 2, 78, 93, 159
    Protestantism and imperial identity 141
    religious talismans 46

INDEX

requests for prayers 43
RGM as Christian hero 42–3, 110
RGM donates Bible 78
styles of farewell 38
support for Jewish community 210–11
Returned and Services League 107
Reynella Winery 97
Rhodes, Captain 125
Rhodes Motor Company 97
Rhodesia 137–8, 154–5
Richardson, Arthur 77–8
Richardson, Gordon 41
Richardson Report 98, 193–4
Riley, Major 140
Robert Burns commemorations 92
Roberts, Mr 65–6
Rogers, Mrs 34–5
Rowse, AL 60
Royal Caledonian Society 92
Royal Commonwealth Society 134
Royal visits to Australia *see* Elizabeth II, Queen; monarchy

Samson, E 152
Santamaria, Bartholomew Augustus 173
Saunders, Thelma 38, 172
Savage Club of Melbourne 94–5
Sawtell, Michael 56, 191–2, 221–2
school students, requests from 50
Scott, James C 23
Scottish Australian Company 137
Scottish connections, claims of 90, 92–3
Sears, Guy 156
Second World War, after-effects of 219–20
secretarial staff 8, 68 *see also* Craig, Hazel;
 Heseltine, William; Linehan, Eileen G
 Frank Jennings 8, 52, 70
 Geoffrey Yeend 8, 69–70, 100, 164
 Les Moore 8, 74
 letters addressed to 36
Shaile, Mrs J 121
Shakespeare, William 52–3, 97
Shayler, Miss 43
Short, James 70
Shute, Neville 206
Siamese cat, named Ming 48
Siegel, Leonard 58
Simpson, Bob 4
Skerman, Mr 43
Skues, Fred 109
Slessor, Kenneth 53
Smart, AJH 198
Smellie, Arthur 63

Smith, Edna 88, 131
Smith, Ian 155
Smith, Nance 183–4
Smith, Waldron 184
Smuts Memorial Lecture 44
Solling, Wendy 101
South Africa
 apartheid in 124, 150–2
 gifts from 46, 135
 letters from 63, 137–8, 146
South Australia, British atomic testing in 126–7, 145, 207–8
Southern Rhodesia 137–8, 154–5
Soviet Union *see* Cold War
Speech is of Time 42–3
spelling errors 33–4
Spickett, Gladys 84, 126–7
St David's, Scotland 92
Stalin, Josef 171, 221
stamps, requests for 99
Stanger, Beth 46–7
Stanhope Hotel in New York 18
State Housing Commissions 122
States of Australia
 Aboriginal affairs relegated to 221–2
 letters originating from 30–1
States of Australia, letters originating from 30–1
Stewart, Mary 85
Stubbs, John 111–12
Suez Crisis 142–4
Sukarno 183
Sundfors, Joy 145, 203
supplicatory letters 18, 99
Sutcliffe, Herbert 136
Suttor, Mr 195
Sweeney, Mrs 126
Sydney
 media critical of RGM 98
 Peace Convention 207
 Plast meeting in 132–3
 poverty in 5, 110–13
 RGM speaks at synagogue 207
 Royal Visits to 132–3
Sydney Morning Herald 98
Sydney University 160

Taiwan Strait crisis 181
Tasmania, quarantine regulations 100
telepathy, claims of 216–17
'Ten Pound Poms' *see* Assisted Passage
 Migration Scheme
Tennant, Kylie 175
textile mills 97

265

texts, letters as 22 *see also* correspondence
Think and Grow Rich 83
Third World War, concerns over 168, 206–7
Thisseu, Mrs 66
Thomas, Edith 49
Thomson, Mr 101–2
Thorley, Graham 176–7
Thornley, Jean 112–13
trade unions, opposition to 165–6 *see also* anti-communism
'tribune letters' 18, 201–4

Umfreville, F 208
United Association of Women 226
United Australia Party, Menzies elected for 2
United Kingdom
  applies to join EEC 143
  Assisted Passage Migration Scheme 136, 138–41
  Australian pride in 186, 224–5
  'British Justice' appealed to 21
  cultural and political links to 20, 123–5
  letters originating from 30, 39, 66, 100
  perceived religious significance 209
  RGM in War Cabinet 69, 126
  RGM visits 2–3
  support for atomic program 126–7
  trade with 126
United States 30, 159

van Ginderachter, Maarten 7
Vandenberg, Adele 67
Vardy, John 170–1
Vernon, EW 128, 212
Victor Emmanuel, King of Italy 188
Victoria, letters originating from 30–1
Victorian League of Rights 186
Vieglais, Ed 86
Vietnam War 159

Walker, Arthur 120
Walker, David 149, 158, 211
war veterans
  letters from or about 20, 95–6, 219–20
  rhetoric of sacrifice 107
Wardenship of the Cinque Ports 69, 130
Warner, Frances 198
Waten, Judah 175
Waterside Workers' Federation 166–7

Webster, Muriel 91
welfare benefits 104 *see also* pensioners
Wentworth, WC 176–7
Wesley College, Melbourne 2, 91
Western Australia 221–2
Western, Timothy 74, 160
White Australia Policy *see also* immigration; racism
  in operation 139–43
  increasing criticism of 124
  letters about 148–62
  maintaining 13
  under RGM 4
White, Mrs 207
White, Richard 224–5
white supremacy, RGM approached to support 137–8
widows' pensions *see* pensioners
Wilkinson, Everil
  direct responses from 76, 80
  on antisemitism 210
  on request for recipes 48–9
  on secretariat 8
  replaces Linehan 69
Williams, Mr 204–5
Williams, Mrs 84, 112, 114
Wilson, Harold 155, 161
'wind of change' speech 153
Wingenter, Anne 7
Woman's Day magazine 174
Women's College, University of Queensland 48–9
Women's Mirror 48
Wright, Edward 78
Wright, Harold 39
writing *see* correspondence
'writing upwards' 5–10 *see also* correspondence

Yeats, Valerie 188
Yeend, Geoffrey 8, 69–70, 100, 164
yoga, letter promoting 38
Young Conservatives of the City of London 126
Young, George 110, 120
'Your Majesty', RGM addressed as 35
youth, opinions of 119–20

Zadra, Camillo 10
Ziegler, Oswald 73, 79
Zymantis, Mrs 171–2

www.ingramcontent.com/pod-product-compliance
Lightning Source LLC
Chambersburg PA
CBHW030339240426
43661CB00052B/1681